Under The Fifth Rib

By the same Author

Matter, Life and Value
Philosophical Aspects of Modern Science
The Present and Future of Religion
Thrasymachus, or The Future of Morals
Samuel Butler
etc.

Under The Fifth Rib

A Belligerent Autobiography

by

C. E. M. Joad

'And . . . Joab took him aside in the
gate to speak with him quietly, and smote
him there under the fifth rib.'
2 Samuel iii. 27

London
Faber & Faber Limited
24 Russell Square

FIRST PUBLISHED IN MCMXXXII
BY FABER & FABER LIMITED
24 RUSSELL SQUARE LONDON W.C.I
PRINTED IN GREAT BRITAIN
BY BUTLER & TANNER LIMITED
FROME AND LONDON

Author's Note

Part of Chapter VIII originally appeared in the form of a pamphlet issued by the Hogarth Press under the title of 'The Horrors of the Countryside'. My thanks are due to the Hogarth Press for permission to reproduce it here.

Contents

CHAPTER   PAGE

I   HOW I BEGAN   9

II   HOW I HAVE DEVELOPED   39
     FOOD AND WOMEN

III   HOW I BECAME A PACIFIST   63
     THE LAST WAR AND THE NEXT

IV   WHAT I AM   98
     LITERATURE, MUSIC, THE COUNTRY

V   DISLIKINGS I   130
     THE CULT OF UNREASON

VI   DISLIKINGS II   146
     UNREASON IN TALK, POLITICS AND THE NOVEL

VII   DISLIKINGS III   167
     UNREASON IN ACTION. FEAR OF SCIENCE

VIII   DISLIKINGS IV   188
     THE HORRORS OF THE COUNTRYSIDE

IX   DISLIKINGS V   226
     MUSIC AND ITS INTERPRETERS

X   DISLIKINGS VI   248
     THE WICKEDNESS OF THE BODY AND THE OLD

XI   MORALS AND MY LACK OF THEM   264

XII   ON BEING NOT SO BLACK AS I HAVE
     PAINTED   288

Contents

I HOW I BEGAN

II HOW I HAVE DEVELOPED

III HOW I BECAME A PACIFIST

IV WHAT I AM

V DISLIKINGS I

VI DISLIKINGS II

VII DISLIKINGS III

VIII DISLIKINGS IV

IX DISLIKINGS V

X DISLIKINGS VI

XI MORALS AND MY LACK OR THEM

XII ON BEING NOT SO BLACK AS I HAVE PAINTED

CHAPTER I

How I Began

Education. I left my public school in 1910, an intelligent young barbarian. I had an extensive knowledge of Latin and Greek literature, could write reasonably good Latin and Greek verses, had 'done' mathematics as far as conic sections and the differential calculus, and knew a certain amount of Greek and Roman history and French grammar. On the strength of my knowledge of Latin and Greek I gained a scholarship to Balliol. I went there a good classic but a complete ignoramus. Looking back I am astonished at the nature and extent of my ignorance. I was, I must presume, one of the most successful products of our public-school system of education. For a year and a half I had been the head boy in the Classical Sixth. Whatever they had to teach me I had assimilated. Admittedly I had learned nothing for myself; but then I had never been encouraged to think that learning for oneself was either possible or desirable. As a result I went up to Oxford ignorant of the major events that have determined the history of the Western world and made our civilization what it is. My acquaintance with the physical sciences was confined to their smells. I had never been in a laboratory; I did not know what an element was or a compound. Of biology I was no less ignorant. I knew vaguely that the first Chapter of Genesis was not quite true, but I did not know why. Evolution was only a name to me and I had never heard of Darwin. Of botany, geology and astronomy I knew absolutely nothing; I had never heard of psychology and the existence of the so-called social sciences was unknown to me. Among great men I knew a little of Plato and Socrates, in so far as they were figures in Greek history; but beyond the information derived from the *Apology* that Socrates had been put to death for not believing in the country's gods and corrupting its youth, I did not know what their teaching was or why it was important. Aristotle was just a name, and of the great philosophers Descartes, Spinoza, Locke, Berkeley, Hume, Kant, Hegel and Goethe I had not heard at all. Of the discoverers and inventors whose original insight has changed the face of human life I knew nothing; I had never heard of Copernicus or Galileo or Harvey or Lister or Faraday or Pasteur. Newton was, however, known to me through the incident of the apple.

History was an abyss of darkness in which there glowed three little points of intense light: Greece from 500 to 380 B.C., Rome from about 200 B.C. to 100 A.D., and the period of English history from the Norman Conquest to the end of the Middle Ages. Why I had knowledge of this last I cannot say; it must have been just chance that set us studying it in the sixth during my two years of membership. In the cycle of recurring periods this obscure tract of English history had come round again about the time when I entered the sixth. But at no time did the cycle go beyond the battle of Waterloo. Had I stayed in the sixth until Doomsday, I should never have learned anything about the nineteenth century. Of the existence of pre-history I did not know.

My conception of the Industrial Revolution was limited to stories about James Watt, George Stephenson, Arkwright and spinning jennies, which I had inherited from my preparatory school. Of the history of the last fifty years, of the origin of the forces that lay behind the movements of my own times and of those movements themselves I knew nothing at all.

As to economics I was not aware that such a branch of study existed. But I had a cursory acquaintance with the Protection-Free Trade controversy, and had astonished and alarmed the school by becoming a Liberal on my own initiative and introducing that class-conscious, revolutionary paper the *Daily News* into the school library, where it fermented dangerously, an irritant leaven in the otherwise untroubled dough of school Toryism. Besides myself there were only two Liberals in the school, and, consciously forlorn, I had written as the lone supporter of an unpopular cause to Mr. Lloyd George for material for a School Debating Society speech in defence of the famous 1909 Budget. It came abundantly accompanied by a courteous note from L. G. himself, and on the strength of it I made a successful speech against overwhelming odds, converting two boys in the process.

My knowledge of literature was confined to an acquaintance with some of the reasons which have led people erroneously to suppose that Bacon wrote Shakespeare, our head master being a Baconian enthusiast, who was unable to discourse on any literary subject for five minutes without making off in the direction of the loved controversy from which he never returned. I had also some knowledge of Sheridan's *The Rivals* and *The School for Scandal*, through having acted the parts of Bob Acres and Charles Surface in school plays. But outside the literature of Greece and Rome, my reading was to all intents and purposes non-existent. I had never read for pleasure a single book worth reading. Of the writers of my own times I knew nothing, and, when I went up to Oxford in the autumn of 1910, I had not so much as heard the names of Hardy or Bernard Shaw.

Looking back upon my education I am not only astonished at its irrelevance but indignant at its inadequacy.

How I Began

To-day I would give all my classics for a knowledge of the rudiments of the physical and biological sciences; yet, a middle-aged man, I have lost the capacity of easy learning and fear I shall never acquire it. It is to my mind nothing short of a scandal that while our knowledge of life and mind grows yearly more astonishing, and the physical universe revealed by modern science is as fascinating as a fairy tale and as mysterious as a ghost story, young minds should still be drilled in the syntaxes of dead languages, and young curiosities stifled by a dead weight of verbs and declensions. Lists of unimportant dates and names blunt the faculties, while the process of acquiring the horrid skill in the writing of Latin Elegiac verses commended at Public Schools dulls and finally extinguishes the instinct to find out. I recently read *The Science of Life*, by H. G. and G. P. Wells and Julian Huxley. I would give all the pages of Latin accidence and syntax that I ever committed to heart, for a knowledge of one single page of this great book. Yet my middle-aged mind can no longer assimilate facts with the old assurance, and the nature and workings of life are destined to remain very largely unknown to me, because of my useless acquaintance with the nature and workings of Greek verbs.

I have often seen it argued on behalf of a classical education that the knowledge of Latin and Greek is a key to a treasure house in which are stored some of the most priceless jewels of the world's literature, and that the languages must be learned in order that these may be enjoyed later in life. It may be so, but I can honestly say that, once I had finished with Mods at Oxford, I never read a Latin or Greek author in the original for pleasure, and since I left Oxford, I have never read one in the original at all. Now this is odd, for I am very fond of literature and have read all the great English writers in my time with avidity.

I know half a dozen men, contemporaries of mine at Oxford, who were also good classics, and, as far as I can see, they read no more Latin and Greek than I do. Of course they may read Virgil and Homer and Cicero and Demosthenes and the rest privately, but, if they do, they keep very quiet about it, and take great care that nobody ever finds them out. My own belief is that of the vast numbers that are yearly given access to these priceless treasures very few ever do take advantage of them, and this for the very good reason that the treasures are for the most part not treasures at all but poorish stuff not fit to hold a candle to the literature of our own language. But grant that Latin and Greek authors are the most wonderful in the world, the languages are so infernally difficult that only one man in every hundred, whose feet are set on the straight and narrow way of Latin and Greek grammar, ever attains sufficient proficiency to read them, so that, even if the contention were true, it would have no relevance to the case of ordinary people. As for extraordinary people like myself and my friends, who actually managed to *read* Latin and Greek, we forgot what we knew as soon as we conveniently could. My belief is that the classics continue to be taught for no other reason than that a great many people's salaries depend upon their being thought valuable enough to be worth learning. Most of what is good in them, that is to say, the thought of Plato and Aristotle, can be understood as well in translations, and for the rest, it is not worth so much as a single week subtracted from the mastery of things worth knowing or the enjoyment of books worth reading.

I am not less resentful of the many wearisome hours I spent over Scripture. It is astonishing that we should still require young minds to absorb those elementary legends about the universe which science has shown to be untrue, merely because God is said to have compiled them. Not only are they untrue; most of them are disreputable to boot; yet the morals of temperate twentieth-century England are still in theory founded upon the exigencies and expediences of a nomadic Semitic tribe travelling in the torrid zone. The Ten Commandments have always struck me as particularly irrelevant. I felt, even then, that they should be prefaced with the remark which appears at the head of examination papers: 'Candidates are warned that only six questions should be attempted!'

I achieved considerable proficiency in Scripture, a squalid accomplishment which, so far as I can see, did me no good at all, and which I had much sooner be without. Almost all the agnostics I know have distinguished themselves at Scripture in their youth. This, I suppose, is only to be expected, for it requires intelligence to be an agnostic, or did, and intelligence to win prizes even at Scripture. I have a clever cousin who for the last two years has won prizes for Scripture at his public school. The prizes take, as usual, the form of books, but the school being an enlightened one, the prize-winner is allowed to choose his books for himself. My cousin, an atheist and a communist, who holds outrageous opinions on all subjects, chooses the works of Shaw and Wells, Karl Marx, James Joyce and D. H. Lawrence, and has now by dint of his expertness in Scripture obtained a fairly complete set of the works of these writers elaborately bound in morocco leather, embellished with the school crest, and duly inscribed in the handwriting of a bishop, who, I suppose, must have signed 'blind'. The books in their strange bindings are altogether a remarkable sight. Looking at them one wonders whether bishops were ever so perverted from their proper uses.

Now this is something like! If the study of Scripture is to make available for poor boys the best literature of our time, then by all means let Scripture be studied. But in my day it was not so, and the prizes I won were as dull as the works that I had mastered to win them. It may be doubted, moreover, if the study of Scripture is usually commended for this reason.

How I Began

This completes the survey of my public-school education, a monument of wasted activity, devoted to ends that were neither useful nor beautiful.

Balliol. It is impossible to exaggerate the change from the intellectual climate of a public school to that of a university; its effect upon me was like that of transferring a delicate plant from an exposed position in an east wind to a shelf in a conservatory. The conservatory was admirably situated, and in the bracing but genial air of the best of colleges I underwent a process of rapid and continuous intellectual expansion.

Balliol is the only institution with which I have been connected for which I have an affection, an affection founded on admiration and kept alive by gratitude. Balliol achieved the supremely difficult task of securing liberty without licence and order without discipline. It was the first, and, I think, the last, completely tolerant society which I have encountered. Men of many different types and interests went their way and did what they pleased, nor was any man the worse for the pleasures of others. My way lay chiefly along the paths of intellect. I worked hard and achieved a first, the fruit of a real liking for history and philosophy. I shall never forget the thrill with which I first read *Plato's Republic*; it introduced me to a fundamentally congenial world. Reading for Greats I found for the first time that work could be a pleasure, and acknowledged a motive other than that of the desire to do better than my fellows as a stimulus to effort.

But side by side with the interest in philosophy, and for a time transcending it, there was a growing interest in politics. I had discovered the existence of contemporary society; I knew what its problems were, and knew too, or thought I did, where their solution was to be found. In those four years at Oxford I became an ardent Socialist.

I do not know how it may be at the Universities to-day—

How I Began

I rather gather that they are swept by alternate waves of æstheticism and science—but in my time politics was the thing that mattered. Politics was in the air, and it was difficult to escape the contagion. The Fabian Society was in its hey-day, and most men at Oxford with any pretensions to be thought advanced were members of it. Complete with statistics we confounded Liberals and Tories in debate, read papers on State management, wrote articles on 'workers' control', and introduced socialist theories into academic essays. The years 1910–14 were years of great industrial unrest; even in Oxford there were strikes, and at strikers' meetings we had our first taste of the joys of political oratory. I remember being fined for leading a procession of Oxford tram strikers to the Martyrs' Memorial where I addressed them in a revolutionary speech of blood, fire and thunder. Then, as always, public speaking went to my head. The spectacle of an audience helpless before you, the knowledge that for the time it is a passive receptacle to be filled with the content of your ideas, the feeling that you can make it thrill to the sound of your voice, vibrate in sympathy with your every mood, these things were, and to me they still are, the closest approximation to the sense of power that I have ever experienced. In my youth they intoxicated me. I spoke in season and out of season at College debating societies, took a pride in being the licensed buffoon of the Oxford Union, and practised the arts of orgiastic demagogy at meetings of discontented workers.

I also at this time helped to run a club for errand boys in the Oxford slums. I had not yet extricated myself from the toils of the sentimental Christianity which had wound themselves about my feet at my Confirmation. My emancipation did not come until my third year at Oxford; meanwhile I thought it my duty to turn working-class boys into Christian prigs and imitation middle-class snobs and held revivalist meetings in working-class

How I Began

streets on a Sunday afternoon. My religion was a very drastic kind. Either, I held, you must take the Bible literally or not at all. I took it literally, insisted on the reality of Hell and preached terrifying sermons about unbaptized babies frying in their own blood. I also attended on Sunday evenings a small chapel near the Union where I went into ecstasies over converted Kaffir boys. Looking back over my intellectual vagaries, there is none for which I feel more disposed to blush.

Socialism. But, as I have said, the dominating interest of my University career, an interest which has largely shaped my subsequent outlook on life, was Socialism. And my Socialism was by no means the mere undergraduate pose which what I have said hitherto may have suggested. Admittedly I and my Socialist contemporaries talked a good deal of inflated nonsense; admittedly we played with theories as a child plays with toys from sheer intellectual exuberance. But we also did a considerable amount of hard thinking.

Like most of my contemporaries I am accustomed to think of my generation—I am forty—as one of iconoclasm and revolt. We grew up in a world still littered with the lay figures of Victorian morality; delightedly we punctured them, and out came some sawdust and a little bran. Shaw and Wells, the gods of my generation, were like men opening the windows of a rather stuffy room, letting in air and light and laughter, and those of us who as young men tried humbly to follow in their wake, thought of ourselves as tremendous iconoclasts breaking down the false idols of Victorian prudery and convention and respectability. And that our revolt might not be deemed a purely academic affair, we did a little defiant free loving—strictly on principle, of course—shocked our elders and gained our latch-keys. And the fact that the forces of the times were with us gave us a supreme self-confidence. As a consequence we were vigorous, cheerful and energetic. We were neither morbid nor introspective; we were more interested in the outside world than in ourselves, more anxious for the reform of society than for the salvation of our own souls. Some of us looked forward to leading what in our wilder moments we conceived to be Socialist revolution. We were ridiculously optimistic no doubt, but, looking back upon our activities and our hopes, I am surprised and a little pained to find ourselves regarded by the contemporary young as a generation of simple-minded rather credulous young men, so simple-minded and so credulous as to belong to what, in the eyes of the moderns, amounts practically to an age of faith.

In all this activity our leader was G. D. H. Cole. He had recently published *The World of Labour*, the first book of its kind on the subject, which speedily became a standard work. Cole's Socialism in those days—for all I know, it has been so ever since—was what it is customary to call Left Wing. Already he was finding the Fabian Society timid and slow; soon he was to break away from it and become, with S. G. Hobson, the joint originator of Guild Socialism. Meanwhile he advocated a new militancy in labour disputes, urged that workers should strike in and out of season, if only because of the salutary training and the added class consciousness that came of striking, and became the protagonist of what was called 'The New' or 'The Industrial Unionism'. The distinctive feature of The New Unionism was its tendency to regard strikes not merely as devices for raising wages or shortening hours, but as levers to undermine capitalist society. When the undermining process was sufficiently advanced, the last and greatest strike would effect its downfall.

Of these more ambitious projects I was only a luke-warm supporter. I was ardent enough as a Socialist, but I was an orthodox Socialist, drinking the pure milk of the Fabian doctrine on which I had been nourished.

How I Began

Shaw. My reluctance to follow Cole out of the Fabian fold was, I think, largely due to the influence of Shaw. I read his plays together with the novels of H. G. Wells during the summer vacation of my first year. I had joined a reading party at a small island off the coast of Brittany, where I encountered for the first time contemporary literature. Literature in those days was a very exciting business. The sociological novel was in its heyday. Writers dilated upon the sores in the body public and employed their talents to produce in their readers a sense of sin in relation to the social anomalies for which they were, so they were assured, collectively responsible. The novels of Galsworthy and Wells and in a lesser degree of Bennett not only opened up for me a new world; they imbued me with a passionate desire to soften the heart and to sharpen the brains of society. Nor was this preoccupation with social questions an eccentricity on the part of a few novelists; all the literature that mattered was concerned with the same theme.

The theatre, for example, had become an arena for the discussion of social problems and the presentation of social abuses. A score of first-rate plays, Galsworthy's *Strife*, *Justice*, and *The Silver Box*, Granville Barker's *The Madras House*, Stanley Houghton's *Hindle Wakes*, and the plays of Zangwill, not to mention Shaw, enabled the drama to make a serious contribution to contemporary thought, and, in becoming serious, the theatre was at the same time infinitely more amusing than it has ever been since.

The effect of all this ferment upon my mind was tremendous. The impact of Shaw and Wells in particular gave my system a shock from which I have never recovered. Shaw, and in a lesser degree Wells, came so to dominate my mind, that they may be said to have formed it. And what they made it, that with unimportant modifications it has been ever since.

Shaw became for me a kind of god. I considered that

he was not only the greatest English writer of his time (I still think that), but the greatest English writer of all time (and I am not sure that I don't still think that too). Performances of his plays put me almost beside myself with intellectual excitement. I remember that I had to leave the theatre the first time I saw *Fanny's First Play*—I was too excited to sit still in my seat—and, when I first met him in the flesh at a luncheon party at Oxford given by Sir Gilbert Murray, I felt like a third-rate curate meeting an incarnation of his deity. I trembled at the knees, sweated at the palm, and my tongue was so dry that I could not speak.

As the influence of Shaw was chiefly responsible for my becoming what it is customary to call an 'intellectual', I shall try to indicate what the main factors in that influence were. I do not mean that I am going to enumerate the main points of Shaw's teaching—it is conceivable that he might repudiate much of what I shall say—I want to describe only what chiefly came home to me. As he would put it himself, what I got from him was the nearest thing to his doctrine of which my mind and temperament were capable.

In the first place, there was a view of modern society as essentially inequitable. It was a society in which the wealth and luxury of the few outraged the poverty and misery of the many from whom it was derived. The government was in the hands of a small privileged class which legislated in such a way as to perpetuate the anomalies on which it throve, and so-called social reforms were mere sops to take the revolutionary edge off the worker's discontent, concessions, the least possible, deliberately made by the governing classes as an assurance and a guarantee of their continued tenure of power. The main ground for objecting to this state of affairs was not so much emotional as rational; it was unjust, but it was more than unjust; it was foolish. It was foolish of society to organize its affairs on this basis, when by dint of a little hard thinking it could organize them much more to the satisfaction of its members on some other basis, and it was particularly foolish of the workers to put up with a state of affairs which it only required a little unity and determination to remove. Why, then, did they not achieve the necessary unity, and display the necessary determination? Partly because their movement was rent with jealousy and dissension; even more because they were not sensitive enough to feel the degradation of their position, class conscious enough to conceive a policy of class abolition, or far-sighted enough to plan the various stages of its evolution, had they conceived it.

Intellectual Priggishness. In the second place, there was born in me a contempt for the ordinary man, for his stupidity in thought and timidity in action, his inability to look beyond the end of his intellectual nose, his incapacity to be swayed by anything but the stomach and pocket view of life. Compared with the self-conscious intellectual he was, I considered, little better than an animal. I was a Socialist, I maintained, not because I admired and liked the working-classes, but because I despised and disliked them; and it was the strength of my contempt and dislike which impelled me to make the efforts necessary to change them. I was a democrat not because I thought people were fitted to vote, but because it was only through their possession of the right to vote that I conceived they would in time become fit to exercise their right.

This intellectual arrogance conceived in the sphere of politics presently extended to that of personal relations. To a young mind nourished in the intellectual atmosphere of Balliol, enriched by three years of philosophy and sharpened and stimulated by Shaw, the conversation of ordinary people could not but seem intolerably boring and silly. And not only their conversation but their pursuits. The men spent their time hitting small round bits of matter with long thin ones in the shape of cues, bats, rackets, golf clubs, croquet mallets or polo sticks; the women in talking self-importantly about themselves and maliciously about one another. Also they were, I considered, far too interested in the methods of satisfying the duller appetites of the flesh, interested, that is to say, in food and drink. (As opposed to food and drink I considered sex to be one of the exciting appetites of the flesh.) I doubt whether middle-aged and elderly people realize how intolerable their preoccupation with eating and drinking often seems to the young. They rarely read books and never remembered or talked about what they read. . . .

I conceived myself to be a different and altogether superior creature; different in interests, superior in tastes, and developed an attitude of intellectual detachment and aloofness which, considerably modified, has persisted ever since. I came to believe that what most people said and felt and thought must almost certainly be wrong, and, except in regard to games and food, I have seen little reason to change this opinion. I no longer believe that I am superior to the great mass of my fellow human beings merely because I am intelligent, although I still hold that the world would be a happier and a better place if most human beings were more like me than they are.

Thirdly, Shaw gave me a passion for ideas, or rather he evoked a passion which had existed independently and justified it. Not only did I think the life of the mind the best kind of life, but I thought that a person's mind, more particularly the reasoning part of his mind, was the most important thing about him, more important than either his character or his conduct. And because of this belief in the importance of mind I placed a trust in the efficacy of ratiocinative processes expressed in argument and advocacy as methods of influencing other minds, which, I am afraid, subsequent experience has done little to justify.

Psycho-analysis with its insistence on hidden prejudices and resistances not discernible in consciousness as yet lay dormant in the mind of Freud, and, innocent of psychology, I really believed that people could be persuaded by reason, and that, if you argued skilfully enough in defence of true propositions and were sufficiently patient, you could convince them that the propositions for which you were arguing were true. What was more, I believed that, once convinced of their truth, they would act accordingly, that is to say differently from the way in which they would have acted, if they had not been reached by your arguments. If one failed to persuade, it was because one had not reasoned cogently or persuasively enough, not because of any inefficacy on the part of reason as such, or any inability on that of one's audience to be influenced by reason. Thus I believed that, if the reasons advanced on its behalf were good enough, people would in due course be led to embrace Socialism, and the world would in consequence become a better place.

Personal Relations. Conceiving my main purpose in life to be the influencing of people's minds in the direction of my own opinions, of making, in other words, converts to Socialism and general enlightenment, I paid little attention to people in themselves. 'Personal relations' says Mr. E. M. Forster in *Howard's End* 'are the real life for ever and ever.' I have a particular admiration for Mr. Forster, and in general am strongly predisposed to credit any statement he makes, but I cannot say that I have found them so. Being intelligent, lively and not unamusing, I made plenty of friends even if I also made plenty of enemies; but I cannot say that at this time I placed much value upon friendship, or took trouble to cultivate my friends or to keep them. Many men of my acquaintance are exquisitely

sensitive in this matter of personal contacts. They cultivate a relationship as a gardener will cultivate a hot-house
plant, and are continually pulling it up to see how it is
getting on. My general view was, and still with modifications is, that this is all very well for women and for men
who have nothing better to do. But, for myself, it has
always seemed that there is too much work waiting to be
done in the world by thought and action and word, to
justify a man in wasting overmuch time in personal relations. The personal contacts I wished for were with those
who shared my objects and were engaged with me in their
pursuit. And I have always found that the companion-
ship that comes most freely and easily and that ripens
most naturally and pleasantly into friendship, is that of
people who are thrown together as a result of their par-
ticipation in some common undertaking, and do not seek
one another's company for its own sake. Friendship, like
other valuable things, is a by-product; it springs up between those whose interests and enthusiasms are centred
upon something else, and, the more hazardous the undertaking, the keener the friendship.

The best way to make friends is not to have leisure
enough to wonder whether those with whom you are
thrown into contact care about you or not. My own
friendships have been mainly formed with those engaged
in socially doubtful and forlorn causes, in Socialism, in
rationalist propaganda, or in the advocacy of an unpopular
Pacifism during the war. I have justified myself for the
somewhat casual attitude to my fellows implied by this
view of them with the reflection that, in devoting my interests and energies not to personal relations but to the
improvement of society in the sphere of action and the
advancement of new ideas in that of thought, I was at
least placing my happiness in something distant, definite
and durable, rather than upon what was near, fluctuating
and unstable. Thus progress in realization was always

possible, while the pleasure of pursuit could never be cut short by attainment. Thus, although I am exceedingly attached to a few people, I have always thought of my fellow human beings as necessary adjuncts to the good life, rather than as its main constituents, as means rather than as ends.

Whether as cause or result of this attitude I do not know, I was, and still to some extent am, psychologically very obtuse. Insensitive to a psychological atmosphere, I rarely knew or even cared to know what others were thinking or feeling, and, as a consequence, made gross mistakes in my estimate not only of people's character, but of their attitude to myself, frequently continuing to regard as my friends persons who felt for me nothing but contempt and dislike. This comparative indifference to the feelings and sentiments of others has incidentally gained me an undeserved reputation for magnanimity. My tendency to forget injuries and to forgive slights has been ascribed to generosity of spirit, when, in fact, I have not cared sufficiently to deserve other people's good opinion or to avoid their bad, to think it worth my while to nourish personal animosities or to maintain continuing feuds. I really do forget how rude Mrs. X has been to me, which, I suppose, must be very insulting to Mrs. X. Even if I remember, I no longer feel an animosity which Mrs. X hardly seems important enough to deserve.

Feminism. As my views in general were derived from books rather than from life, so in particular and inevitably were my views of women. I conceived myself to have learnt from my reading that women were the equals of men, denied their proper place in society by the same selfishness embodied in vested interests as impeded the realization of Socialism. Those were the days of the agitation for women's suffrage, which was culminating in attacks upon property and the harassing of eminent persons.

How I Began

I joined the Men's Political Union for Women's Enfranchisement, hobnobbed with emancipated feminists who smoked cigarettes on principle, drank Russian tea and talked with an assured and deliberate frankness of sex and of their own sex experiences, and won my spurs for the movement by breaking windows in Oxford Street for which I spent one night in custody. But perhaps the most vivid memory of these feminist experiences is that of courting surreptitiously the daughter of an Oxford landlady, prevailing upon her, after immense difficulty, to come with me to Brighton for the week-end, planning the necessary arrangements with the most elaborate secrecy, concocting an ingenious alibi to enable her to explain her absence to her mother, and then finding the mother at the railway station to see me off, where I duly received her blessing for my enterprise in assisting to emancipate women from the shackles of convention.

I only mention this simple-minded advocacy of feminism as an extreme example of the academic rationalism which in these days characterized my opinions. I had had, it should be noted, practically no experience of women; I did not in the least know what women were like. But my reason, countenanced and encouraged by Shaw, told me that their difference from men was limited to a difference in function touching the procreation of children, a difference which, I was assured, was not relevant to the performance of functions appertaining to the other departments of life. Politically, socially and intellectually women were the equals of men; this equality should, I thought, inform personal relations and receive explicit recognition from society. My reason, supported by Shaw, further assured me that there was no reason why I should abstain from sexual intercourse with a woman merely because we had not been through a preliminary ceremony in the shrine of an obsolete religion where an incantation had been pronounced over us by a priest; it also told me that

26

it was natural for me to desire to have sexual intercourse. Accordingly on strictly rational grounds, in pursuance of principle rather than of passion, I went away for a week-end with a woman I did not love, and, I suppose, on strictly rational grounds, although much to my embarrassment, her mother, as I have already explained, came to see us off.

The fourth important thing I got from Shaw was a style, a style of talking and also at one time of writing. The style of talking was dialectical, provocative, argumentative. To eke out my arguments and embellish my dialectic I kept rows of statistics in my head. When hard put to it I used to invent those that I could not remember; I also reproduced from memory many of Shaw's witticisms, thus tending to rely upon my imagination for my facts and my memory for my jokes.

The style of writing was intended to be moulded on that of Shaw's prefaces. Among other things I considered Shaw to be the greatest living writer of English prose; in fact I regarded Swift alone of all writers as his equal. The outstanding merit of Shaw's style is effectiveness of assertion; taking my cue from him I endeavoured, by vigorously asserting, to supply the place of the literary arts and graces of which I knew myself to be largely incapable. Poetry, for example, I could not read as a young man, and I have come to it slowly and much against the grain as a middle-aged one. As for writing it, I can honestly say that, alone among the intelligent young of my acquaintance, I have never committed a line of would-be serious verse to paper. I also tried to copy Shaw's immensely complicated interlocking sentences in which the device of stating what is in effect a series of separate assertions by means of relative clauses cunningly fitted into the structure of the sentence by dependence on a remote main verb, secures an implicit assent for propositions which, stated explicitly, would immediately be repudiated. I can well remember writing a letter to my father from France asking for more pocket-money, on the ground that a fisher-boy had stolen the loose cash out of my trouser pocket when I was bathing. The incident occurred during the height of my Shaw period and was described in the language of a Shaw preface, with the result that I received by return of post a new pair of trousers in the belief that I had lent mine to the hotel proprietor who had burnt a hole in them!

Finally, I obtained from Shaw the germs of my subsequent philosophy. This is a form of Vitalism based on the ideas which, originating in Samuel Butler's special brand of Lamarckianism, were later developed as the doctrine of creative evolution in *Back to Methuselah*. This book is, however, not concerned with philosophy, and I shall not attempt to state these ideas here.

Zeal for Opinions. Looking back upon myself as I was at that time, I see a young man witty, argumentative, provocative, exasperatingly rational and professionally zealous for the public good. My public zeal expressed itself in an enthusiasm for advanced creeds and causes of all kinds. I was not only a Socialist, I was a humanitarian, a suffragist, a pacifist, even for a short time a vegetarian. I see myself fraternizing somewhat unsuccessfully with working-men, and spending week-ends with bearded clerks who wore sandals and knickerbockers and lived on green food at Letchworth, nibbling it delicately like rabbits with their front teeth. Whenever some social disturbance occurred—and they occurred fairly frequently from 1910 to 14—I hailed it joyfully as a portent of the coming revolution. Whenever I could, I took part in it. In addition to my championship of the Oxford tramway-men, I went to and fro from Chipping Norton daily for several days to address meetings on behalf of the wood-workers who were striking against the intolerably low wages which

in 1913 were paid to workers in comparatively unorgan-
ized trades. I particularly remember the Chipping Norton
strike from the fact that the first day on which I was
asked to speak was also the occasion of that visit of Shaw
to Oxford to which I have already referred. Shaw was to
lecture in the Examination Schools on the origin of the
drama, and all Oxford was there to hear him. I have
never known the Schools so crowded; never, indeed,
either before or since have I seen so many people gathered
to hear a lecture. I stood on tiptoe at the back of the hall
to get my first glimpse of the great man, and when
punctual to the minute amid tumultuous cheering his
spare figure appeared walking briskly up the aisle, I
thrilled with an excitement that I can remember to this
day. But why was I at the back? Because I had to leave
in the middle of the lecture to catch the train to Chipping
Norton to address a mass meeting of the strikers. The
occasion has remained memorable because it enabled me
to represent to myself the conflict between public duty
and private inclination in its most vivid colours. I wanted
to stay and hear Shaw; I ought to go and help the strikers.
It was only by dint of asking myself what Shaw himself
would have done in the circumstances that I eventually
managed to secure a victory for public duty.

But although vaguely excited by the prevalent industrial
unrest, stimulated by the growth of Labour, interested in
anything and everything that could be conceived to bear,
however remotely, upon Socialism, I maintained an
attitude of aloof indifference to foreign politics, an indifference which was to stand me in good stead when the
war came. Patriotism filled me then—it has done so ever
since—with a kind of puzzled distaste. Why, I used to
ask, should people be required to love a country which
condemned them to live penned together like sheep in
overcrowded tenements, which stunted their bodies and
starved their minds, offering them as a substitute for the

fully developed life which a citizen of an enlightened modern community had a right to expect, a choice between idleness and starvation on the one hand and a bare existence in return for nine or ten hours' boring drudgery on the other? Why should they be expected to defend it, until they had a stake in it worth defending; why, indeed, sacrifice to it anything at all until they had first got something out of it to justify the sacrifice? And under Capitalism, I argued, they never had or could get anything out of it. The real struggle for me was the struggle between Capital and Labour; all others were artificial, and seemed only to disguise the real fact of the situation, the fact of class war.

Now I do not want to suggest that these opinions of mine were not seriously held. On the contrary, they constituted at that time the main body of my intellectual convictions and oriented my outlook on society. Ambition and desire to excel I had in abundance, but zeal for what I believed to be the good of society was a perfectly real and quite distinct motive for action. I wanted to go into politics because I believed that by politics the world could be made better. Yet looking back I can now see that my zeal was at that time mainly a zeal for certain speculative opinions. It was felt for the results of certain academic exercises, rather than for oppressed and struggling humanity; it sprang rather from the pride of the intellect than from the sympathy of the heart. It is interesting, perhaps a little saddening, to realize in middle age that, while my capacity for sympathy has widened, so that I now feel imaginatively the ills of mankind and feel them intensely, my zeal for their alleviation has correspondingly diminished. I no longer desire so continuously as I did to help my fellows, although I realize more vividly that they suffer. But perhaps it is not my zeal for betterment that has diminished, so much as my confidence in my ability to effect it. The world is not for me so simple as it was,

nor do I now regard an inevitable Socialism as a panacea
for all ills.

Being Disliked. I had not yet learned to control my
intellectual combativeness, and my constant display of
it in support of provocative opinions was apt to get me
heartily disliked. I was good at argument and took pleasure in the exercise of my skill, delighting to produce
reasonable arguments in support of what were thought to
be outrageous opinions. Unable to resist the arguments,
people revolted in horror from the opinions, and were apt
to vent upon me the dislike which was the inevitable
result of their intellectual discomfiture.

Thus I was at one time a warm adherent of Egoistic
Hedonism, and firmly believed that all human actions were
prompted by the desire to obtain pleasure for their agents.
With cheerful iconoclasm I went to and fro among my
acquaintances proving to them that unselfishness was
only a hypocritical form of selfishness, religion far-sighted
prudence, respectability the habit of being intimidated by
threats which society considered honourable, martyrdom
pig-headed obstinacy, self-denial masochism, and morality
in general a rationalization of the impulse to blame.

Everybody, I was fond of pointing out, did what he
wanted to do most; if he did not want to do it most, he would
not do it. Some of us, however, were so constituted that
we got more pleasure out of pleasing other people than
by directly pleasing ourselves. Hence, for those of us who
were thus fortunately disposed, doing what one wanted
to do most automatically involved giving pleasure to
others. Such conduct was naturally applauded by society,
which did its best to encourage it by dignifying it with
the names of the moral virtues. It was none the less
selfish, as selfish in fact, neither more so nor less, as
all conduct. Take, for example, courage. Everybody, I
pointed out, had a natural instinct to flinch from the

mouth of a machine-gun raining bullets; the fact that men
nevertheless, conquered their fear and faced the gun wa;
due to the influence of a greater fear. Society, in fact, hac
contrived to make men more afraid of their own con
sciences, the contempt of their fellows, and the shame o
letting their comrades down, not to speak of the fear of ;
court-martial in the background, than of the bullets o;
the machine-gun, with the result that soldiers on th
whole preferred to face the bullets. But it was significan
that Society always took care to reinforce these moral anc
spiritual fears with a more tangible one in the shape o
discipline. Discipline was simply a device for substituting
the certainty of being shot if you did not go over the to]
for the probability of being shot if you did. The ordinary
man, preferring the risk to the certainty, went over th
top and was called brave; but he was nevertheless impellec
by fear just as surely as the coward. As for those whe
went to the stake for their opinions, martyrs, I pointec
out, were notoriously pig-headed people with a strong
sense of histrionic display; they gloried in the centre o
the stage and were prepared to pay for the honour. Bu
the price was not as heavy as it seemed, for most martyr
were convinced that fifteen minutes' torment in an earthl
fire was the only way of avoiding an eternity of tormen
in an infernal one. If you have got to be burned anyhow
the shorter the burning the better. Hence the martyr
like every one else, was merely aiming at his own greates
pleasure, or rather at avoiding his own greatest suffering
And so on, and so on. . . .

You see the sort of thing; and you can see, too, how i
was calculated to annoy, especially when presented witl
a good deal of vivacity tricked out in imagery and spicec
with wit. At that time I regarded any conversation o;
even the most trivial topic as a diving-board from whicl
to plunge into the sea of controversy. Perpetually going
off the argumentative deep end, I was as perpetuall

irritating, and acquired the reputation of being rather a dreadful young man.

There are some men to whom the world gives prizes without asking, men eligible and electable, who never offend anybody and who get put on things, committees, governing bodies and so forth, as a reward, I suppose, for their inoffensiveness. There is no post in the country which a man cannot hold if he can only hold his tongue. I have never been the sort of man to whom the world gives anything away. Nobody has ever shown a disposition to elect me to committees or wished to appoint me to positions of emolument and power. People always prefer the rabbits, rabbits being so much safer. Accordingly I have had to work for and to take whatever I have managed to get, and at this time I was first being schooled in the necessity of 'taking' what the world did not freely give.

This 'taking', by the way, was the source of most of my 'wit'. I am occasionally witty, but not so often as I would like to be, and I have been accustomed to make good the deficiency by remembering the wit of others. I defended myself by pointing out that appropriate remarks are meant to be appropriated, and that originality is little more than skill in concealing origins.

Fortified with these aphorisms I came in conversation to rely upon my memory for epigrams as habitually as I relied upon my inventiveness for my facts. To assist my memory I kept an 'epigram' book in which I recorded for future use the better remarks of authors and friends. To make a good remark seemed to me in those days to be almost the most important thing a man could do, so important that I subsequently wrote two books of alleged fiction, a novel and a book of short stories, to see how many 'good remarks' I could fit into them. The method was simple enough; I would take a sheet of writing-paper, write an epigram somewhere in the middle, and then introduce comment in the form of explanatory matter to string the epigrams together. Thus my essays in creative literature were neither the fruits of inspiration nor the product of observation. They were dictated largely by the necessity of making a number of different epigrams relevant. The result was exceedingly brilliant but had little relation to literature. The novel, however, which was in part autobiographical, was spiced with an element of malicious reminiscence of eminent persons which gave it a certain *succès de scandale*. At the height of the novel's success, such as it was, a kind friend circulated among my acquaintances an annotated copy, in which all the 'appropriate remarks' were underlined in red ink, and notes inserted in the margin indicating their origin and authorship.

Belief in Reason. In all this intellectual posturing and exhibitionism, there was, I still maintain, an element that was rather fine. This element I want to emphasize, because it is less common to-day than it was, and I believe that its comparative rarity in the modern world is a source of danger.

I really believed and cared for the things of the mind. I was rational myself, or tried to be, and, as I have already said, I believed that other people were rational too in the sense that you had only to make them see that an opinion had reason in its favour to cause them to embrace it. In this respect my outlook on life was thoroughly Victorian. So great was my reliance on the influence of reason over the minds of men whenever it was allowed to reach them, that I considered that people had only to be given access to all sorts of opinions for the truth to be perceived. Hence education, liberty of thought and freedom for discussion, were in my view sufficient in themselves to produce an improvement in the state of the world, and, if long enough maintained and sufficiently widespread, ultimately capable of introducing a millennium in human affairs.

How I Began

Hence, what I principally set myself to do was to alter people's opinions, seeking to cause them to believe in accordance with the evidence, and to realize things as they were. And to effect this result the instrument of rational argument addressed to the formation of opinion was, in my view, adequate.

This, as I say, was the nineteenth-century view of reason; emphatically it is not the twentieth. To-day reason is regarded as a feeble shoot springing from a deep and insecure foundation of instinctive tendencies and unconscious strivings. Reason so conceived is not free; it is dominated by the trends of the unconscious, whose expression it is, and its operations are determined by the necessity of arriving at conclusions which are congenial to its master. Thus reason is in the twentieth-century view a mere tool of the unconscious; its function is to justify its desires and to rationalize its beliefs.

Many people have, it is obvious, brought their reasons to a great pitch of perfection in this respect. They will never admit that they do anything because they want to do it; nor is it only other people whom they deceive as to their motives.

This question of the freedom and function of reason seems to me to raise important issues, and to have a considerable practical relevance. To a consideration of these issues and of their bearing in the modern world, I shall devote three later chapters. For the present I content myself with saying that I am an unrepentant rationalist. I do not, myself, subscribe to the modern view of the subservience of reason, and it is because I do not that I call myself an intellectual. I still hold the view—although I realize how much harder it is to hold than it was twenty years ago—that reason can on occasion function freely, issuing in action which is resolved upon because on a calm and *reasoned* survey of all the circumstances, it is seen to be the best thing to do in those circumstances,

and forming conclusions which are reached as the result
of an impartial and *reasoned* survey of all the available
evidence. It is because I believe these things, because,
further, I believe that it is in the spread of reasoning of
this type and an increase in the number of rationalists,
that the chief hope of the world lies, that I call myself
an unrepentant rationalist. I do not, however, wish
to minimize the importance of instinct and unconscious desire in influencing reason, and I am quite
prepared to admit the extent to which as an intellectually
arrogant, argumentative young man, believing that you
had only to convince men's reasons to alter their beliefs, I
did minimize it.

I can remember, for example, an argument which in
the interests of Shavian Socialism I used to address to
young married women, with a view to persuading them
that their children ought to be brought up by the State.
The argument was a perfectly reasonable one: if you want
to build a bridge or a town hall, you don't, I would
put it to them, pick up a chance collection of persons out
of the street and ask them to undertake the job. You call
in an expert engineer and an expert architect. But if you
want to build what is after all more important than a
bridge or a town hall, a modern citizen, you leave the
job to any chance couple of persons who are able to
produce one. Now any pair of persons, provided they
be of opposite sexes, are capable of producing a citizen—
the job is, indeed, all too fatally easy—but the ability to
produce does not connote an ability to educate, to build
up a character, to guide an intellect, to develop a personality. Very much the contrary! And it is just because we
leave the task of making citizens to chance couples of
ignorant women and average men instead of entrusting
the job to experts, that our bridges are so much better
than our citizens, and we ourselves are on the whole the
grubby, unworthy, ill-shaped, ill-mannered and meagre-

minded lot that you see around you. The argument, I repeat, was perfectly reasonable; I, at least, have never heard it adequately countered; yet it never seemed to carry conviction. Irritation and resentment at the immorality of the suggestion, yes; but conviction, no. Now I could never understand this; I could not then—I cannot even now—take it for granted that people's convictions should not be formed by their reasons, but that their reasons should follow their likings as the feet of a hungry dog follow its nose; and I could not take it for granted, because I failed to understand the resistance which our unconscious natures put up to any conclusions which threaten their interests or antagonize their desires. But because I realize that as a young man I grossly underestimated people's rationality, it does not follow that, like so many moderns, I now deny it. I content myself with affirming that reason can on occasion win free of distorting influences and function independently, and that it is only in so far as it does do so that man can be called a reasonable being.

Nature of Book. But this, I see, is a lie. Not only do I not content myself; I seek perpetually to protest against the floods of unreason which, since the war, have overwhelmed the world. Of this protest the present book is an expression. I have tried to show in later chapters how some of the ills from which we admittedly suffer are due to insufficient rationality. Man, I hold, is not wicked, but he is stupid. I should define him as a reasonable being who spends most of his time in protesting against the dictates of reason. Nevertheless he is reasonable, and being so he can sometimes be made to see things as they are. So to see them is admittedly unpopular; for it is impossible so to see them without finding oneself at loggerheads with most of one's fellows, voicing an impotent protest against the catchwords and movements of the time. One is, for example, a 'highbrow'; one is a Socialist; one is a Pacifist. I confess to being all three; and it is as an unrepentant highbrow, proud of my 'highbrowism' and convinced that in the increase of this despised characteristic lies man's chief hope for the future, that I have written this autobiography of highbrow tastes and ideas.

But before I come to them I must supplement this account of how I began with a description of how I have developed and what I have become. This brings me to the influence of the war, and, following it, to that spread of irrationalism in the modern world to which I have already referred, topics which demand separate chapters to themselves.

CHAPTER II

How I have Developed
Food and Women

Pre and Post-war Generations. I have described as best I can the influences which went to my making. At twenty-three, when I came to London to take a post in the Civil Service, I was a fairly efficient reasoning machine, with many enthusiasms but no judgment, a good head and a poor heart. My mind, formed as I have recounted by Shaw and Wells, entertained emancipated views on sex and advanced views on politics. I was, in fact, an 'intellectual' in every sense of the word, which meant that I was hopelessly out of touch with the aims and interests of the great mass of my fellows. Inevitably I laid this remoteness to their charge rather than to mine, and salved my self-respect by despising as a herd the genial throng of ordinary folk I seemed unable to enter. What I was at the age of twenty-five, that I still very largely am. People's minds do not, in my view, change appreciably after the early twenties. They do not, that is to say, readily incorporate new material; their mental activity consists rather in re-arranging, adapting to new conditions and in general making the most of the material which they already possess. The middle-aged mind does not grow; it merely organizes itself in the most effective way. Most middle-aged men are unaware of this and insist on parading their opinions upon issues which, having arisen since their own formative years, they are precluded from understanding. This is why the middle-aged merely bore the young whom they believe themselves to be enlightening out of the stores of their experience.

In the case of the present generation the war has made the gulf wider than usual. My mind is not only middle-aged; it is also pre-war, and, as such, out of touch with the minds of those who have come to maturity since the war. I can neither sympathize with post-war movements, nor subscribe to post-war literary and artistic reputations. Because I am aware of this deficiency and try to allow for it, I am regarded by contemporary young men and women as quite remarkably understanding and sympathetic. Nevertheless, I am poles asunder from them; I reprobate their conduct, pick holes in their thinking and share neither their admirations nor their dislikes. It has been my lot as a teacher of philosophy to make contact with the minds of a large assortment of the contemporary young, and I know that this is so. I would, therefore, ask the reader to bear the point in mind, should the presumption with which elsewhere in this book I pronounce upon modern developments seem to him intolerable.

My attitudes and opinions, preferences, prejudices, predilections and sympathies are, then, with certain modifications, much what they were when as a young man of twenty-three I came to London and proceeded to do my best to ignore the war. In this chapter and the next I propose to describe the modifications; they may be summed up under three heads, food, women and the war. The war will demand a chapter to itself.

Food

As a young man I took little account of food. It was not that I despised it as unspiritual, or regarded an appreciation of it as inconsistent with high endeavour. I simply had not had time to notice it. I ate what was put before me without paying much attention to what I ate. All I asked was that it should be enough in quantity. This attitude of indifference has ceased; to-day I regard food and drink as two of the major interests of life, and my meals are among the most important events of the day.

Lectured on Food. Looking back, I can date the change from a meal which I had with Mr. H. D. Harben in the autumn of 1914 and the homily which it provoked. H. D. Harben was a Socialist; he was rich, he was a gentleman, and he had a large place in the country. He was also an ardent suffragist. Suffragettes, let out of prison under the 'Cat and Mouse Act', used to go to Newlands to recuperate, before returning to prison for a fresh bout of torture. When the county called, as the county still did, it was embarrassed to find haggard-looking young women in dressing-gowns and djibbahs reclining on sofas in the Newlands drawing-room talking unashamedly about their prison experiences. This social clash of county and criminals at Newlands was an early example of the mixing of different social strata which the war was soon to make a familiar event in national life. At that time it was considered startling enough, and it required all the tact of Harben and his socially very competent wife to oil the wheels of tea-table intercourse, and to fill the embarrassed pauses which punctuated any attempt at conversation.

Harben took a fancy to me, regarding me as one of the coming young men in the Labour movement, and asked me one evening to dine with him in Town. The dinner was at Kettner's, where we sat at a table for two lit by a discreetly shaded red light, and a very good dinner it was. To me, however, all courses came alike. Uncompromisingly from the hors-d'œuvres to the savoury I discoursed.

How I have Developed

I talked of Socialism and the war, of women and books. I remember getting very excited over the question, whether anything, and if so what, would be lost in a journalistic paraphrase of a lyric of Shelley's. I also talked about the Minority Report of the Poor Law Commission. . . .

As I talked I forgot what I was eating, forgot, indeed, that I was eating at all, refused dishes that were offered to me with a gesture of annoyance at the interruption, and flicked cigarette-ash into my Chateau-Yquem. At the end of the meal H. D. H. asked me if I had enjoyed my dinner. I replied casually that I had enjoyed it very much and went on with the Minority Report. Then it was that my host, genial man that he was, turned and rated me, dubbing me savage and barbarian for my loutish, my criminal indifference to good food.

I forget the exact words he used, but their substance made a lasting impression upon me. 'My good young fool,' he said in effect 'give to this matter of food a little reflection. In the first place consider that you have four meals a day. On these meals you spend, or can spend with care, some three hours. Now let us suppose that your active waking day lasts for fifteen hours; then one-fifth of it will be spent in eating and drinking. Assume your length of life to be the average span of seventy years. Then you will spend in all some fourteen years continuously in shoving solid and liquid substances through an ugly little hole at the bottom of your face. What could be more bestial? What more absurd? Yet rightly treated, this bestiality can be transformed into an art, this absurdity into a source of solid satisfaction, one of the greatest that life has to offer. For man has contrived to make a grace of necessity and to found upon the satisfaction of a need the cultivation of an art. In this he chiefly shows his difference from the animals. And who are you, pray, to disregard the example of our ancestors, and in pride of intellect and dullness of spirit to neglect to cultivate this

42

art which the wisest of our race have had the wit to derive from the necessities of their bodies, this flower that blossoms on the dunghill of men's appetites? There are not so many pleasures upon which human beings can count that they can afford to neglect even one of them, still less one which is so reliable and so punctually re-current. One day you will learn this, unless of course you marry badly, or live in a boarding-house!'

English Food and French. H. D. H.'s arguments appealed to me on my most susceptible side; they appealed to my intellect. As an intelligent man I did not see how I could well ignore them. I did not ignore them, and now at the age of forty I have a pretty taste in food and quite a respectable one in clarets. I think, nevertheless, that it is questionable whether, in spite of what H. D. H. said, to cultivate a taste for food is the part of wisdom, at any rate in this country. A sensitive palate is more likely to be outraged than grati- fied. Travelling recently from Aberystwyth to London in the middle of the day and finding no dining-car on the train, I asked for a luncheon-basket. One was duly prepared for the price of 3*s*. 6*d*. Opening it I found that it contained two slices of fattish ham with a glaze on them, a slab of edible soap miscalled Cheddar which in most parts of England is the only cheese obtainable (this particular piece was mouldy and slightly furred in one corner), a tomato, three slices of bread (stale), two pats of butter and a juiceless orange! The example, I admit, is sensational—I have rarely if ever paid so much for such abominable fare—also it is not quite fair to England. It is only in Wales that the extreme depths of culinary barbarity are plumbed; yet English food, although not sensationally bad, is bad enough. England, indeed, stands to Wales in this matter of food almost in the same relation as that in which France stands to England. To point the contrast, the week before I had had lunch on a French train. Hors-d'œuvres there were, and then a kidney omelette of just that right consistency between liquid and solid which seems to elude even the best English cooks. Veal followed with salad and a purée of potatoes. Then a chocolate bombe, delectable delicacy, and a choice of four different kinds of cheese with fruit and coffee to round off the meal. The quality was no less admirable than the variety. But this, you will say, was a served luncheon, not justly to be compared with an *ad hoc* luncheon-basket. Passing by the significance of the fact that food in Wales is not thought sufficiently important to justify the provision of luncheon cars for long-distance travellers, I will now compare basket with basket. A few days before the French train lunch just recorded, I informed the hotel where I was staying that I wished to go on an all-day expedition and asked them to put me up some luncheon. They did. We unpacked a bewildering variety of comestibles arranged neatly in little parcels. First there were slices of sausages with crisp new bread and butter. The next thing we came upon was a long thin loaf. 'Why all this bread?' we asked ourselves. But the loaf was no loaf at all, but only a husk. It had, we found, been split down the middle, the inside was scooped out and there had been inserted a long, thin and wholly admirable ham omelette. There were slices of veal with salad in a little cardboard box; there were cakes, sardines, peaches and a bottle of white wine. And this was the ordinary picnic lunch of a hotel charging the equivalent of 5s. 10d. a day!

It is a great trouble to me, this business of food. I love England, and, were it not for the unparagoned brutality of its diet, would never leave it. As it is, I go to France at least once a year to feed. The visits are gastronomically memorable—there is, for example, a whole series of feeding places in Périgord of which I could speak. . . . Memorable also are the returns. The last time I was in

44

Food and Women

France I stayed at a little hotel in the Basque country, only a mile or two from the Spanish border. The cooking was admirable, and a point was made of consulting and, so far as possible, meeting the wishes of the guests. The cook, who was also the proprietor, would appear in the morning and discuss at length the details of lunch and dinner, soliciting suggestions with so expert an air that their acceptance seemed an honour, their rejection a rebuke. Trout was his speciality, and he was very earnest with us touching the different ways of preparing and cooking trout according to the season of the year and the precise local variety of the fish. Arrived in England we motored from Folkestone to London, and stopped for a meal at a fair-sized hotel at Ashford. The waiter, a depressed-looking individual, approached and I asked what was for lunch. The waiter seemed a little bewildered by the question, but finally said that there was soup. 'Soup?' said I. 'Yes! But what kind of soup?' The waiter looked more puzzled than ever. Presently he shrugged his shoulders and 'What kind of soup? Well, soup! Just soup,' he said. And 'just soup' it was. So with the fish. Again forgetting momentarily where we were, we asked for particulars of the fish to be supplied to us, and again the waiter replied, this time with a certain irritation, that the fish was 'Just fish', as if all fish were the same. And he was quite right. At that sort of hotel all fish is the same, a slab of utterly tasteless white solid floating in a colourless liquid. Whatever it is called, it all tastes alike, that is, it all fails to taste at all, and, whatever it is called, it is almost always cod.

I have never been able quite to fathom this English indifference to food. Sheer culinary incompetence lies, I suspect, at the bottom of it, an incompetence which finds in the traditional Puritanism of these islands a convenient excuse behind which to shelter itself. The English are adepts at making a merit of their deficiencies. The flesh

is sinful and should be mortified; too much attention to
things appertaining to the stomach argues, it is thought,
a neglect of those appertaining to the spirit. The flesh,
I repeat, is sinful and should be mortified; our cooks take
advantage of the injunction and mortify with a will. Now
I suggest that the aroma of virtuous self-discipline with
which the resultant assaults upon the stomach, the prunes,
the boiled puddings, the hashes and the chops are invested
is merely a cloak to hide our lack of culinary skill. I have
not noticed that English Puritanism requires us to outrage or to atrophy our other senses. Picture galleries are
not regarded with disfavour; on the contrary, they are
the legitimate prey of girls' schools. Yet what are pictures
but an open and shameless indulgence of the sense of
vision? The English again are notorious lovers of nature;
nor do they think that any excuse is necessary to justify
the deliberate and unashamed gratification of the sense of
hearing by the varied sounds of a concert. It is only the
palate which is discriminated against in this way; it is only
against the sense of taste that Puritanism vents its displea-
sure at the pleasures of the senses. But then we can paint
at a pinch, we can even compose music, or could once.
Hence we are under no necessity to prove to ourselves that
it is wicked to cultivate the arts of seeing and hearing. But
we cannot cook and the palate is censured accordingly.

Prodigy among English Cooks. Of course there are
exceptions. In these later years I have by God's grace
happened upon one of them, and through her beneficent ministrations I hope to go down in gastronomic
comfort to the grave. It is not only that she can cook,
that she has imagination and knows the virtues of
variety, that she can mix a salad like a French-woman
and make pastry like a traditional Yorkshire-woman,
though these things and many more like them are added
unto her. Nor is it merely her negative virtues, her

scorn for prunes and custard in all their forms, for moulds, for cold mutton, for tapioca and for rice, her failure to take the taste out of vegetables by boiling them in water, her refusal to regard lettuce and beetroot drowned in oil and vinegar as a salad, that entitle her to respect. It is in her complete understanding and mastery of all the adjuncts and incidental appurtenances of the culinary art that her greatest merit lies. Like all masters she delights in the exercise of her skill. She has the Frenchwoman's gift, a gift amounting almost to magic, of preparing an elaborate and varied meal out of nothing at all, and she does this with a speed and absence of fuss which are the admiration of all who are privileged to behold her. I have seen this prodigy among English women play tennis until six forty-five, enter at six fifty an apparently empty kitchen, and produce therefrom by seven fifteen a perfectly cooked meal of four courses for seven people. Incredible, you will say, or point out, if you are a grudging and envious woman, that the dinner had really been prepared in the morning, that the kitchen was not, in fact, empty at all, but was bursting with maturing food which, hidden away in saucepans and ovens was boiling and roasting and stewing and simmering away, and had been since twelve o'clock that morning. No doubt; I am sure that all my women readers know how the trick was done, and will be quite ready to prove to me that it was no trick at all. Agreed! But why, if they do know it, cannot they reproduce it themselves, instead of, after hours of preliminary grumbling and fussing, peevishly outraging their miserable tables with the tasteless muttons, the overdone beefs, the manufactured custards, the dank moulds, the brick pastries, the milk puddings and the enormous dingy company of stewed fruits week in and week out, until the overtaxed stomachs and congested guts of their unfortunate dependants rise in revolt and their owners pay in dyspepsia, chronic constipation, gastritis, colitis, or some one or other of the hundred ills that come from bad cooking and inappropriate feeding, the price of their wives' lazy contempt of the household arts?

Women

I see that I have come inadvertently to the subject of women, and this seems as good a place as any in which to describe the modifications which my attitude to them has undergone. Everything that it is possible for men to say about women has already been said much better than I can say it. I shall, therefore, be brief and as matter of fact as possible.

Early Theorizings. As a young man I was, as I have explained, a member of advanced movements. Prominent among them was the movement to secure the vote for women: and not only the vote, for the vote was regarded merely as a symbol of that feminine emancipation which was to be the great achievement of the age. Women were, it was held, by nature the equals of men; capable of playing their part in the world of affairs, in art, in politics, in industry and commerce, they demanded the right to do so. It was only tradition and circumstance that had kept them back. Alter the tradition, remove the circumstances, and the true capacities of women would become apparent. So ran the argument of the times and I subscribed to it heartily. Not only did I regard women as my intellectual equals, but believing their tastes, their interests, their emotions, their desires to be fundamentally the same as my own, I looked forward to marriage with a beautiful blue-stocking, at once soul mate, bed-sharer and thought-communicator, with whom I should spend an absorbed lifetime in the intellectual discussion of matters of abstract interest. That most women had neither talent nor taste for such a programme I was, I think, even then dimly

Food and Women

aware; but there must, I conceived, be some who even now could reach the level I required, intelligent among women even as I was intelligent among men, while potentially I held that most women were capable of the higher intellectual life. Educate women and give them a fair chance, and the world would, I believed, teem with females anxious and fitted to discuss with me the problems of abstract philosophy and millennial Socialism.

An element of irony was added to a situation already sufficiently absurd by my susceptibility to the physical charms of women, a susceptibility incapable at that time of being aroused without implicating in its excitement my emotions and my sentiments, which impelled me to invest a pretty face and a good figure with all the virtues of character and intellect. I had a penchant, moreover, for child wives and little baby faces. Intimidated by women of character and individuality, I was attracted by feature-less dolls, clean slates for the writing of whatever my instincts impelled me to inscribe. What I fell in love with was not a woman but the aura of fictitious qualities with which my sentimentality invested her. Thus I imagined myself to be penetrating the depths of woman's nature, when I was, in fact, discovering myself. Character in a woman, the hard core of an alien personality, impeded the process of self-projection, and threatened the satisfaction of an egoism, which in intercourse with another sought only the fulfilment of itself.

Hence the women to whom my instincts impelled me, were the antitheses of those of whom my reason, hag-ridden by feminist theories, approved. The head was at war with—to call it by a polite name—the heart, and their opposition afforded a pleasant field in which the Comic Spirit might disport itself. The Comic Spirit was not slow to take advantage of the opportunity. Of the ensuing adventures, of the ecstasies with which they began and the disillusion in which they ended, of the unsuspected

How I have Developed

violence of my instinctive self and the terrible humiliations to which it subjected my reasoning self, of the awful boredom, which, after the first transports were over, remains the outstanding memory of my affairs with women, I do not intend to write. Each of these affairs has followed a more or less uniform course, in which, having overcome every obstacle to make a lover's Paradise, I have ended by discovering only a wilderness of ennui. I have begun by behaving unforgiveably to everybody in order to achieve a *tête-à-tête*, and ended by behaving unforgiveably to the woman in order to end it. The recollections are humiliating to me and I have no reason to suppose that they will be diverting to others. I therefore omit them.

Later Discoveries. The effect of these encounters has been considerably to modify the views of women which I inherited from my feminist youth. I have not been able to avoid the conclusion that, in spite of the wide opportunities which the modern world offers to women for a fuller and more varied life than has hitherto been possible, it has made many of them singularly unhappy. I doubt, indeed, if the general level of instinctive happiness among women has often been lower. Whereas the human being who is performing reasonably useful work and is reasonably suited to his environment is contented unless he has some positive reason for discontent, the average woman, as I have met her, seems to be discontented unless she has some positive reason for contentment. She endeavours, therefore, to create positive reasons in the shape of amusements; and being unable to amuse herself, she hires other people to do her amusing for her. Hence arises a constant search for pleasure and excitement, a conception of entertainment as something for which one pays, and a vast expenditure of time and money in the endeavour to buy from others the happiness which no longer comes unsought. There is an immense industry in this country devoted

Food and Women

solely to the amusement of women. The film, the dress-maker, the theatre and the Church are its most important branches.

The theatre and the Church are institutions which are kept going almost entirely by women; they flock in crowds to matinées, chatter like magpies whenever they get the chance—for example, during overtures and *entr'actes*—come in late, leave early, and chink with their tea-cups all through the second act. They obtain emotions of a rather different order from the services of the Churches, where they talk less and look about them more. There is also a large and spreading growth of substitute religions, Theosophy, Spiritualism, Christian Science, and so forth, which appeal to those women who are said to think freely because they do not think at all. In the intervals of being entertained by films, theatres, Churches, parties, dances, golf or tennis, unemployed women of the middle class suffer intolerably from restlessness and boredom.

Women in the Home. There is a controversy perpetually revived in the cheaper Press on the question of whether women should go back to the home. What is not usually realized by participators in this controversy is that for the middle-class woman—and it is over the middle-class woman that the controversy rages—there is no home to go back to. A home may be defined as a centre of interest, activity and influence in which the housewife has traditionally per-formed important functions which demanded skill and merited respect. Growth of transport facilities, increase in mechanical and electrical appliances and the encroach-ments of the municipality have stripped the home of the majority of these functions and left of its manifold and varied duties only an automatic routine. The middle-class woman neither brews nor bakes; she does not wash; she has no skill in the making of conserves and regards cooking as on the whole a nuisance. To mitigate this nuisance she does not cook so much as warm up food that others have cooked for her; she does not prepare meals; she takes out of tins meals that are already prepared. She has no skill in shopping, but orders from the stores by telephone, or from the tradesman's van that calls at the door. She gets her gas from the gas company, her water from the municipality. Thus the once-varied duties of the home have dwindled into washing up, cleaning, sweeping and bed-making, a round of boring routine duties which the woman of average intelligence can perform in a couple of hours in the morning, leaving her with energies unused and interests unawakened to get through as best she may the great tracts of unoccupied time in the afternoon and early evening. As for children, she has one, at most two, and often none at all; and, when she can, she hires other people to look after them for her.

Women in the World. If she complains, and rightly, that such a life is no life at all and turns to the outside world for scope for her energies and employment for her faculties, she finds a curious position. In theory the barriers which man has erected against women are down; practically no occupation is now closed to her; she may enter where she will. In fact, however, the world persistently refuses to organize itself in such a way as to make room for her, or it makes room for her only at the bottom. It opens the doors of its offices and exhorts her to enter the professions; but it offers her dull and drudging work, and when by dint of sheer ability or gross conscientiousness she forces herself into the same positions as those held by men, pays her less for doing what they do. How often have I seen women of first-rate intelligence and some culture, replete with all the accomplishments which a University education can bestow, glad to take down the letters of illiterate boors, who cheerfully paid them three or four pounds a week for the privilege of ordering them about, pestering them with their attentions and picking their brains.

On the whole I cannot help thinking that there is some method in the world's churlishness. Women seem to me unsuited to the world of affairs. I do not mean that they cannot perform difficult and responsible tasks, and perform them well; but although they may perform them well, they do not perform them easily. Women in responsible posts are fussily and unnecessarily conscientious; there is a sense of strain, a creaking of machinery, and too often they achieve efficiency at the cost of losing not only their womanhood but their humanity. They never master a subject or a task sufficiently well to be at play with it, and one finds it difficult to resist the conclusion that they are condemning themselves to function in a medium other than that for which life intended them. Put them in positions of power and authority and they are intolerable. How well one knows them, those principals, head mistresses, women staff clerks, supervisors and manageresses, conscientious and bad-tempered, polite to superiors, rude to inferiors, maintaining a pedantic adhesion to the letter rather than to the spirit of rules, afraid to bend for fear they may break. They are unjust; they behave abominably to young women who are pretty; they are swayed by prejudices, given to favouritism, and inspire hatred in those who are unfortunate enough to be governed by them. For these vagaries sex starvation is, no doubt, partly to blame. In my view nobody should be put in a position of authority over his or her fellows who does not lead a normal and satisfied sex life. Those who are sexually starved almost inevitably find compensation for frustrated desires in the abuse of authority and the tyrannical exercise of power. They are driven by an urge to feel important, to throw their weight about, to make themselves felt. Often they are sadists moved to cruelty by unconscious envy of those whom they believe to be sexually satisfied.

How I have Developed

It is only right that at this point I should make public avowal of what is, indeed, already sufficiently apparent, that I am prejudiced on this subject. Whenever I have had dealings with women in positions of authority, they have turned out badly; whenever I have been so unfortunate as to be subject to their power, I have been made to suffer. Powerful women always dislike me and their reasons are well drilled in respect of their capacity to invent justifications for giving vent to their dislike. I have always found women to be very good rationalizers; they think what they think because they feel what they feel, but their reasons are never at a loss for arguments to justify the indulgence of their feelings.

Humiliated as I have been at the hands of women whose authority has enabled, whose dislike has predisposed them to humiliate me, I am naturally prejudiced against women in authority. I know, as I said above, that most of them can do certain things very well, and that there are no things that some of them cannot do reasonably well. I know, for instance, that women are more efficient telephone operators than men; they put you through more quickly, forget less readily, get fewer wrong numbers, take more trouble. Yet I am always glad to hear a man's voice answer when I take down the receiver, and look indulgently upon mistakes by a male operator which, if the offender were a woman, would evoke a flood of irritable curses culminating in a diatribe upon the inefficiency of the sex.

Having admitted the prejudice and indicated its cause, I feel that the full explanation of the bad temper and taste of the preceding paragraphs is still to seek. The Freudian, no doubt, will be ready with a host of suggestions, but for reasons which it would be indelicate to give, I cannot accept them. The root of the trouble lies, I suspect, in the commonplace fact that I don't like women's company. I do not mean that there are not individual women with whom I would as gladly be as with any man, and, of

54

Food and Women

course, when I have been in love with a woman, nobody else would satisfy me at all. But taking them by and large, they are not, I submit, such good companions as my own sex. They are not as interesting, as amusing, as well informed, or as even-tempered; they are apt to take offence, they sulk, they nourish strange grievances, feel incomprehensible slights and are over-given to quarrelling. I once heard somebody ask Shaw at a public meeting whence he derived the insight into women that enabled him to create the heroines of his plays? Candida, it was said, and Lady Cicely in *Captain Brassbound's Conversion* were women more real and more lifelike even than the heroines of Shakespeare. Shaw replied that his recipe was perfectly simple, 'I think what I would have done and said in the particular circumstances of the situation, and then I make my women characters do and say the same. I assume, that is to say, that women are exactly like myself.' There was never a more flagrant lie. I have not found women in the least like me (and if they are not like me, still less are they like Shaw); so little, indeed, have they turned out on examination to be like me, that I cannot better describe the change that has characterized my views of women since I was an ardent young feminist than as an increasing realization of their differences from myself.

Boringness of Women. One of the chief of these differences is a comparative absence in women of objective external interests. My chief interests are outside myself; they are in philosophy, politics, music, literature, food, games and the countryside. I concern myself with these things more than I do with people. In fact, although I care for a few people immensely, I think about people comparatively little. Now women do not seem to me to be interested in things for their own sake; they are interested in them only in so far as they react upon people. They are interested, for example, not in music but in

55

its composers, its interpreters, and the reactions to it of particular individuals. Above all, they are interested in themselves, in the effect which they are making, in other people's attitude towards them, in the subtle changes and *nuances* of a psychological atmosphere. A woman will notice a dozen changes in the reactions upon one another of a group of people, when I notice none at all. It is this psychological preoccupation which, I think, makes women so infernally dull, so boring as companions.

The self, like any other organism, must, if it is to be fruitful, be crossed with things other than the self; it must be fertilized by experience and harrowed by a diversity of interests. It chiefly thrives upon an absorption in external things, the word 'things', of course, being intended to include ideas and intellectual pursuits. Denied these 'things', the soul grows poor and thin—some people's souls can be heard to rattle like dried peas in a pod—and presently withers away altogether. Or a soul cut off from a healthy interest in outside things may grow rank and lush; it ceases, in fact, to be a soul and becomes a temperament. As such it monopolizes its unfortunate possessor, diverts all nourishment to itself, and judges everything by its ability to minister to its own appetites. Thus persons with artistic temperaments are always taking their artistic temperatures. In this respect most women are artistic. A good soul like a good body should be as unobtrusive as possible; in so far as it functions properly, it should not be noticed either for good or for ill. It is only when one is unhappy that one thinks about oneself, and the extent of their self-absorption may be the measure of women's fundamental discontent. Whatever be the reason, I find them on the whole dull, trivial and vain. With unimportant exceptions, I would always sooner be in the company of men, and women themselves seem to be of the same opinion. Few of the women I know have any women friends. Their apparent friendships with each other will usually be found to hinge upon their relationships with men. Normally two women tolerate one another because they are respectively attached to men who happen to be friends, and this they often do the better to destroy the friendship. When this end has been effected, the women's acquaintanceship lapses.

I have been in the habit for many years of spending occasional week-ends in the country with a couple who cultivate week-end entertainment as an art. Very carefully they select their guests. The chief qualification in a guest is that he or she should be a prominent person, with the reservation that the kind of prominence should vary as much as possible from guest to guest and from week-end to week-end. For example, if there are prominent politicians one week, there will be prominent painters the next. If famous people cannot be had, they will stage a week-end consisting entirely of the relations of famous people. Inevitably, the English social system being what it is, wives have to be asked with their husbands. On a recent occasion *à propos* of the eternal and eternally renewed discussion of the position and prospects of women in the modern world, we went through the names, carefully preserved in the visitors' book, of all the women who had visited that house for week-ends during the last few years. Our object was to discover how many had been invited on merits, how many had come merely as appendages of men. The word 'merits' as applied to women we defined as including not only prominence in some particular department of life or letters, but the possession of some special gift or talent, some social *flair* or personal charm, in virtue of which a woman might be considered an acquisition to a party and so invited for her own sake. We came to the conclusion that of only about five per cent of the women could it be said that they had been included on 'merits'; the remainder had come as male attachments. I believe this result to be not unrepresentative. There are many charming and intelligent women in the world, but they are very few compared with the number of those who are stupid and boring. And even where there are both charm and intelligence, they are not always in the ascendant. Let the waters of these easily ruffled temperaments be ever so slightly disturbed and the charm is dissipated, the intelligence obscured, and the cultivated woman becomes an offended chit.

Women in Work and Talk. For these reasons my present view is that women on the whole are better excluded from the normal activities of life, at any rate of my life. For special purposes, for holidays, for the refreshment of the spirit, the relaxation of the mind, or the illnesses of the body, for occasions when one's wounded spirit demands the balm of flattery or the solace of apparently perfect comprehension, one's intelligence the stimulus which only a slightly inferior intelligence can give, they are admissible, even necessary. But for the ordinary usages and purposes of life, for the hatching of schemes, for the organization of undertakings, for administration, for joint endeavour, for intellectual discourse, for shared activity whether in work or in play, I demand the company of men. Above all, I demand it when there is work to be done. The influence of women is, I have found, inimical to work; there are too many women who make it their business to see that none of the world's work is done while they are about. How often in moments of irritation induced by exasperated desire have I vowed that they ought not to be let out at all, and that a return to the Seraglio system is a condition of the further advance of civilization.

And, since the best conversations are those that accompany feeding, I would, if I had my way, exclude them from the dinner table. Women, I think, ought not to sit down to table with men; their presence ruins conversation, tending to make it trivial and genteel or at best

Food and Women

merely clever. With women present there are bound to be topics at which faces lengthen and voices drop. There will be closed subjects and spades which must be called by other names. But, if there is to be good conversation, none of the chambers of the mind must be locked; if the mind is to play its prettiest games, it must have all heaven and earth for its playground. Close one door in the house of the universe, and intellect sits hobbled and sulking in the lobby, with the result that instead of epigram, paradox and wit, you have only reminiscence, anecdote and pun.

And, should it after all manage to be born in their presence, intelligent conversation only puts ideas into the heads of the women. Now women are rarely at ease with ideas; they do not know how to play with them, to take them lightly and naturally, appraising them as one appraises a flavour or a piece of old china, and putting them away again when one has done with them. Women do not so much have ideas as experience a rush of ideas to the head. Arrived there they become invested with an emotional content; they are either wicked or noble, shocking or refined; the best that one can hope is that they should be accepted as merely true or dismissed as merely false. As if any idea were *merely* true or false! No! from good company and good talk women should be absent.

I am quite aware that women have been among the best and wittiest talkers in the world. They lived in eighteenth-century France and possibly, I speak from hearsay, in the Athens of the late fifth and early fourth centuries. I am also prepared to concede that women may again talk well and learn to mix in society as human beings with free reasons, and not merely as women. But I am speaking here not of what women have been and may be, but of women as I have found them. If you tell me again that the position of women to-day is transitional and difficult because it is transitional, that they have got one foot out of the home yet do not know where to put it, and that they have not yet found themselves in the larger life which opens out to them, I am prepared to agree. No doubt there are very good reasons for the state of affairs I have described, but that does not alter the fact that it is as I have described it. While it remains so, I shall rate cheerfulness, good temper and good cooking above all other virtues in a woman—thank goodness, I have found them at last; for intelligent discourse and the life of the spirit, for the jolly march of mind with mind, for good company and good fellowship, I shall be content to look to men.

My Prejudice and its Causes. If you tell me finally that I am prejudiced, I have already told you that and can but agree again. I started my adult life, as I have recounted, with such high hopes of women, that the process of disillusionment has left a bitterness behind. If I was never sentimental enough to expect women to be soul mates, at least I thought to treat them as intellectual equals. It was a shock to find that the equality had been imposed by myself upon unequals who resented it. If only women could have remained at the silent-film stage, all would have been well; but the invention of talking has been as disastrous in women as it has in the cinema.

Another reason for my prejudice is my clothes. I am an incurably slovenly and ill-dressed man; clothes, I regard, not as an adornment, not even as a necessity, but as a nuisance. When I have been 'hard up', I have always insisted on having luxuries such as music, books and travel, and dispensed with so-called necessities such as decent clothes, washing and hair cuts. Nor is this attitude to clothes without its social uses. My shabby and ill-fitting garments have proved an admirable touchstone for people, separating out, as it were, the sheep from the goats among potential acquaintances. Persons who show a disposition to turn up their noses at me because of my

Food and Women

slovenly appearance, are *ipso facto* persons whom it is not worth my while to know.

Women, however, do not share my point of view. All the women under whose charge I have come—and there have been several—have taken it upon themselves to take me sartorially in hand. They have made it their business to smarten me up, putting creases into my trousers, starch into my collars and shirts, and oil into my hair. They have succeeded only in producing a passable representation of an unpleasant little race-course tout at the cost of making me feel thoroughly uncomfortable. Sooner or later they have grown frightened at the effects they produced and given me up in disgust as incorrigible. The discomforts I have endured during these periodic smartening-up processes, and the contempt with which I have been visited when they have 'failed', have no doubt coloured my views of those who inflicted them. I have concluded that individuality is anathema to women, and that, not content with looking all alike themselves, they are not happy unless their menfolk are equally indistinguishable.

But after careful consideration I come back to boredom as the root of my prejudice. On the occasions on which I have fallen in love I have been impelled by an over-mastering desire to be alone with the loved woman. I have usually succeeded in this object. There has followed a period of ecstatic happiness, but it has been relatively short; and, as soon as it began to wane, boredom has set in. I do not know that this should be taken to imply an assertion of the greater tediousness of women as compared with men, although I adhere to my view that women are more boring than men in proportion as they are less well informed and more self-centred. It is rarely that women possess specialized knowledge and information, and it is knowledge and information which, properly controlled, constitute the best basis for talk. But it is not of this deficiency that I am thinking, when I remember how women have bored me. I am a person inordinately susceptible to boredom; boredom is, indeed, my chief enemy. I keep it at bay with the weapon of variety. My instinctive demand is for new faces, new sensations, change of scene and change of interest, and I find the society of one or two people, provided they remained the same one or two people, irksome after a comparatively short time. For this reason I have always hated walking tours. Beglamoured by Stevenson and Hazlitt I have set off with a couple of men for a four or five days' tour through rural England, and by the end of the second day I have hated the sight of them. When I have been walking with a man all day, I want somebody else to talk to in the evening. So should he. To be stimulating to or stimulated by a person whose fount of conversation you have already drained dry during the day and would like to turn over to somebody else like a sucked orange in the evening is beyond my powers. If you say that one should not want to talk in the country, I agree; but, if silence is your object, you were better walking alone.

It should now be apparent that my emphasis upon the boringness of women is due to the fact that, having from time to time been impelled by the Life Force to shut myself up alone with them, I have spent far more time in the company of single women than in that of single men. My reason again, as so often where women are concerned, is at war in this matter with my instinct, my reason demanding a company of intellectual equals, my instinct a *tête-à-tête* with a woman. As a result I have been intolerably bored by women, and have come, no doubt unjustly, to blame them for the unfortunate results of situations which, under the influence of the cosmic process, whatever it is, that pitchforks us into life, I have insisted on creating. I suspect that most married men have something of this feeling, although perhaps it is not as consciously realized. They go into Society to avoid a *tête-à-tête*, quite as often as a bachelor does to avoid solitude.

CHAPTER III

How I became a Pacifist
The Last War and the Next

IT IS in my attitude to political and social questions that I have changed most radically since, a young man of twenty-three, I went down from Oxford in the summer of 1914. I left Oxford a revolutionary Socialist, convinced that our social arrangements were contemptible, that they were not so of necessity but could be improved, but that nothing short of a change in the economic structure of Society would improve them. Such a change, I considered, would inevitably involve violence and in all probability an armed conflict between classes. This conflict, therefore, I believed—I suppose that I must have believed it; it seems incredible enough to me now—desirable.

I 'go down'. I had hardly 'gone down' when the war broke out. I was at the time taking the Civil Service examination, and on the day on which war was declared was writing for several hours on the dimensions of the stage in the Attic theatre, while excited crowds thronged the streets and cheers and counter-cheers rang in my ears. I succeeded in obtaining a reasonably high place in the examination, and chose a post in the then Labour Exchanges Department of the Board of Trade, which subsequently became the Ministry of Labour, in the erroneous belief that Labour Exchanges and Unemployment Insurance might have something to do with Socialism.

How I became a Pacifist

During the first few months of the war my employ
ment was no less irrelevant than the examination b
means of which I had obtained it. On the day on whicl
the news came of the battle of the Marne I can remembe
writing a long and carefully thought-out minute on th
subject of whether the desk which it was proposed t
requisition for the use of the secretary of the Bootl
Advisory Committee for Juvenile Employment shoulc
have sixteen drawers or eight. Much is written on th
suitability of a classical education as a training for mem
bers of the governing class. I have already indicated m
views on the subject and shall not repeat them; but
cannot refrain from pointing out the almost Gilbertia
commentary which this early employment of mine offer
on the issue. For ten years I had learned Latin an
Greek and little else; for the last three, since I had com
to man's estate, I had made myself acquainted with wha
great men had thought and written memorably about th
universe and the purpose and destiny of human life, an
had obtained a fairly extensive knowledge of Greek an
Roman history. All this rather impressive preparation le
up to what? The writing of minutes on the number c
drawers which should properly be contained by the desk c
the secretary of a Committee dealing with the employmer
of boys and girls under seventeen belonging to Bootle. An
apparently to little else. For many months I languishe
miserably in the Civil Service doing practically no work.
was not a satisfactory Civil Servant and people were apt fc
a time to give me no more to do than they could help. It wa
only during the last two years of the war that I was give
a substantial job and like everybody else was presentl
overworked. Meanwhile I resolutely ignored the war.

Attitude to War. I had never had any illusions abou
the war, and for this I had to thank my early Socialisn
Whatever else it had done or not done for me, it ha

inoculated me against war-fever. I had always regarded war as criminal, but believing war among civilized nations to be practically impossible, had never given the subject much thought. I was not alone in this belief, which most of the intellectuals of my generation shared. When the war came, I never for a moment thought of it as other than a gigantic piece of criminal folly; the nation, I considered, had simply gone mad, and it was incumbent upon a wise man to stay quiet until the fit had passed.

Never for a moment did it occur to me that it was my duty to participate in the madness by learning to fight. On the contrary, I thought that I ought to do whatever I could to avoid being implicated. I was, therefore, a potential conscientious objector from the first, my objection being based not on religious grounds but on a natural reluctance on the part of a would-be rational and intelligent individual to participate in an orgy of public madness. So far as concerned any moral obligation I conceived myself to have in the matter, I thought it my duty to try and stop the war by any means in my power. I did, in fact, write a number of violent anti-war articles in Pacifist papers and took part in Pacifist meetings which were almost invariably broken up by persons who believed themselves to be fighting, among other things, for free speech. I emphasize this attitude of mine not because I am particularly proud of it, but because it may help to render intelligible my astonishment that it was adopted by so few of my fellow-intellectuals, who disbelieving like myself in the possibility of war until it came, condemning it as an outrage on civilization when it did come, nevertheless with very few exceptions either went out to kill themselves, or more frequently hounded on young men to do their killing for them.[1]

[1] Anybody who doubts that this was, in fact, the attitude of Liberal intellectuals, of Wells and Galsworthy, Gardiner and Spender, Massingham at first and even Shaw, is recommended to read *England's Holy War*. by Irene Cooper Willis, which contains extracts from their public pronouncements.

How I became a Pacifist

It seemed to me then, as it seems to me now, that the attitude of repudiation was the only possible one for a would-be rational and intelligent being, and, as I say, I never had any doubts about it. It was only gradually that I realized that the line I was taking was unusual, and that my sentiments were quite unrepresentative of those of the majority of the *intelligentsia* in my own or any other country. Men for whose intellectual capacity I had profound respect, men whose motives I could not doubt, were, I was painfully compelled to admit, convinced of all the things of which the statesmen and the papers wished to convince them, and were evidently feeling the emotions of hatred and ferocity appropriate to their convictions. They believed that the war had been forced upon England by a militant and intransigeant Germany and that it was the outcome of a deliberate attempt to impose German culture upon the world; they believed that we had no alternative but to take part in it and that there would be no peace for the world until Germany had been irretrievably crushed. And at the same time as they were making pronouncements expressive of these beliefs and vibrating with patriotic loyalty and belligerent enthusiasm, hurrahing with the best and obviously having the time of their lives, they were nevertheless convinced that England's policy had always made for peace, that they, like all right-minded Englishmen, desired peace and nothing but peace, and that the war was a terrible necessity, which had been thrust upon them in spite of this continuing will to peace and the pacific policy in which it had found expression. I have before me as I write a book, *England's Holy War*, which describes the attitude of the English Radicals and intellectuals at the beginning of the war. As one reads their speeches and notes their behaviour at the time, it seems incredible that they should have been so taken in. Writers like Wells and Bennett, life-long Radicals like A. G. Gardiner and J. A. Spender, Socialists like Blatchford and Hyndman, who were certainly not remarkable for loyalty to the existing Capitalist State, all threw themselves into the war with enthusiasm. Reading some of the things that Wells wrote one almost blushes, and it is only my respect for a great man which prevents me from quoting them. I did not understand this gross self-deception then, and I do not understand it now.

Bewildered and shocked, I did my best to ignore what was happening. For a time I succeeded, but gradually the war forced itself upon my unwilling, my almost disdainful attention. It was impossible to shut one's eyes to the terrible suffering and misery it involved. I never went to the front; I never even went to prison, so that my direct contacts with the war were very few, but nevertheless towards the end I found it possible to think of little else. And insensibly it effected a change in my political outlook, making me realize that of all the things that can happen to a civilized community armed conflict is immeasurably the worst.

The Great War of 1914–18, breaking out as it did when I had just reached manhood, has played so large a part in forming my views of human nature and of human society, it has contributed so largely to the formation of my deepest political convictions, that I feel I must say something of the considerations which have made me an uncompromising Pacifist. I believe that war is the greatest evil that afflicts mankind; I believe that the next war will destroy our civilization, and I believe that nothing but the refusal of a sufficient number of human beings to fight, whatever the circumstances may be, can prevent it. These beliefs I hold with considerable emotional intensity; in fact, I feel so much more strongly about them than about any others, that the whole of my attitude to politics is coloured by them. I must try, then, to say in some little detail why I hold them. I propose to consider first the various arguments of those who hold that war, although always regrettable, is sometimes necessary, who hold even that the necessity may sometimes do good, in the light of my own experience of the Great War.

Motives of War-makers. I will consider first some of the grounds on which war is advocated or is said to be necessary. It is sometimes said that war is undertaken from creditable motives. The *professed* motives are undoubtedly creditable. Nations fought in the last war to make the world safe for democracy, to preserve the rights of small nations, to uphold the integrity of treaties, to protect the Fatherland, to defend the virtue of their women. But the concept of the nation is a figment; the realities are Governments and peoples. So far as the Governments were concerned, their motives were not such as I have mentioned. They were composed mainly of fear and pride, fear of the superior force of other nations, which was felt equally by those who were the objects of it, and pride which refused to make the concessions which reason suggested from fear of lowering national prestige. These were the main motives, but there were subsidiary ones; of these the desire for money and power were the most important which, under high-sounding names such as economic necessity, the White Man's Burden, or the duty of protecting undeveloped peoples, created a situation which sooner or later was bound to issue in armed conflict. It is certainly a fact that, once the conflict was joined, numerous financial and manufacturing interests benefited from the expenditure which it involved, and men grew rich as never before. Nor can we suppose that these results were unforeseen or unintended.

These motives by which Governments and governing classes were inspired were not, of course, avowed. Man, as is well known, is a moral being, and it is necessary to appeal to his highest instincts, to inspire, in other words, his idealism before he will consent to do murder for you.

The Last War and the Next

For this reason it was thought desirable to invent a moral case for the war; the real aims of the belligerents were concealed and the professed aims announced. Thus deception must be added to the other factors which were involved in the causation of the war. For this, indeed, is the chief difference between civilized Governments and savages, that the former are under the necessity of using their reasons to invent moral justifications for the gratification of instincts of cupidity and aggression in which the savage permits himself to indulge without hypocrisy.

The motives of the *peoples* on the other hand, in so far as they fought voluntarily, were very largely those which were professed by the Governments. They fought to save their countries from wanton aggression and to protect their homes. Thus war is a device by which decent people are induced to further the schemes of scoundrels by virtue of an Idealism which enables them to be duped into the belief that they are fighting for all that they hold to be sacred.

War and Religion. It is sometimes argued that circumstances arise in which war is the course which religion dictates. So far is this from being the case, that war violates every principle of the religion in which Western civilization professes to believe. During the last war this became so obvious that every effort was made to suppress the teaching of Christ and to prevent it from being known. Persons who drew attention to the precepts of the Sermon on the Mount were persecuted, while conscientious objectors who endeavoured to act in accordance with them were abused, imprisoned, placed in solitary confinement and tortured. The record of what was done to conscientious objectors during the war does not make pleasant reading. Meanwhile the Christian religion remained, as it had always been, the official religion of all the belligerent countries, the assistance of the Almighty was simultaneously invoked by all the combatants, and atheists were looked upon with disfavour as being likely to cause Him offence. Piety and professions of respect for the Almighty were, indeed, very marked during the war. Women were assiduous in their attendance at Communion, and heartfelt prayers were offered for success in the slaughter of Germans. It is a suggestive fact that nothing so effectively promotes the belief in the goodness of God as some large-scale calamity such as a war, a pestilence or a volcano eruption, which brings death and suffering to thousands of people. For these and other reasons the Almighty's stock during the war was high except, perhaps, among the troops. To decry or to denounce either Him or His Son was a crime, so that people were actually in prison at the same time under the Blasphemy laws and as conscientious objectors, thus demonstrating that it was equally illegal to throw suspicion in public upon the divine source of Christ's teaching and to say what that teaching was.

The uncompromising directness of this teaching upon the subject of non-resistance was less of a stumbling-block than might have been expected. Those who were paid to expound it overcame the difficulty by the simple device of forgetting all about it, or cheerfully identifying the enemy with the devil or with Anti-Christ converted his destruction into a Christian act and their pulpits into amateur recruiting offices. 'You ask, Is Christ a God of War?' wrote a Welsh minister to one of my friends, a conscientious objector, in prison. 'Look up Joshua v. 15; vi. 1–3, and you will see that Jesus Christ came to be the Field-Marshal of the armies of Israel; and the character of Jesus Christ has not changed even to-day.'

As for the 'Sermon on the Mount' with its inconvenient suggestion that Christ was partial to peace; it was summarily disposed of. 'The Sermon on the Mount' continued the clergyman 'was for the new kingdom, but since the world has rejected that kingdom, *God has been obliged to go back to Old Testament methods.*' [1]

The identification of the Germans with the devil, miraculously multiplied for war-time purposes into several million personages, was sanctioned by the most formidable array of ecclesiastical organizations. The following extract is interesting as presenting within a short compass a number of the official Church positions of the time, including the spiritual element in the war, its sanction by God, and the incarnation of the devil in the enemy.

DAY OF NATIONAL PRAYER

'At a meeting of united thanksgiving and intercession arranged by the World's Evangelical Alliance yesterday the Organizing Secretary said the question of a national day of prayer had been under the consideration of the Archbishop of Canterbury and the Free Church Council. In a few days there would be a deputation to Mr. Lloyd George to discuss the matter. What they desired to impress upon the Prime Minister was that throughout the Empire, not through fear or cowardice, or any such desire for peace, except peace through a victory over the devil incarnate, there was a feeling that until there has been an official acknowledgment of God on the part of the nation and of the spiritual element in this war, so long would the conflict continue.'

Presumably the acknowledgment was duly made, for presently we find Bishops busily thanking God for the war. For example:

BISHOP PREDICTS A LONG WAR

'In dedicating at Ilford yesterday a motor-ambulance for the use of wounded soldiers, the Bishop of Chelmsford predicted that the war would be a long one. He

[1] My italics.

71

thanked God,[1] he said, that the war was going on, for it would be a folly and a crime to put aside the sword until the purposes for which we had drawn it had been secured.' (Extracts *Daily News.*)

Inspired by their own teaching, clergymen did not hesitate to exhort their congregations to kill Germans directly, when they could, and vicariously by prayer and the 'giving of sons' when they could not. Thus those who were unfortunately prevented by sex or age from carrying out God's work themselves, were asked to invoke God's assistance for those who were doing their killing for them. It must be admitted that they took full advantage of the opportunity. Dowagers mewed for blood; the suburbs yammered and the boarding-houses of the South Coast vied with each other in the ferocity of their sentiments.

As a further act of piety clergymen proposed tarring and feathering such Pacifists and conscientious objectors as ventured to disagree with their interpretation of the divine will. In a remarkable speech delivered in Johannesburg on Saturday, April 14th 1917, Dr. Furse, Bishop of Pretoria,[2] 'suggested that the Government should appoint two independent tribunals to deal with single men who were not doing their duty. One should be composed of Government officials, who would go through every business in the place, and say what business was essential to win the war, and what individuals were essential to that business. And when they had said that such and such a man should stay, he would be dressed up in red and purple so that there should be no doubt that he should stay. Every man not so dressed he would make his life such a burden to him that he would get out somehow or somewhere.

'The other tribunal should be composed of business

[1] My italics.
[2] What follows is a verbatim report from the Johannesburg *Sunday Times.*

men to go through every Government Department, and say how many people in these Departments were necessary and how many were not. Also he would paint the essential people red, and to every man who was not painted red he would give such a time of it that he would get out of the Government service, wherever he went to. (Laughter and cheers.) Get everybody exempted who is essential to stay, and as to anyone not essential, give him a week to get to the front or to the Potch,[1] and if he did not get there in that period, tar and feather him.'

'Every man who kills a German is performing a Christian act,' said another patriotic bishop, and, in order that there might be no doubt about the matter, proclaimed that God had decided temporarily to approve of murder when the victim happened to be born in Germany.

The view that the killing of Germans was a noble and a necessary act was, indeed, regarded as so self-evident that those who disagreed with it were thought to be mad, and persons serving in the army who occasionally felt doubts about the necessity of continuing the war were treated as mental cases and placed in 'Homes'. This, of course, only applied to those of good connexions; the socially insignificant were doubtless shot out of hand.

War and Civilized Behaviour. That war is not a mode of activity appropriate to civilized human beings will, I think, be generally conceded. The belief that, when your country has a quarrel, the only method of showing that it is in the right is to kill off as many of the other side as you possibly can, is a belief appropriate to savages and children. It is only by the aid of hypocrisy that it can be held by the ostensibly civilized. Those who are most succesful in killing, that is to say the victors in the war, demonstrate, it is obvious, not that they are in the right, but that they possess the might. Thus the resort to war

[1] Potchefstrom, a military training camp.

to settle disputes rests upon the implied identification of might with right, an identification which, indignantly repudiated in peace-time, is hypocritically assumed by those who are prepared to accept successful violence as evidence of the rightness of a cause.

That the effects of war upon civilization are uniformly disastrous, nobody who has taken the trouble to find out what the effects are can doubt. In the last war masses of mankind were reduced to a condition which was indistinguishable from savagery, while among those who were only indirectly affected by the war, credulity, intolerance, uncharitableness, bitterness, anger and every kind of childish superstition from the grosser forms of spiritualism to palmistry and the belief in the second coming of Christ and the imminent end of the world grew and flourished. The mob, stupid and intolerant, was all pervasive; one has only to look through the files of the baser and more popular journals of the time to see how stupid, how intolerant and how pervasive. A perusal of the *John Bull* of the period is a sobering corrective to those who believe in the rationality of our species.

Here, for example, is an extract from a public letter to Mr. Bottomley, which appeared in the paper towards the end of the war:—

'There are two kinds of boil, one that comes to a head and one that simmers below the surface and is called a blind boil. There is no room in the body politic for blind boils. For God's sake, Mr. Bottomley, come to a head now and relieve the situation!'

I give five further examples from the thought and literature of the period. The first is from a letter in the *Morning Post* signed W. H. D. Rouse on the subject of those societies which were thought rightly or wrongly to be desirous of peace.

74

The Last War and the Next

'Union of Democratic Control, No-Conscription Fellowship, Freedom of the Seas, League of Nations. . . . These titles are false every one, and the men who are working behind them are false as hell, although they work through innocent and honest people who are their dupes. They are like the outward appearance of the educated German himself. Those blue eyes seem to be full of candour; that unwrinkled and smooth countenance shows no sign of care; the ingratiating smile must please; yet behind them lurks the mind of a devil and the personal predilections of a herd of swine.'

The second is an extract from the editorial comments on the possibility of peace printed in the paper of the parish in which I was living at the time, St. Jude's on the Hill (Hampstead Garden Suburb):

'To me last Sunday was—what shall I term it?—a peculiarly distressing day. I mean to see the eagerness and the hope expressed in so many people's faces and voices at the prospect of an immediate peace. Well, it was painful. I tell you that *any* parley with the enemy at this moment is a crime before God, and an armistice a cruel mockery of the dead—and of the living. America fights by our side. And on the shoulder-straps of her men are three letters. Those three letters must be America's only answer to Germany as they are ours—Unconditional Surrender—Absolutely. Let Hindenburg and Ludendorff publicly surrender their swords and the Allies occupy Berlin and Vienna. If this be refused, then, by all that is holy, Fight on! Fight on!

'When the other day people of this country chuckled over Bulgaria's retirement from the war they little knew! That act was Germany's latest triumph. Bulgaria . . . has been permitted to extricate herself with ease from her precarious position. Instead of being annihilated as she deserved, she has been granted an Asquith peace—i.e. a peace which does not leave the victim sore!! Well, we may thank God that this Empire still has a few—precious few—men whose eyes are not quite blinded by German dust. Two of them are going to speak at the Albert Hall on Nov. 5 at 7.30 p.m.—Mr. W. H. Hughes and Dr. Ellis Powell.'

The third example is from a speech by Mr. Bonar Law, quoted in headlines in all the papers. The purpose of the speech was to convince people that we must win the war in order to prove that war does not pay. This is done as follows:

MR. BONAR LAW'S REPLY TO LORD LANSDOWNE

WAR AIMS LETTER DESCRIBED AS A 'NATIONAL MISFORTUNE'

No security by a peace got now

'We have got to show the German nation in the only way in which they can be made to realize it, that war does not pay, that their military machine cannot get the results which they want; *and that will only be obtained by victory*.' [1]—MR. BONAR LAW.

The fourth example tells what a Lord who was also an Admiral did when he found that he was dining off German plates:—

' "We have actually been dining off German plates!" said Lord Beresford. A succession of crashes followed, a number of guests hurling their plates to the floor. The Manager of the Savoy remarked after the luncheon . . . "I at once gave instructions to the staff to search among the plates, and only one has been found bearing the German stamp." '—Report in the *Daily News*.

The fifth example consists of a few typical extracts from a book, *Women and Soldiers*, by Mrs. E. Alec Tweedie,

[1] My italics.

76

which enjoyed enormous popularity towards the end of the war; deservedly, since it faithfully represented the views and outlook of a number of women of my acquaintance, and probably of masses of women up and down the country.

'Let us put the whole nation from sixteen to sixty under conscription——men and women alike, so that babies by dozens may be born into a better-disciplined world.'

'It is a strange anomaly, by the way, that while men from overseas were flirting with typists, they were marrying domestics.'

'The question of butter for tea is not climacteric.'

'Alas! some really nice girls are afflicted with an unintentional "glad-eye" that attracts the worst side of the worst men.'

'Bachelors from twenty to forty should be taxed 25 per cent. on their incomes.'

'Let the Minister of Reconstruction start by putting all feeble-minded persons on farm lands, where there is no possibility of offspring.'

'Tawdry finery is the hall-mark of the usual working-class girl, while the factory-hand has been known to pull out her mirror, puff-box and rouge in the middle of a twelve-hours' night shift on a fourteen-consecutive-nights' job.'

It would be a pity to soil such perfect things with comment, and I refrain.

The extracts I have given are not untypical of the thought of the period. Admittedly they are rather sillier than most public pronouncements, but the slight added silliness is accidental and does not indicate a radical difference of outlook. Anybody might have written and said such things, and many people did.

For the lowered level of public sense from which such

utterances sprang and to which they appealed the war was responsible.

The war brought about a general decline of rationalism, and for a time there was a real danger of a lapse into the fears and superstitions of a pre-scientific age. From the effects of this decline of rationalism we are still suffering, as I shall try later to show.

War and Morals. It is sometimes said that war is morally beneficial. War, it is alleged, braces nations grown slack and pleasure loving, and ushers in a return of the old-time virtues of courage, endurance and simplicity. War on this view is a purge, cleansing the community from the vicious humours bred of too long a peace, and restoring it to a more wholesome way of life. Take for example, the following from the speech of a popular novelist, Mr. John Oxenham, at the City Temple:—

'If we had won the war two years ago it would have been a bad thing for us, in spite of all the horror and suffering. For we had not learned our lesson, and I am not sure we are ready to win yet. I believe that all this suffering is intended to turn us back to God. Are we learning our lesson? Until we do so the suffering may have to continue. No statesmanship of man can save the world. The only way is to come back to God.'

'War' said the Bishop of London 'brings out all that is best in our men,' referring, presumably, it was surmised at the front, to their entrails, which when their stomachs were ripped up by a shell were 'brought out' plain for all to see.

Peaceful progress, it is said by those who take this Condy's fluid view of war, is impossible, and, even if it were possible, it would be ignominious. For victory in war is the only method by which a nation can realize itself, fulfil its destiny, achieve its historic mission, release ts dynamic force, confirm its manhood and maintain its place in the struggle for existence, to quote only a few of the catchword phrases which, from Hegel through Nietzsche to Bernhardi and Mussolini and from Henley through Stevenson to Kipling and Sir Arthur Keith, have issued from time to time like gnats from the languid summer of the minds of those who are duped by their own moral or physical weakness into a romantic admiration for men of energy and will, and are betrayed by their own incompetence in action into lauding the life of dangerous action in others.

No set of beliefs could be further from the truth. War provides an outlet for all the worst elements in man's nature; it enfranchises cupidity and greed, gives a charter to petty tyranny, glorifies cruelty and places in positions of power the vulgar and the base. Persons whose only passport to favour is the strength of their lungs, the blatancy of their self-advertisement, or the overbearingness of their demeanour, win the attention of the nation, and staking out a claim upon the public ear, close it to the counsels of reason and justice.

A visit to the Grill Room of the Savoy Hotel during the last war afforded an interesting commentary upon the moral cleansing of the nation. There were visible for all to see those to whom the war had brought power, prominence and wealth. Profiteers rank and lush, and uniformed Jacks in office guzzled and swilled and chattered of the profits the war had brought them. 'If this war goes on much longer,' I remember hearing one of them say 'I shall be able to retire.'[1] The daughters of the aristocratic poor

---

[1] The extent of the private fortunes made out of public calamities was prodigious. The following extract reporting a speech in the House by the inconveniently honest Mr. Bonar Law shows just how prodigious. 'Mr. Bonar Law spoke as a shipowner to the shipowners in the House of Commons yesterday, and made a sensational statement as to the profits being reaped by this particular class of profiteers, which is loud in its pro-

How I became a Pacifist

paraded their attractions before the fishy eyes of the newly enriched. . . .

'Pacifism', I read recently in a book, *The Soldier's Testament* by one René Quinton, 'is an outrage on the dignity of man; it would deny him his only majestic quality, the knowledge how to die.' I do not think that I quite know what this means, but, with the vision of the war-time Savoy Grill Room before my eyes, I find it difficult to resist the temptation of pointing out that in war the dying is done by the young and the noble, the surviving by the old and the base. It is this fact no doubt which produces the conviction of war's 'majestic quality' in middle-aged authors.

Nor was it only vulgarity and grab that the war enthroned; mere silliness had the time of its life. The idle and frivolous elements of society, supported and encouraged by the sense of public duty born of hospital visiting, flag selling, entertainment organizing, and unstinted patronage of the bereaved and the wounded, indulged in an orgy of pleasurable excitement. Young women 'gave themselves as a public duty to those who were fighting to preserve their virtue, and to many who were not, and the London stage was visited by a series of farces whose unashamed pornography made it impossible to doubt the 'liberating' effects of the war on public morals. Meanwhile a stream of hypocrisy and cant poured from pulpit and Press, the old assuring the young how noble it was of them to get themselves murdered to protect the old, and the professional journalists who spoke for the young, in-

tests against the excess profits tax. He himself, he declared, held fifteen investments in small shipping companies, amounting in all to £8,100. At 5 per cent. this would produce £405 a year. In 1915 he received as interest, not £405 but £3,624, and last year this grew to £3,847. One of the ships in which he was interested was "sold or sunk", and for the £200 which was his share in it he received more than £1,000. Yet another investment of £350 brought him £1,050. No more damning exposure of profiteering was ever made from the Government benches.

forming the old that the young found the war as amusing as their fathers found it morally edifying.

War and Truth. Meanwhile public lying was at a premium. Northcliffe, while arranging for millions of leaflets to be dropped behind the German lines assuring the Germans that the victory of the Allies would not mean the destruction of Germany but only the dethronement of the Hohenzollerns and their own welcome into the comity of nations, was simultaneously instigating his papers to inflame the public by declaring that the Germans were fiends, who tortured babies and made meals out of the corpses of their dead, and insisted that there should be no peace until their country was dismembered and they themselves destroyed as a nation. Anyone who favoured a milder peace was denounced as a defeatist, a Pacifist and a traitor. Nobody apparently but Mr. H. G. Wells, who resigned from the Ministry of Propaganda rather than continue to act there as one of Lord Northcliffe's lieutenants, questioned the morality of this double-faced procedure.

Popular journalism has still to recover from the inundation of moral bilge with which the war-time Press was flooded; indeed, it is doubtful if in my lifetime it ever will. As for public morality, its level is lower in all belligerent countries than before the cleansing process was applied to it. Crimes of violence are more common, there is less respect for human life and, according to the judges, less trust in human veracity. The cruelty of war and the brutalization of humanity that cruelty engenders are an endless theme. Nor do I propose to dilate upon it. As I write, I have before me an article which appeared in an English newspaper which commanded, and still commands, one of the largest, if not the largest, circulation in the country, which advocated the killing of German women in order that fewer little Huns might be born in the future. British delegates went to the Peace Conference with a mandate conferred upon them by a delirious electorate to squeeze the German orange 'until the pips squeaked'. . . . These instances must be enough to show the effect of war upon the general level of man's humanity and culture.

The Aims of War. But, it may be said, 'The war at least produced a settlement'. In the narrow sense, the sense in which a foe who has been beaten to his knees is then beaten to the ground in order that he may be kicked into helplessness, the Germans were certainly settled; but in no intelligible sense has the war settled anything at all.

It would be easy to show that no single one of the aims which the war was professedly fought to achieve has in fact been achieved. It was fought, for example, to make the world safe for democracy, with the result that at the moment of writing we are enjoying military autocracies in Turkey, Italy, Roumania, Hungary, Bulgaria and Poland. It was fought, again, to protect the rights of small nations. As a result some small nations have disappeared altogether, large slices of nations, removed from the parent body to which they belonged, have been artificially grafted on to arbitrarily abstracted portions of their similarly mutilated neighbours, while the Conference of Versailles, called to concert a crime which each of its members had an equal interest in committing, has left Europe more fundamentally restless than at any time within living memory. The perpetual irritation produced by this unsettlement makes inevitably for another war.

Another aim for which the war was fought was to end war for good and all. None appears in retrospect more ludicrous. The war proved to demonstration that, if you only pile up a sufficient number of armaments, sooner or later they will be used. Europe for fifty years had devoted all its savings to the storing up of explosives; it was, to

The Last War and the Next

say the least of it, a little ingenuous to show surprise when they went off. If ever the inadequacy of war preparations as a means of preventing war could be demonstrated, one would suppose it to have been done seventeen years ago. So effective, indeed, was the demonstration of 1914, that the victorious nations, having disposed of the German army and navy, solemnly pledged themselves to disarm in order to reduce the chances of war. Yet schoolboys are still writing their inevitable essays on the theme '*Si vis pacem, bellum para*', many school O.T.C.'s have dropped all pretence of being optional, while others, which remain optional in name, complacently announce that 'all the boys in the school are at present members of the Officers Training Corps'. Meanwhile the nations, so far from showing any disposition to end war as a result of the successful realization of their alleged war aims, pile up armaments on an unprecedented scale, while the pledge to disarm is dishonoured at Geneva by a series of interminable discussions carried on by a system of committees so complicated that the outsider's irritation at finding that it is quite impossible for him to discover what is being done is only rendered tolerable by his conviction that nothing is being done at all. Upon the sincerity of these discussions the sums spent in preparation for the next war form a fitting commentary.

To take English expenditure alone, roughly a hundred and twelve million pounds a year are now spent on armaments, or nearly forty millions more than was spent in any year before the war to end war was brought to a successful conclusion. The total world expenditure is something like two and a half million pounds a day.

The Next War. There is no need to dilate on the efficiency of these preparations. Instruments of warfare are now being perfected which will enable human beings stationed in positions of complete safety to kill other

83

human beings from a greater distance and in larger numbers than ever before. So efficient are these weapons that the next war on a large scale will almost certainly see the end of our civilization. France, for example, is estimated to possess 1,300 first-line war aeroplanes. A tithe of this number would suffice to wipe out London in a night. The following calculation culled from the work of an expert on air warfare vividly illustrates this possibility. In the last war the number of enemy aeroplanes that were brought down was 4·6 per cent. As the war proceeded, the arrangements for defence grew more efficient and in the last raid six out of twenty-two invading machines were disposed of. Let us suppose, says the writer, that at the beginning of the next war the provisions for defence are twice as efficient as they were at the close of the last war and account not for six but for twelve out of every twenty-two invading machines; this would be equivalent to six hundred out of the eleven hundred which an hour after the declaration of war might be expected over London. Why, asks the writer, should this fact be expected to console us for the reflection that a single bomb dropped by any one of the surviving five hundred would lay waste practically three-quarters of a square mile of London?

It is in prospects of this kind that one of the few grounds for hope is to be found. The next war will be the first in which there are no non-combatants; the home front will be the front line. Thus for the first time in modern history those who are responsible for preparing and declaring war will be exposed to the dangers it brings. Previous wars have been made by the old and fought by the young, but this eminently satisfactory arrangement under which the young suffer in the trenches while the old egg them on to slaughter from a safe background will not recur. The old will never again enjoy the safe background, a fact which may give them pause.

The Last War and the Next

Meanwhile, however, the international stage seems set for war. It is not only that the nations spend a large part of their means in protecting themselves by accumulating those instruments of warfare which make war inevitable; no less significant is the fact that in the second decade after the war to end war the psychology of the peoples grows once again manifestly bellicose. As I write, Mussolini has just made a speech, typical of many such, from which I quote the following sentence. 'The reality is that the whole world is arming. Every day the papers publish the accounts of the building of more submarines, cruisers, etc. The number of guns and bayonets is for ever growing.' The speech ended with a demand for a million more Italian babies, in order that Italian women might not suffer the reproach of falling behind the women of other nations in the supply of cannon fodder.[1]

Now it is pretty obvious that this kind of talk does not horrify other people as it horrifies me. On the contrary, they regard it as a healthy sign of natural virility, and take pleasure in contemplating their own nation's war preparations. They approve of guns, tanks and battleships, and regard them as a source of pride. There is a cinema theatre in London, the Avenue Pavilion, which at the time of writing devotes the whole of its programme to the weekly news. The screen depicts events from all over the world which the proprietors regard as being of topical interest, whether as bearing witness to the march of civilization, as portraying new and startling events, or as otherwise contributing to the pleasure and edification of the audience. Having watched this weekly gazette on a number of occasions, I have estimated that at least 40 per cent of the pictures shown represent military preparations. All over the world, in states large and small, from Albania to Hawaii, from China to Peru, one sees soldiers drilling,

[1] (Added twelve months later on going to press.) The demand, I understand, has been complied with.

How I became a Pacifist

aeroplanes bombing, cannons firing, warships manœuvring. Everywhere human beings are seen achieving efficiency in the art of elaborately killing each other. The most civilized communities are those which exhibit the most soldiers, the biggest cannon, the most destructive bombs! Nor, as far as I can see, is there any reason to suppose that the audience does not share the views of the producers and proprietor in regard to the interest and praiseworthiness of these displays.

In the summer of 1928 King Amanullah of Afghanistan visited England, and for several months was fêted and entertained at the expense of the nation. Pictures of him appeared in all the papers, seeing tanks at Lulworth Cove and bombing aeroplanes at Hendon. He was photographed 'enjoying' a trip in a submarine and firing a torpedo off Spithead. It was after his trip in the submarine that King Amanullah exclaimed, 'I shall soon be the complete Westerner now,' implying no doubt that the Western European is never so happy as when in a submarine. There was, however, no record of his being taken to see the Poet Laureate, Sir James Jeans, Liverpool Cathedral, or Bernard Shaw. Looking back upon the episode in a hundred years' time, the Afghans will no doubt conclude that the English were an exceedingly warlike nation with little time or inclination to cultivate the arts of peace. Whether this is so or not, I leave others to judge; but that we take more pride in exhibiting to the world our skill in war than our proficiency in the arts of peace, and prefer to be known for our cannons rather than for our poets is the only moral one can draw from the incident of King Amanullah. No, assuredly, the great war did not achieve the aims it professed!

Suffering and Cruelty of War. And bearing all these things in mind, remembering that war promotes cruelty and enfranchises all manner of evil, that it enthrones vulgarity and gives power to the greedy and the base, that it is contrary to our 'holy religion', that it achieves none of the ends which it is professedly fought to achieve, that it leaves all belligerent nations incalculably worse off than it found them, and bequeaths a legacy of humiliation, bitterness, and desire for revenge which only the sheer physical exhaustion of the combatants has hitherto prevented from breaking out in a fresh conflagration, it is impossible to resist the temptation of asking whether, whatever may be the nature of the goods that war is said to secure, they are really worth it? In the last war some ten million young men were killed, and some twenty million permanently maimed and mutilated. More terror and agony were experienced in the space of four years than in the hundred years that had preceded them. Men were burned and tortured; they were impaled, blinded, disembowelled, blown to fragments; they hung shrieking for days and nights on barbed-wire entanglements with their insides protruding, praying for a chance bullet to put an end to their agony; their faces were blown away and they continued to live. . . . But this appalling tale of sheer physical agony was only a part of the suffering the war involved. Discomfort of every kind was the lot of millions of men for four and a quarter years. There was the discomfort of ill-fitting clothes and boots, the discomfort of coarse food, the discomfort of never being alone, the discomforts of damp, of mud, of rats and lice. Above all there was the discomfort of unspeakable boredom. Many men, looking back on the war, will tell you that the sheer boredom of it was its most terrible feature. I do not believe that they are right in this—there is a convention that it is discreditable to confess to fear or pain; but nobody minds admitting to feeling bored—yet if the tale of all the varied miseries inflicted by the war could be told, the waiting, the lack of reasonable occupation, the being packed up and sent hither and thither as if you were a bale of merchandise, the appalling squandering of knowledge and skill and the wasted talents of mind and body will be a heavy item in the account.

I have spoken thus far only of the combatants. What the war involved to those who suffered at home, to mothers and lovers and wives, the partings, the breaking up of homes, the loneliness, the ever-present dread, the still ache of hope deferred, the sharp pain of hope extinguished . . . these things require a more eloquent pen than mine, and I do not propose to do less than justice to the theme by a treatment that falls short of what it deserves. And bearing in mind just how much of suffering and misery the war did involve, it is impossible to refrain from again putting the question I asked above, is it worth it?

The Figment of the Nation. It is difficult to believe that it is. Even if war achieved every single one of the aims which it professes to achieve, even if it conferred every one of the goods which its apologists claimed for it; if it settled disputes, cleansed the national life, left the world happier and more vigorous, restored manliness and courage, gave security and laid the foundations of a lasting prosperity, even if it did all these things, I doubt if they would be worth the price that must be paid for them. In fact, as we have seen, it does none of them, and the ocean of suffering and misery and boredom which the last war entailed was completely wasted.

I would go further and maintain that even if the suffering that war involves were enormously and incredibly diminished, so that it fined itself down to the suffering of a few, a very few people, of one family even, that still those things for the sake of which the suffering was endured would not be worth the endurance.

The ends for which wars are fought are not concrete but abstract; they are such ends as national prestige,

national honour, national security, ends begotten of pride
and born of fear. And these nations whose prestige must
be flattered, whose honour must be safeguarded, whose
security must be guaranteed, are not real things at all but
figments. They are the embodiments of a debased Hegeli-
anism, which holds that the State is a real entity and that
its well-being is more important than that of its individual
citizens. To it individuals, generation after generation,
must be subordinated, and to its alleged welfare men and
women must be sacrificed.

The growth in power of these national States is one of
the greatest menaces to man's happiness. Like the gods
of old they are jealous, violent and revengeful. They bear,
indeed, a frightful resemblance to the Jehovah of the Old
Testament whom they have supplanted. To them belong
the energies, the thoughts, desires, the very lives of their
citizens. They are the Gods, the officers of the army and
the navy are their high priests, the people their sacrifice.
In war-time they claim to be omnipotent, and would make
the same claim, if they dared, in peace. Yet in spite of
their power and prestige, these States are figments, own-
ing no reality except by virtue of men's belief in them.
There is, in fact, no political reality except in the individual, and no 'good of the State' other than the good of
the living men and women who call themselves its citizens.
And because they are figments and because living human
beings are realities, the alleged good of the State as
such is not worth the suffering of a single individual.
Those abstract ends of the State for which wars are fought
are of less value than a single man's blood or a single
woman's tears. How long, one cannot help wondering,
will men continue to sacrifice their lives and happiness on
the altars of a non-entity? This much at least is clear,
that, until mankind has outgrown the worship of these
idols, curtailed their powers and transferred their jealously
guarded sovereignties to some supernational authority,

there will be neither peace nor lasting progress in the world.

And so it is that I have come to see in war not only the ultimate evil but the ultimate folly of mankind. Whatever the situation, nothing that can possibly happen through not going to war seems to me to be of an evil comparable with what will certainly happen once war is begun. Hence of all possible alternatives war is always the worst. War settles nothing, achieves nothing, creates nothing. The evils of war, the physical and mental agony of living human beings, are undeniably evil, the goods are at best problematically good. And while the evils which it involves are certain, the goods at which it professes to aim do not accrue.

The Evil of Physical Pain. I have come to think—partly, perhaps, as the result of the war—that, of all evil things in the world, physical pain is by far the worst. There is a convention to the effect that physical pain is not so great an evil as mental or spiritual suffering. According to most novelists and all moralists the worst evil in the world that can happen to females is that they should lose their honour. This is simply not true. Far worse than losing your honour is to be tied up naked to a post and jogged at nicely calculated intervals in carefully chosen parts with the end of a red-hot poker. I am convinced that any female would prefer to lose her honour a hundred times over, if this is not a contradiction in terms, provided only that the process of stimulation with the poker would stop. Similarly with male honour. There is a convention among men which requires them to make light of physical suffering. They are not so successful in this as women because they feel pain more intensely. Women, as is appropriate in less highly developed organisms, have a less delicately adjusted nervous system than men, and consequently are less sensitive to pain. In the small things of life the difference is easily recognizable. Women, it is well known, can hold hotter plates, stand in picture galleries without fatigue and stay in cold water for longer periods than men; their success in the one sport in which they really excel, swimming, is indeed, largely due to their greater imperviousness to physical cold. (It is interesting, by the way, at a seaside resort to notice how the women always want to stay in the water longer than the men, and the shifts to which the latter are driven to excuse themselves for coming out first.)

Hence I infer that women's vaunted superiority in the endurance of pain, as evidenced, for example, by their greater hardihood under the hands of the dentist, is due not, as alleged, to greater courage, but to smaller sensitivity. There are many savages who bear for hours and without a murmur a degree of apparent pain which would make a civilized human being faint in a couple of minutes!

In spite of their manifest inferiority in this matter men, especially brave men, pride themselves on their ability to endure pain. While nobody minds confessing the pains of bankruptcy or despised love, and the ability to feel emotionally miserable is regarded by many with approval as a sign of sensibility, to confess that one is being physically hurt is thought to be unmanly. Hence the convention which requires us to pretend that physical suffering is not really to be feared, at least, by the brave. The convention is a foolish piece of hypocrisy. Nothing, I repeat, is comparable in evil to the physical pain which human beings can be made to suffer, and which they have, in fact, made one another suffer.

I have acquired a fairly considerable and detailed knowledge of the history of torture. To convince the doubting I should, perhaps, regale my reader with some of this knowledge, but I cannot bring myself in the interests of my argument to sully these pages with a hint of even the milder of the appalling things which human beings have

How I became a Pacifist

done to each other.[1] And so I will content myself with my previous example, and defy any male, however brave, after five minutes' treatment with the poker, not to choose any evil that I could name that was not a physical evil in preference to a continuance of the treatment.

The chief bringer of pain in the modern world is war. All wars, especially modern ones, are, as I have tried to show, fought in 'a good cause'.

Stimulus of 'a good cause'. Now it is an interesting fact that human beings are never quite so diabolically cruel as when they have 'a good cause'. Examples of 'good causes' are the defence of the virtue of white women from lustful blacks, and the saving of heretics from everlasting torment in hell. Many of the lynchings of blacks in the United States have undoubtedly been undertaken in support of the former of these two objects, but by no means all. During the thirty years period 1889–1918, less than one-fifth of the coloured men done to death by lynching mobs were accused of the 'usual' crime; and although 264 negroes were lynched in the United States between 1914 and 1918, I read that 'in only twenty-eight cases . . . was rape assigned as the cause'. Thus when white women travel in special excursion trains for the privilege of paying enormous prices for front seats, from which they may see a negro's tongue torn out before he is slowly burnt alive, it is apparently only on rare occasions that they find it necessary to persuade themselves that they are acting in defence of their virtue.[2]

As for the saving of heretics from eternal torment, there

[1] Those who are interested are recommended to read *The Pleasures of the Torture Chamber*, by John Swain, published by Williams and Norgate.

[2] In case any reader is in doubt as to what a lynching involves, the following extracts taken at random from a number of similar accounts, will enlighten him:

Davisboro (Georgia), Friday. 'A 15-year-old negro, named Charles Atkins, who had been arrested in connexion with the murder of a rural

The Last War and the Next

seems to be little reason to doubt that the activities of the Holy Inquisition were on the whole animated by the best motives. They were correspondingly more fiendishly cruel than those of any other organized body of living beings, animal or human, known to history. Ancient Rome was bad, the Dark Ages were worse, mobs in all times have been savage and brutal; but for large-scale cruelty of the highest quality the Holy Inquisition is unexcelled. As to quantity, in twenty-seven months, 1482–4, two thousand persons were burnt in Seville alone, while in the same city seventeen thousand persons were taught the elements of Christianity by suffering punishments which ranged from torture to fines, confiscations, imprisonments, deportations, dismissals from employment, and that comparatively benevolent penalty called civil death. As to quality—but I really cannot soil the pages of this book with even a bare mention of the things the Holy Inquisition did to people, in the endeavour to make them share its views about the supernatural government of the universe.

I have no reason to suppose that, given a sufficiently good cause, for example, another war for liberty and freedom, or even a proletarian revolution, people's behaviour would be radically different from what it has been on similar occasions in the past. Our civilization is only *sin* deep; once disturb the surface tenor of our lives and we become, as the last war showed, the cruellest of the beasts.

mail carrier, named Mrs. Kitchens, was to-day burned at the stake under horrible conditions.

'In the first place he was tortured over a slow fire for fifteen minutes, and then, whilst shrieking with pain, was questioned concerning his accomplices, as a result of which he implicated another youth.

'The ringleaders of the mob, which consisted of some 2,000 people, then proceeded to chain Atkins to a pine-tree and relit the fire. While the tortured boy was burning some 200 shots were fired at his body. The mob are now searching for the other lad.'—Reuter. *Daily News,* May 20th, 1922.

How I became a Pacifist

Pacifism first. I have summarized as best I can some of the considerations which have made me for good or ill a Pacifist before all things. I have imbibed such a horror of violence and physical suffering, that I have come to regard the primary object of all political activity as the prevention of those situations in which they occur.

I am still a Socialist and believe that a reconstruction of society involving the communal ownership of the means of production and distribution would be an immense improvement. I am also convinced that equality of income irrespective of services rendered to the community is an essential pre-requisite of a civilized society. In Russia, when I visited it in 1930, to all intents and purposes there was such equality. There were no rich and in the towns no poor; all citizens were living on incomes ranging from about £100 to £250 a year. What is more, the Bolsheviks had succeeded in establishing a society in which the possession of money had been abolished as a criterion of social value. The effects were far-reaching, and, so far as I could see, entirely beneficial. The snobbery of wealth, which is so important a factor in the social life of Anglo-Saxon communities, was absent. There was no ostentation and no display, and the contemporary fat man, complete with fur coat, white waistcoat, champagne and cigars, was missing. It was only when one returned to England that one realized by contrast the vulgarity of wealth. The first English 'fat lady' 'featuring' jewels, lap dogs and cosmetics, whom I saw on return seemed an outrage. The Russians, admittedly, are poor and live badly, but the sting is removed from poverty if it is not outraged by the continual spectacle of others' wealth. I cannot believe that complete equality of income would not produce similar effects here, and, if snobbery and vulgarity were eliminated from English society, the gain would be incalculable.

But, although I still desire most of the ends which

Socialists advocate, I no longer believe that revolution is the only method of securing them. On the contrary, I believe that, so far as Western European countries are concerned, it would preclude their achievement for many generations to come by destroying such civilization as we possess. Finally, I do not believe that, even if a revolution were able to achieve an economic millennium and did in fact achieve it, the result would be worth the price in human misery and suffering that it would involve. Thus I have learned to curb my expectations and to modify my demands in respect of the future of our society. Socialism I still think a good, but I am less certain that it is realizable in its old form than I used to be. In many moods I am inclined to think that the Marxians are right in holding that the difficulties involved in the supersession of Capitalism are too great to be overcome without a violent struggle; and this violent struggle it seems to me essential at all costs to avoid. If its avoidance means that Socialism must be regarded as impracticable, then we must get on without it as best we can. I have seen in Russia how nearly war, civil war and revolution destroyed civilization. In England, I am convinced, with our more closely interlocked and economically interdependent society, a revolution would mean death by starvation for thousands.

All this means that I am a Pacifist first and a Socialist second. I am too convinced of the magnitude of human folly and the horror of human suffering to be prepared to provoke the one and risk the other by seeking to improve our obviously defective social system by any abrupt or sudden change. This conclusion, born perhaps of the complacencies of material comfort and the timidities of middle age and in any event allied with them, has radically changed my attitude to politics. It is not so much that I hold different views—ever since I grew up I have been a Pacifist, an Internationalist and a Socialist—but they are differently emphasized. My attitude is now more coolly detached than it was; it dwells upon probable rather than hoped-for consequences, distrusts enthusiasm and sees in most Idealism little more than a device for projecting one's desires into the future and then inventing reasons for supposing that they will be fulfilled. Moreover, I realize, as I did not realize when I was young, the horrors of which human beings are capable when they have a good cause in which they believe.

The world seems to me to have grown since the war increasingly irrational; there is indeed in some quarters a definite cult of unreason. This cult of unreason and the consequences which flow from it, will be the theme of succeeding chapters. In face of it, it seems to me to be the first duty of a would-be reasonable being to hold fast to reason at all costs, and to pin his faith to the possibility of achieving realizable goods rather than to imperil the whole structure of our civilization by insisting upon an economically equitable but doubtfully attainable society.

A Charter for Rationalists. Examples of such goods are the following. I put them in the form of a programme which twentieth-century rationalists might do well to adopt.

(1) Repeal of the divorce laws; it should be made as easy for people to get divorced as to get married.

(2) Repeal of the laws against what is called unnatural vice. I have never been able to see that sodomy does harm, or to understand why it should be persecuted with such malignant ferocity.

(3) Diffusion of birth-control knowledge, including the provision of information and advice with regard to birth-control at all Government and Local Authority clinics and of birth-control appliances at all chemists' shops.

(4) Repeal of laws penalizing abortion as a criminal offence.

(5) Sterilization of the feeble-minded.

(6) Abolition of the censorship of plays, films and books.

(7) Abolition of all restrictions on Sunday games, plays, entertainments, etc.

(8) Disendowment and Disestablishment of the Church. If people want priests and churches to put them in, I do not see why they should not be expected to pay for their upkeep.

(9) Preservation of the amenities of the countryside, including compulsory town and country planning, restriction on ribbon development, access for walkers to mountains, moorlands and wild places, and the provision of national parks.

(10) Prohibition of exhibitions of performing animals.

(11) Abolition of all licensing restrictions.

(12) Complete disarmament. Involving the abolition of the army, navy and air-force.

These are the main points in a modern rationalist's charter. If they were embodied in legislation, the general level of public health and happiness would, I am convinced, be sensibly improved. For my part at any rate, soft middle-aged man that I am, with a status to maintain and goods to lose, I am prepared to abjure revolutionary activity and to devote my energy to the task of persuading my fellow-beings of the desirability of such measures as I have enumerated.

CHAPTER IV

What I am
Literature, Music, the Country

On having a closed Mind. I have described as well
as I can the influences that went to my making.
By the time I reached the age of twenty-five my mind
was to all intents and purposes formed; formed and,
as I have hinted in Chapter II, closed. I have told how
in respect of the three important matters of food, women
and politics I was led to modify my earlier outlook,
but with these exceptions, I was thinking at thirty much
what I thought at twenty, and at forty I am thinking
the same still. The ability to conceive new ideas, to
adopt new attitudes, to respond with new reactions, to
experience new sensations, ceased in me nearly twenty
years ago. My mind, in short, is in all respects essentially
a pre-war mind.

I am not claiming any peculiarity for myself in this
matter; I do not believe that I am a case of arrested
mental development. On the contrary, I think that my
case is the common case of almost every man who advances
from youth to middle age. As I look round at my contemporaries, I see that their reactions too are determined
and stereotyped, that they too have ceased to think, that
their minds also are closed. I even think myself superior
to them in that I know what has happened to me, while
they for the most part still retain the illusion that their

minds move and that they are open to new ideas. Yet to any unprejudiced observer it is manifest that this is not the case, the views of the average middle-aged Englishman on art, literature, politics, morals and life being as fixed and immutable as those of Almighty God.

Having said so much in dispraise of myself, I have to add that in my heart I consider that my mind is not so completely closed as my reason makes out. That it is closed in almost every direction save one or two I know well enough; but I flatter myself that this knowledge helps me to keep it open in just those one or two places where it is not quite closed. The job admittedly is a difficult one and is only accomplished at the cost of perpetual vigilance. It requires a considerable expenditure of energy to keep any part of the mind open after the age of thirty, and, in order to economize this energy, I have found it a good plan deliberately and ceremoniously to close a few extra doors every year in order that I may the better keep open the one or two that really matter. Thus I hope and believe that my mind is still receptive to new ideas in philosophy, and my palate sensitive to new flavours in food and drink. I am even capable of an occasional new orientation in politics, and not long ago changed my political party.[1] Until quite recently I tried to be sympathetic to new forms of expression in art and literature, but I found the effort too much for me, and have had to give it up as a bad job. I am now frankly a conservative in these matters.

Literature. In literature my gods are still, as they were in 1912, Shaw and Wells and Bennett. Of the stars who have risen in the literary firmament since the war, although some, J. B. Priestley for example, Sinclair Lewis,

---

[1] I went back to the old one again after six months, but that was not my fault.

What I am

Virginia Woolf and Aldous Huxley, win my unstinted admiration, none shine with a brilliance in any way comparable with those earlier luminaries. Most post-war literature, as I shall try later to tell, seems to me to be definitely retrogressive; it makes not for but against civilization, and emphasizes the forces of unreason in human nature. In this respect post-war literature is representative of the times, since recent developments in psychology encourage the mood to which literature gives expression. The world, I believe, is less reasonable than it was, or rather it is more disposed to use its reason to belittle reason and exalt emotion. The literature and art of to-day seem to me to be at once the prop and the mirror of this tendency, catering for tastes which they have in part created. But I am trespassing on matters which belong to the next chapter.

To return to myself, my literary tastes were formed by the sociological plays and novels which were in vogue in my early twenties. I like my plays and novels to be topical, to deal, that is to say, with the concerns of contemporary society; and not only with what concerns it, but with what does not but should. Social evils admittedly exist, and it is, I conceive, the business of the dramatist to bring them to light, dragging the dirt of society from under the table where the official housemaids have swept it, and rubbing the noses of the audience in what they are accustomed to pretend is not there. People live dull and thwarted lives through no fault of their own. Capacities are wasted, personalities remain undeveloped, children go into factories at fourteen, husbands beat their wives, families live ten to a room, the bank clerk's soul rattles like a dried pea in its pod. . . . It is, I suggest, the duty of all citizens to examine these sores in the body politic for which we are collectively responsible.

Literature, therefore, should in my view be regarded primarily as an artistic device for calling attention to aspects of life which would otherwise pass unnoticed. Its object should be not to stir our emotions for the sake of stirring, but so to stir them that as citizens we may learn to conduct ourselves differently and as human beings to feel differently. To do this it must arouse our senses of pity and fear, enabling us to see more beauty, more passion, more scope for our sympathy and understanding in life than we saw before. Thus tragedy should portray sufferings caused by social injustice rather than by individual wickedness, and wit spring from the ridicule of social convention rather than of personal peculiarity. To the latter I am particularly partial, and the social satires of writers like Shaw and Butler and Swift and Anatole France have always given me the keenest pleasure.

Style. The function of literature being for me essentially propagandist, I have never had much value for pure literature or literature proper. Style, for example, I consider a nuisance. There are many writers, as Samuel Butler pointed out, who have sought to cultivate a style as a preliminary measure before they begin to write, much as a swordsman will practise the use of his weapon before fighting a duel. This seems to me a misconception of the whole business and purpose of writing. For me, the object of writing is to convey meaning by asserting something, and style, I agree with Shaw, is simply effectiveness of assertion. As such it cannot be divorced from the matter it seeks to convey. He who has nothing to assert has no style and can have none. He who has something to assert will go as far in point of style as its momentousness and his conviction will carry him. Disprove his assertion after it is made, yet the style remains. In other words, conceive a thesis clearly in your mind, if possible feel strongly about what you have conceived, be at pains to say what it is as simply and briefly as possible and have done with it, and good style will automatically result. Try to adorn a passage with literary ornaments which do not spring naturally from the development of the subject, to make up, in other words, by the effectiveness of your manner for the thinness of your matter, and you will bring to birth some literary monster like the style of Pater or Meredith, who when, as frequently happened, they were at a loss for a construction to decorate, proceeded to supply the deficiency by constructing a decoration.

Rhetoric I dislike and I have never been able to make anything of symbolism. A symbol I understand to be a sign for something else. Either the symbolist knows what the something else is, in which case I cannot see why he should not tell us what it is straight out, instead of obscurely hinting at it in symbols, or he does not, in which case not knowing what the symbols stand for he cannot expect his readers to find out for him. Usually, I suspect, he does not, and his symbolism is merely a device to conceal his muddled thinking. Whether it is so or not, I have no patience with it; I am bored by allegorical and metaphysical poetry, as I am bored by ceremonial and ritual religion, while works such as Maeterlinck's *Blue Bird* or Rutland Boughton's *The Immortal Hour*, in which the unutterable purports to be discernible behind a veil of homely symbols and obvious melodies, seem to me merely pretentious nonsense.

In art generally I like things clear cut, simple and precise, and dislike blurred edges, hinted meanings, overtones and obscurely indicated 'beyonds'. If people have experienced the unutterable, then, I feel, they should not try to utter it. I admire the classical virtues, of poise, symmetry, balance and clarity. Reason, I feel, should never be far absent from any work of art. The heart, they tell me, has its reasons of which the reason knows nothing; very possibly, but I wish that the heart would keep them to itself. In any event the heart, I feel, is never an adequate substitute for the head. Thus I am partial to eighteenth-century writers, to Hume and Gibbon, Swift and Pope; I love *Tom Jones*, and, although I dislike Dr. Johnson, think Boswell a great book. And by the same token I find myself out of sympathy with romance and the romantic. The romantic writer purports to dive below the obvious surface of life to imagined depths beneath. That there may be such depths I do not deny; but too often he imagines himself at life's well spring, when he is merely stirring up the mud of its shallows. I admire but am not moved by the Gothic in architecture, and am faintly bored by the Gothic in literature. Shakespeare is the one really romantic writer, if, indeed, he is romantic at all, that I can read with pleasure. Shakespeare and the Brontës. I think *Wuthering Heights* and *Villette* two of the most thrilling books in the world.

Nineteenth-Century Novelists. But here I must enter a disclaimer against this vilification of myself. I have been describing what are at most tendencies and see that in doing so I have been led to exaggerate them. My taste is not really as narrow as the account I have given of it would suggest. I like other kinds of literature than sociological novels and eighteenth-century essays. I like, for example, novels of most kinds and particularly, although I do not know how to square this with the previous account, do I enjoy the great nineteenth-century novelists.

I had the good fortune to be brought up in a philistine household, with the result that works of great literature were not for me, as they are for many children, spoiled by being stuffed down my literary throat, while I was still too young to assimilate them. I came to them in the late twenties with a fairly mature mind after I had completely soaked myself in the works of my own times, and in six years read most of Dickens, Thackeray, George Eliot, the Brontës, Mrs. Gaskell, Charles Reade, Trollope, Mere-

What I am

dith and Hardy. Between them these great novelists
have given me an enormous sum of pleasure. I think
their virtues admirable—chief among them is the virtue
of being able to tell a story—and to their defects I am
comparatively blind. Even upon Dickens's sentiment I
am apt to look with a less censorious eye than most of
my contemporaries. As for Trollope, he has become a
stand-by for life, and I am eternally grateful to him not
only for writing such good novels, but for writing so
many of them that there is no likelihood of the supply
giving out in my lifetime.

This admiration for Trollope, this addiction to Victorian novelists in general, is, no doubt, highly inconsistent. Perhaps I am a bigger man than I suspect, big
enough to afford and to transcend inconsistencies which
would wreck a smaller. And yet, I think, the incon-
sistency is less real than apparent. I like the Victorians
because they can tell a story and create characters. Story-
telling has always enthralled me, and one of my chief
complaints against the moderns is that they seem no
longer able to tell stories, or no longer to wish to tell
them, if they are able. Story-telling and character-drawing
provide me not so much with an escape as with a rest
from life. I can best illustrate what I mean by trying to
analyse the attraction of Trollope. At first sight it is a
standing mystery. Trollope—it is obvious—was not a
great man; he does not write from the motives which
inspire great writers, and his novels do not produce the
effect of great books. Yet they have a stronger hold on
the affections than most works of acknowledged genius,
and the man himself comes as near to greatness as is permitted to mortals without genius. These facts are generally admitted; yet, reading the novels, it is exceedingly
difficult to explain them. The ordinary standards of what
constitutes great writing when applied to Trollope's
novels are ludicrously inappropriate, while, according to

the ordinary conception of the great artist, Trollope is no artist at all.

You can think, for example, of the great writer as a person sent into the world to give conscious expression to life's instinctive purpose. He is the vehicle of a direct inspiration from life, a forerunner of the evolutionary process, his mission to point forward to a new and higher level of thought and conduct than that which humanity has hitherto reached. In this guise he is the legitimate descendant of the preacher and the prophet. Conscious of a world order, driven by an irresistible urge, he is too absorbed in what he has to say to care overmuch how he says it. His preoccupation, in fact, is moral rather than artistic; he writes to give the world a piece of his mind, and regards his art only as a device for serving it up as attractively as possible. 'No doubt' says Mr. Shaw 'I must tell my story entertainingly, if I am to hold the wedding guest spell-bound, in spite of the siren sound of the loud bassoon. But for art's sake alone I would not face the toil of writing a single sentence.' These, or something like them, are the motives which inspire the work of such men as Swift, Ibsen, Bunyan, Blake, Tolstoy and Shaw. And, reading them, inevitably one is changed; one's mind is stretched, one's outlook widened and, even if one does not share the convictions and enthusiasms of the author, one is nevertheless profoundly affected. Now think of Trollope with his few simple ideas expressed in competent prose, flowing in well-calculated lengths of 2,000 words for three hours every morning before breakfast and the Post Office claimed him. What could be more unlike?

Or you may think of the great writer as an expert in the art of life, one who enhances the business of living, enabling you to find significance in the trivial and the dull, and to see more beauty, more passion, more scope for your sympathy in the world than you saw before. In this connexion one thinks inevitably of Dickens or of Balzac. To read them is not to escape from life, but to be introduced to it. And not only to life but to yourself. All great books, it may be said, force the reader by one method or another, by contrast or sympathy, to discover himself; and one thinks again of Henry James or Proust.

Trollope for the Middle-Aged. But no man was made introspective by Trollope. When one has finished the Barchester Novels one knows a vast deal about Barsetshire, but nothing at all about oneself; in fact, one has not once been reminded of oneself, a circumstance which brings me to an enlightening point. Trollope is essentially an author for the middle-aged. Young people like to be reminded of themselves; their personalities intrigue them; much of themselves is as yet unknown, and there is much for them to discover. Moreover, they are still under the illusion that their selves are important. But the middle-aged who have found out, or think they have, all that is to be known about themselves, who have, or think they have, no illusions left, and have lived long enough with themselves to be thoroughly bored with themselves, ask nothing better than to have their thoughts directed elsewhere; they like, as they put it, to be taken out of themselves and are grateful to an author who will do this for them.

It is the same with the moralists and the prophets. Young people are interested in ideas; they want to know what has been said and thought memorably about life; moreover, they believe in the efficacy of thought, and read the great authors in the hope of coming upon the solution of the riddle of the universe, or a creed to regenerate the world. But with the middle-aged it is not so; they know, or think they know, most of the things that can be said or thought about life, and they are distrustful, supremely distrustful of what is new. Their minds, like their bodies, are set; the mental furniture is all in its proper place, and to admit a new piece would put them to the trouble of re-arrangement, involving discomfort, overcrowding and, in extreme cases, a painful jettisoning of highly valued antiques. In a word, the only ideas the middle-aged want are those they expect, and from Trollope they may be sure of getting them.

He introduces us to a world of people (I am speaking for the middle-aged) whom we welcome as being exactly like ourselves. It is a bustling, vigorous world, full of colour and incident, through which move real live characters, so real and so alive that if you were to meet Mrs. Proudie and Mr. Slope, Mr. Harding and Archdeacon Grantley in the street, you would recognize them on the instant. But, though Trollope's characters are as large as life, in life they were never large. His folks are wise and foolish, irritating and complacent, pleasant and disagreeable and little just like ourselves; the emotions by which they are moved, rivalry and ambition, love and jealousy, are the emotions we know, and their way of taking life sober and moderate and level-headed, a little dull maybe, but fundamentally English (Trollope is the most English writer who ever lived) and fundamentally decent, is our way. You can understand the characters in a Dostoevsky novel, but your understanding is the fruit of imaginative insight; it demands an effort. For these frantic Russians, although in some profound and spiritual sense they may be true to life, are—and you cannot help feeling glad that they are—creatures hopelessly different from yourself. But one's understanding of the people in Trollope is different; it is more familiar, more homely like one's understanding of a well-loved friend. And it is because these people are so like ourselves, because page after page and novel after novel they give us the answers and behave in the ways we expect, because of our complete assurance that Trollope will never for one moment 'let us down', that to read about them is to know at last that literary peace that passeth all understanding.

What I am

To reach the close of a Trollope novel is like coming to the end of a humdrum, busy, happy day. Joy and grief, ecstasy and suffering, poetry and romance have not visited us; but how often, after all, do they visit our own busy humdrum days?

And so it is that, when I look forward to old age and remind myself that a time is coming when I shall have to read books instead of writing them, there is no author in the prospect of whom I feel gladder, or to whose works I look forward with happier anticipation than those of Anthony Trollope. Just think of it, fifty-one novels, all of them good, and some of them very good indeed. And now that I have said why I like Trollope, you will justly observe that these are not the sentiments of a romantic man, it is doubtful even if they are the sentiments of a literary one. I agree with you; I agree too that in so far as the Victorian novelists are literary-romantic, I like them in spite of and not because of their literature and romance; I like them, in fact, because of their stories and their characters. The Victorian poets who, presumably, provide the literature without the story, are beyond me, and I have never been able to read the Rossettis, Meredith, Francis Thompson, Tennyson or even Keats without considerable boredom. And if a writer becomes too romantic, if he deals too largely in grand passions, hinted presences and symbols, and relies too much upon his sense of the unseen and the unknown, then, however competent he may be as a story-teller, I find him difficult to swallow. Thus, much as I admire Conrad, I have never been able to read him easily. A sense of duty and sheer admiration of his craftsmanship have carried me through most of his books but I have never enjoyed them with the gusto that I feel unfailingly for Dickens, or Wells, or Hardy.

Poetry. As for poetry, I have already hinted that I can make little of the Victorian poets, and I do not fare much better with the others. I like my poetry to be very simple and direct; for example, I read with pleasure the songs and legends of Shakespeare and the nature lyrics of Hardy. I like it to be about nature, not treated in a high-falutin metaphysical way as by Wordsworth or Coleridge, who address nature with a big N and use her as a diving-board for plunges into the infinite, but simply and un-ambitiously described with catalogues of natural scenes and objects. Thus I like the modern nature poets Davies and Blunden and Ralph Hodgson, and Miss Sackville West's poem, *The Land*, is one of my favourite London bedside books. I like John Clare, I even like Crabbe. Again I like the poetry of indignation, when the poet, inspired with a fine frenzy of revolt, shakes the fist of outraged man in the face of an ungentlemanly God. It is because of the rebellious strain in him that I read Hardy's poetry, while A. E. Housman is perhaps my favourite of all the poets.

But on the whole, I must confess, I have little use for poetry. I like it in company and enjoy reading it and hearing it read aloud; but I rarely take to it spontaneously. I am æsthetically obtuse to poetry, and, although I am capable of seeing the beauties of a passage when some-body takes me, as it were, by the æsthetic hand and points them out to me, I am normally incapable of seeing them for myself. If I were alone in the world, the sole survivor of mankind, with all its literature at my disposal, I am pretty sure I should never read any poetry at all. In fine, I do not take to poetry naturally as a solace and refreshment for the spirit, as so many of my friends aver they do. I say 'aver' because, although I do not doubt the word of these poetry lovers, I regard it as significant that I never by any chance come upon them reading the poetry to which they are so addicted. Time and again I have looked at the books which people read for their pleasure, in the tube, in railway carriages, on steamers, on holidays and in their own houses; yet it is rarely indeed that they are books of poetry. No doubt people still read poetry extensively, but it is odd that they never allow themselves to be detected in the act. Poetry reading, of course, is desperately hard work, and most people, I suppose, are too busy earning their living.

Painting. As with poetry, so with painting; I am æsthetically obtuse to pictures. I do not mean that I do not like pictures; on the contrary, they have given me on occasion very great pleasure; but my liking is neither natural nor spontaneous. Here again I require to be taken by the æsthetic hand. If somebody will go with me to a gallery, point out the pictures that I ought to like, tell me why I ought to like them, what I ought to look for and why; if he will discreetly impart little gobbets of technical information, tell me the school to which the painter belonged, his relation to his predecessors and his successors, if he has any; if he will do all this in a non-boring way as one reluctant to give valuable information, and if, finally, he will prevent me from looking at too many pictures and insist on my concentrating on the three or four he chooses to point out to me, then my eyes may be opened and I may come to see. And, if you object that this is a queer way to approach art, and observe that beauty is not accustomed to yield herself to a little technical instruction, the answer is that it is not with beauty that I am making contact, not at least as yet. But if presently I return and look at the chosen pictures by myself quietly and at my leisure, then the significance of the points to which my attention has been drawn may be revealed to me, and I may come to realize that a picture is beautiful.[1] But, as you will have seen, the process is a slow and hazardous

[1] If the reader wants to know what I mean by that, I am afraid he will have to read some of my philosophy, e.g. *Matter, Life and Value*, Chapter VI.

one, and it is rarely that it has been carried to a successful conclusion.

Moreover, it is conditioned by my bias against the romantic. No amount of preliminary exposition will open my eyes to the beauty, if any, of Turner, and, although I like Leonardo and Giotto, most of the famous pictures of the Italian Renaissance leave me cold. What really moves me are the pictures of the great Dutch artists. Those dark, cool interiors slashed by a bar of sunlight, in which homely men and women are seen doing commonplace things, in which every piece of furniture is clear and distinct, and the whole glows with a rich brilliance as if it were lit from within, are pictures after my own heart.

The pictures of Van Eyck and Franz Hals, of de Hooch and Vermeer, above all the pictures of Vermeer, seem to me to contain and to convey all that life holds of peace and repose. Everything is sharp, clear cut and precise; nothing is hinted, everything is stated. Below the surfaces of Vermeer there are no depths, but the surfaces are themselves deep. Dutch art is a perfect statement of the classical view of life; it enshrines the virtues of order, balance, clarity and poise. And almost unintentionally, as it were, these homely pictures achieve beauty. Apparently coloured photographs of simple scenes, in which every detail is accurately reproduced—it is one of the most interesting and difficult exercises I know to try to state in what respect a Vermeer differs from a coloured photograph—they are invested with a significance which the scenes themselves lack. Or lack for you and me! For Vermeer, I suppose, differs from you or me in being able to see in the scene the significance which we cannot observe save in the picture. What he has done is to drag it forth from the irrelevant setting in which it lurked, and throw into high relief. He does not create beauty; he is the midwife who brings to birth the beauty that is latent

in things, so that even persons as aesthetically obtuse as
I am can see it.

Also I like Monet and Manet, Degas and Renoir,
especially Manet and Renoir. I cannot explain this and
shall not try, except to say that I probably like Renoir
for his girls and the whole group because I was introduced
to them by a woman I passionately loved. Of modern
painting I can make neither head nor tail.

But enough of my limitations and æsthetic obtuse-
nesses. It is time that I spoke of what I know and feel for
myself, of the realms that are my own, where, independent
of the instruction and indifferent to the opinion of others,
I enjoy and am unassailably convinced of the rightness of
what I enjoy; it is time that I spoke of music and of nature.

Music. Whatever reservoir of æsthetic sensibility I
possess has flowed into the channel of music; yet I never
heard, or never knew that I heard, any music that was
worth hearing until I was well over twenty. As a boy I
knew all the popular songs of the time, and whistled them
incessantly. There were better songs then than there are
now with more rhythm and more melody. I suppose that
the final demise of English popular singing, which has
been continuously decaying since the Elizabethan age
when England was a nation of singing birds, must have
set in about 1913 with the invasion of jazz. It is impossible either to whistle jazz or to remember it, and the
first sign of the conquest of England by America is that
the Americans should have made us like themselves, a
songless nation.

But it was no part of my public-school education to
make me aware of the fact that music existed except in
the form of popular songs; and, although at Oxford I fell
for Gilbert and Sullivan, absorbed Sullivan's music and
incorporated it with my being, I cannot be said to have
had any intercourse with real music until my last year

Literature, Music, the Country

I used, I remember, to maintain that all classical music was lacking in 'tune', by which I meant a well-defined melody, and that those who went out of their way to hear it were affected *poseurs*. I can even remember attending occasionally and in a spirit of tolerant detachment several of those admirable concerts that we used to have at Balliol on Sunday night, but I cannot remember that, with the exception of a slow movement in a quartet of Greig's which moved me strangely, they ever made much impression on me.

There came a time at last when it was my fate to hear often repeated the last movement of the Pathétique sonata of Beethoven and Chopin's Raindrop Prelude. They were badly played, in fact they were being practised, but by dint of constant repetition they forced the gate of my soul and I thrilled to a new experience. The entry, once effected, other music was not slow to follow in the breach. The early sonatas of Beethoven came first accompanied by the Nocturnes and Preludes of Chopin. Chopin soon dropped away, but Beethoven became a god. My friends and acquaintances, however inexpert and unwilling, I bullied into playing the sonatas upon the piano—I even went out of my way to cultivate the acquaintance of pianists—and was so worked upon by the Moonlight, the Appassionata and the Waldstein, that, unable to sit still, I used to dance about the room in a ferment of excitement. As the apogee of this phase I remember a concert at the Queen's Hall at which the Kreutzer sonata was played by Adela Verne and Isaye. It was the first time I had heard it, and, as the insistent rhythms of the first movement with their passionately reiterated refrain beat upon my ears and tore at my vitals, I could no longer contain myself, but squirmed in my seat, sweated at every pore, and at last wept uncontrollably, a proceeding so little to the liking of my neighbours that I was forced to go out and take refuge in the lavatory.

What I am

As a result of this concert I wrote to Adela Verne in grateful acknowledgement of the intense pleasure she had given me, praying to be allowed to come and hear her play. It did not matter, I hinted, whether the playing was in private or public, at home or in concert room; whenever or wherever it was, she had only to say the word, and I would come. I forget how she put me off, courteously, I think, but firmly.

Beethoven, Bach, Mozart. I recount these early extravagances, albeit with a certain diffidence, to indicate the intensity of the effect which music in general, and Beethoven's music in particular, produced in me. There was no pose or affectation in my behaviour——these ebullitions of emotion were, so far as I can remember, quite genuine——and, when the next phase came and Beethoven gave way, as in due course he did, to Bach, the emotions were no less intense, although the expression of them was less eccentric. I am still in the Bach phase and expect to remain there. For the last fifteen years I have played the forty-eight preludes and fugues every morning for twenty minutes after breakfast upon the pianola, an instrument in the use of which I am become by continual practice fairly proficient. Bach to be enjoyed to the full should always be played in the morning. His music demands a brain fresh and alert, a sensibility as yet unsullied by the experiences of the day. Exquisitely pure, it requires a similar purity in those who would fully savour its appeal; emotionless, it requires that the emotions of the listener should be dormant. Bach, in fact, should be heard in an emotional clean sheet. Although I must have played the forty-eight preludes and fugues of the Well Tempered Clavichord hundreds of times, my enjoyment of them is still fresh. If I feel an occasional tendency to tire, I have only to play other music for a week and at the end of it I return full of ardour to Bach, like a lover to his mistress.

Bach, I am convinced, achieves in music a supremacy over all-comers unequalled by that attained by the practitioner of any other art. It is a humiliating reflection, which honesty alone compels me to record, that I used to say the same of Beethoven.

Since Beethoven died, practically no music has been written that I wish to hear. It is true that I am fond of Schubert, especially in hot weather; but he died only a year after Beethoven and it is only in the work of his last two or three years that he shows signs of beginning anything more than an immensely prolific writer, very occasionally inspired, with a great gift of melody and a great vice of repetition. He announces lovely themes, and then, not knowing what to do with them, repeats them until they cease to be lovely. Schumann, too, announces lovely themes and then loses them in a cloud of romantic vapourings. The flame of his inspiration, rarely clear, is normally invisible in the smoke of his passions. His music is a standing illustration of the need for discipline. But the A Minor concerto is full of lovely things and achieves greatness.

Chopin is for women, drawing-rooms and twilight. Its delicious woefulness is pleasant enough in its way, but is no more to be taken seriously as music than a savoury or an ice is to be taken seriously as a meal. Since Chopin there has been nobody, at least for me. For the rest I love Handel, admire and perpetually underrate Haydn—I never hear him without being surprised that he should be so good, resolve not to do him the injustice of underrating him again, and immediately forget his merits until my next hearing and next surprise; I do the same injustice to Arnold Bennett—think Purcell the greatest Englishman who ever lived—I would give all the plays of Shakespeare for Purcell's music to 'The Fairy Queen'—and consider their neglect of Purcell, and incidentally of Byrd (composers comparatively ignored even by the patriotic

B.B.C.) to be a convincing demonstration of the hopeless unmusicality of the English, who, unable to discover genius for themselves, can only admire what the Germans and the Italians discover for them. I enjoy Scarlatti and Gluck and worship Mozart only next to Bach.

Mozart's operas are the only operas which I care to hear, the incredible loveliness of the music triumphing even over the intolerable stupidity of the medium. The accompanying music is, indeed, so lovely, that the voice is for the most part to be regarded as an intrusion; one longs for the singer to stop making a noise, that one may the better listen to what the orchestra is doing. It is particularly unfortunate that women should be permitted to attend operas, since their view seems to be that except when somebody is singing there is nothing to listen to. Operas, they know, are musical pieces in which people sing; *ergo*, if nobody is singing, nothing of importance can be happening. Music unembellished by the human voice may be all very well at concerts, but is obviously not meant to be listened to at an opera. As a consequence directly the voices stop they burst out chattering like a flock of magpies. I have known the lovely *entr'actes* in *Figaro* made practically inaudible by women's chattering. But Schopenhauer has said all that there is to say on the subject and I shall not dwell upon it further.

Music is, perhaps, the most important single influence in my life; if I speak no more of it here, it is because I have devoted a whole chapter of this book to its performance, its perversions, its listeners and its interpreters.

Nature. Of nature I find it more difficult to speak. Since I was twenty years old the country has become with every year that passes a more important factor in my life. Yet I do not know what to say of it that has not already been said by others far better than I can say it. Men like Hazlitt and Jefferies, W. H. Davies, John Clare,

Literature, Music, the Country

Edmund Blunden and W. H. Hudson, above all W. H. Hudson, have given expression to the feelings which the English country arouses in me with a beauty of utterance which I cannot hope to achieve. Therefore I had better confine myself to a bald statement of facts.

Until I was twenty-two or three I took little interest in the country. At Oxford I was insensibly affected by the beauty of the place, but hardly realized the influence until I had left it. Then I took to walking and for a dozen years or so was a reasonably energetic cross-country walker. Yet, although I went often into the country, it was for the exercise of the body rather than the refreshment of the soul. I used to go with groups of people numbering from half a dozen to twenty, and it was my pleasure to choose the route and lead, running down steep places, clambering over rocks and taking them, often protesting, through hedges and over fields. Some of the fruits of this phase of my development are gathered into Chapter VIII.

All the time my feeling for nature was growing, but the growth was unconscious. To-day it has reached a point at which I cannot be really at rest away from the country, or at least from such imitation country as Hampstead Heath affords. To spend a night in the middle of a large city is for me a positive discomfort; I cannot bear to wake up in London on a fine morning, and to be in London on a Sunday morning, whether wet or fine, is enough to depress me for the day. If I have to spend the day in the middle of London, I pray God that it will be wet; if the sun shines, I am too restless to go collectedly about my business.

Nor is it only the countryside that I need; it must be the English countryside. Time and again I have been to beautiful places abroad, the Italian Lakes, the Alps, the Mediterranean Coast, the Pyrenees, and been homesick for the English country. It is not that I do not know

117

these places to be beautiful, merely that I do not feel at home in them. The eternal blue sky welcomed for a few days, is felt as a nuisance by the end of a week; the flowers are not English flowers; the grass is coarse and sparse; the rocks jagged and harsh; there is nowhere to lie about. The English country is unequalled in the facilities it provides for lounging and lying about. Whether these are the reasons which really determine my disapproval, or whether, as is more likely, they are merely rationalizations of an instinctive discomfort felt in foreign lands, I do not know. What I do know is that before a fortnight has passed I am afflicted with violent nostalgia and come scuttling back to England.

To say anything new about the beauty of the English countryside is beyond my powers; nor shall I attempt it. I have, however, devoted the whole of a later chapter to a lament on its destruction. In this chapter I propose to permit myself a word on my own reactions to nature which, being personal and private, will at least escape the charge of being a *mere* repetition of the thoughts of others.

Classes of Nature Lovers. It has seemed to me that lovers of nature can be divided into two classes. The first desire to *lose themselves* in nature; they like wide views and big spaces, mountains and moorlands and great bare fields; they like, the more sophisticated of them, flat fenland country, where the sky is the chief feature and where, sensing their own insignificance in the vast prospect, they may forget the nervous little clod of wants and ailments which is the self, by absorption in something greater than the self. This class, then, desire to transcend themselves by fusion with something other than themselves, and they look upon nature as a vast absorbent, a sort of sponge for the swabbing of their own individualities.

The second class go to nature not to forget but to

realize themselves; their desire is that their personalities shall be enhanced not absorbed. Accordingly, they seek not large scenery but small, not downs and open spaces but wooded dells and glades, copses, lanes and meadows, the courses of little streams, or narrow valleys running up into the hills. Mountains they like but for their lower levels, eschewing heights which make them feel insignificant and therefore uncomfortable. People belonging to this second class, as I conceive—and I belong to this class myself, so speak with the more confidence—wish not to lose themselves in nature but to affirm and strengthen themselves by absorbing her. Their instinct is to take up, as it were, the essences of nature into themselves that they may incorporate them with their being. They would know a spot so well that they can conceive themselves to have left the impress of their own personalities upon it. Now this fancy can only be entertained in small homely places, in orchards, at a turn of a lane or in a glade in a wood.

My own natural history has consisted in a gradual widening of appreciation, an extension of affection from scenery of the second type to that of the first. Once I liked only what was small, detailed and irregular. Surrey was an ideal county for me, Surrey and the New Forest part of Hampshire. It was only later that I came to appreciate moorland and mountain and the line of a down against the sky. And, as my feeling for the country has grown more catholic, I have come to see that my earlier classification of nature lovers was not the most appropriate; at any rate I find that in my own experience it has been gradually superseded. I am now inclined to think that a love of the country which is both catholic and discriminating will embody two rather different elements—there are more than two, of course, for the feeling that binds us to nature is a rope of many strands—but two seem to stand out in sharp contradistinction.

What I am

There is a purely instinctive feeling that takes its origin from our remote past. Nature is the mother of our race, and country sights and sounds, above all country smells, touch some ancestral chord that stretches back to our savage, even it may be to our sub-human past. The touch of the bole of an oak, the smell of fallen leaves or new-mown hay, the tang of a mountain brook or the feel of lush meadow grass against the face, these are things to which we respond with an instinctive love that not all the unnatural conditions of an urban existence have been able entirely to stifle. Take a train from London on a spring morning or in autumn and get out at a wayside station. If you are lucky, the sense of the country will descend upon you with such a wealth of association that for a time you are like a man drugged. It is a sense which brings balm to the spirit and rest to the soul. For me the feeling is exactly like that of a home-coming after a long absence; here, at last, I feel, I can relax and be at peace. But there is another element in our love for the country which refers not to the past but to the future, which is less a reminder of what we have been, than a foretaste of what we may become.

I believe that the capacity for æsthetic appreciation is the highest, as it is the most recently evolved, of all human characteristics. The æsthetic emotion which we experience in the presence of great painting or great music is, I believe, the first intimation, fleeting and uncertain, of a type of experience which man will one day enjoy more fully and more continuously. The appreciation of art is thus a foretaste of what is to come; it does not remind us of the experiences that were ours in the dim past of the race; it points forward to those which will be ours in our more developed future. The issues raised by this assertion belong to philosophy rather than to biography; at any rate they fall outside the scope of this book, and I shall not therefore pursue them here, especially as I have written about them at considerable length else-where.[1]

Grant, however, that there may be something in the theory, grant too that there are æsthetic responses involved in our appreciation of nature not fundamentally different from the emotions we feel for a picture or a fugue, and it will follow that there is an element in man's complex relation to nature which points him forward to the consciousness which will one day be more fully his. For example, the emotion we feel for the line of a down, or for an elm in August standing solid and solitary in a field against a sunset sky.

I hope that it will not set the reader against me if I say that my feeling for nature which originally was almost entirely primitive, as instinctive as my desire for food when hungry and for rest when tired, has become increasingly æsthetic. The old feeling still remains—there are certain sorts of wild places, a tiny valley, for instance, in a mountainous country strewn with boulders and great rocks and gay with flowers and small blossoming trees that I never enter without an immediate feeling of home-coming; it is almost as if I remembered being a fawn—but it is not so strong as it was, and increasingly my pleasure in nature approximates to my pleasure in great music or a perfectly proportioned building. Types of country, which I should once have found merely dull because of their lack of detail and richness, now give me intense satisfaction.

The Fascination of Essex. Take Essex, for example. There was a time when I thought of Essex as an uninteresting county. That it was flat everybody knew; it was also, I thought, featureless, without woods, moors or wild places, consisting merely of great tracts of agricultural land stretching to the sea, intersected by the muddy

[1] See my *Matter, Life and Value*, Chapters VI and IX.

estuaries of sluggish rivers. Visiting it constantly, however, as the more obvious country to the south and west of London became increasingly built over, I found there strange and unsuspected beauties.

Essex is a country of great prospects bounded by low sky-lines. Topping a little rise you see the countryside spread out before you like an enormous picture. So viewed it is seen to shape itself into lines of beauty; its forms are significant. It is a land of great trees. I do not mean that the trees are especially large—although there are as fine trees in Essex as in any county in England—as that, owing to their peculiar shape and spacing, they acquire significance. Each tree has a distinct form, an individuality; three or four together stand a solitary group in the empty fields, brooding presences living an inner life of their own, at once a symbol and an enigma. What the symbol stands for is as unknown as the answer to the enigma. . . . Over the wide mud stretches play curious lights, and the horizon has the power, more than any other that I know, of suggesting unimagined mysteries beyond. Almost all the villages in Essex are lovely, and the spire of Thaxted Church, seen from practically any direction over an immense distance, is unforgettable.

Over the whole county there is the sense of an impalpable decay. It is very deserted, and its winding roads, instead of leading you to a village, end abruptly in solitary farm-houses. It is something of a shock to find that the farm-house with its whitewashed walls, mellow tiles and exquisite shape, is derelict. To walk across the Essex countryside is for me a disturbing, almost a frightening, experience. One cannot accustom oneself to the fact that it should be so lovely and so completely deserted. Corn-growing, its one industry, has collapsed, and there is literally nothing left. It seems impossible to believe that there should not be something beyond that immensely significant skyline, something, one knows not what, to give point and purpose to the whole. One reaches it and looks beyond only to see another empty landscape, featureless like the last, stretching to another skyline. The Essex country is like life, in that, without point or climax, it nevertheless perpetually provokes the expectation of both. Of it all that one can say is that it goes on. And how it does go on! There are places near the Essex coast not fifty miles from London which are as solitary and remote as any in England; there is a seaside village eighteen miles from the nearest station. It is as if the English countryside, doomed as it is to ultimate dereliction had, like a disused limb, begun to atrophy in its extremities. The decay has set in in the east, whence it is destined to spread westwards until all the English country is either derelict or suburb.

Now it is impossible to explain the hold which a countryside like that of Essex has over the affections of those who know it as an instinctive response to primitive and exuberant nature. There is nothing exuberant about Essex. The Essex scene is set in a minor not a major key; it is autumn twilight, Debussy's music, Monet's pictures, anything you like that is dim and plaintive; but it is emphatically not a source of rude and primitive life. I am not sure that my love for it is healthy, but I am sure that it is not elementary. A child or a savage would see nothing in Essex; it is the sage or the artist who savours the formal beauty of its exquisite decay.

Admirations. I have sought in this chapter to describe, as well as I can, my tastes and likings. It has not been altogether an easy task, for I find it difficult to praise. The things one loves are not meant to be written about; perhaps they are not meant to be understood. They exist, it is obvious, to be enjoyed. Hence I turn with relief to the task which will occupy me for the greater part of the remainder of this book, the task of enumerating the objects of my dislike. These in the modern world are sufficiently numerous, and I hope I may deal faithfully by them.

Like many modern people, I like to consider that my spiritual home is fifth-century Athens, or, more doubtfully, eighteenth-century France. I admire reason and the free movement of the mind. I like art that is measured and formal, and I think of the good life as an affair of playing games and scrambling over mountains as a relief from the rigours of intellectual effort. This last, I feel, should be the backbone of one's life, intellectual effort and that playtime of the intellect which is conversation and discussion, provided they be abstract. By saying that they must be abstract, I mean that they must deal with matters on which agreement is impossible, and with problems of which the solution must remain unknown.

I am more interested in what people think than in what they do, and regard action only as an unimportant outcome of thought, the necessity for it being thrust upon us by the lowly plane we occupy in the evolutionary scale. For the race, it is obvious, is in its childhood; it craves material things and acts in order to obtain them. Yet material things, rightly considered, are only the toys of children. To grow up is to pass beyond the need to amuse oneself with toys, and to come to rest, like Shaw's Ancients, in the contemplation of changeless realities, such as truth, goodness and beauty.

Meanwhile, the objects of my admiration are those who have best succeeded in embodying these changeless things in concrete form.

I consider Bach and Mozart, Plato and Buddha and Christ to be the best in the way of instruments that life in the process of its evolution has yet been able to devise; they are the world's greatest men, and Shaw and Wells, Einstein and Bertrand Russell among the greatest of living men.

Literature, Music, the Country

Men's Irrationalism. If men's faculties are not to be devoted to discovering truth or revealing beauty, they are, in my view, most appropriately employed in exposing the hypocrisies and castigating the stupidities of society. Most people, I think, are kindly and honest; but they are very stupid. It is from the silliness not from the wickedness of mankind that the evils of the world seem to me to spring. It is not because men are bad at heart, but because they are weak in the head that they so harry and torment one another and make their world a hell. They accord their greatest admiration to those who have been most successful in organizing slaughter on a large scale—all the highest columns in their cities are surmounted by the figures of those men who have shown the greatest ability in depriving other men of life—and their greatest enthusiasms are expended in pursuit of ends, which there is no reason to think valuable, and on behalf of creeds, which there is no reason to think true. So far as creeds are concerned, that the Holy Ghost proceeds from the Father and from the Son, or that he proceeds from the Father only, that bread and wine are or are not body and blood, or that in some mysterious sense they both are and are not at the same time, are propositions in defence of which men have killed one another in thousands, and practised hideous tortures upon thousands. Yet none of these propositions can be shown to be true and, so far as I am aware, not the faintest evidence has ever been adduced in favour of the view that any of them is true. Whereas in defence of the probably true proposition that seven times seven makes forty-nine, nobody, so far as I know, has been anxious to make life unpleasant for anybody.

Just as the intensity with which men have embraced their beliefs has usually been in inverse proportion to their truth, so the self-sacrificing idealism which they have displayed in pursuit of their ends has been usually in inverse proportion to the value of the ends pursued. Men have collectively suffered torments in order to go to heaven or to convert the Jews; but very little for the sake of spreading knowledge, and scarcely at all to promote happiness or to produce beauty. Yet, I repeat, it is not because they are wicked, but because they are stupid that men behave in this way.

In the Middle Ages the respectable burghers who tortured witches did so, not because they were cruel, but because they desired to save witches from the clutches of the devil. The Inquisition persecuted and burnt heretics, not because the inquisitors took a delight in distorted limbs and roasted living flesh, but because they were persuaded that it was only by this means that heretics would escape an eternity of burning in hell. And in modern times it is by appeals, not to their cupidity or to their cruelty, but to their idealism that decent people are induced to further the schemes of scoundrels, in the belief that they are fighting for justice and liberty.

Enlightened persons frequently contrast the hundreds of millions that a modern nation spends on armaments with the paltry thousands that it is willing to give to education, to housing, or to hygiene. But the contrast is not confined to expenditure. Men will not only give more money, they will give more time, more energy, more ardour and enthusiasm to killing and coercing their fellows than to educating them, to housing them, to keeping them healthy, or to tending them when they are sick. To the work of destruction they will bring a nobility, a forgetfulness of self, a truly religious spirit which the work of construction is powerless to evoke. Thus, were it not for the good in men, most of the evil in the world would have remained undone.

War in my opinion—and I am aware that I have already laboured the view to the point to tedium—is the greatest single evil that afflicts mankind. Yet war, as its apologists are never tired of telling us, has called forth more courage and endurance, has enlisted in its service more nobility and unselfishness, than any other human institution. The suffering and sacrifice and uncomplaining heroism which war alone has demanded, had they only been given to causes which mankind deems ignoble, could in the million years of man's existence have eliminated the need for suffering anywhere within his sphere of activity. War alone can make men trained in the school of self-assertiveness forget the good of the individual in the good of all. War is the one thing that can unite men; it is also the one thing they all know to be wrong.

Religion of Matter and Speed. To a species which is at once so noble and so foolish no greater service can, in my view, be rendered than the exposure of its stupidities. Hence among writers those whom I most praise are those who have most used their reasons to try to make men reasonable. Shaw and Ibsen and Swift, Voltaire and Gibbon and Anatole France, seem to me the most admirable of writers. The world wrongly classes them as literary men, who succeed in producing more or less good plays and novels. Rightly considered, they are propagandists, who seek to give the world a piece of their minds. Their efforts, it is alas only too obvious, have met with little success. The world as it is to-day is given over to unreason not less notably than at any previous period in its history. Since the war a fresh wave of irrationality has swept over Western civilization. Its chief expression is to be found in the worship of matter and the worship of speed. If these two idols can be combined, they evoke a sentiment which borders upon religious ecstasy. Contemporary standards recognize as the supreme test of a man's ability the number of miles he can cover in an hour, and the most infallible sign of human intelligence the number of revolutions it can make

a propeller turn in a minute. The rapid movement of
pieces of matter from one place to another may thus be
defined as the highest end recognized by civilized man.

It is in America that the religion of matter and speed
can be seen in its most advanced form. In New York
there exist all the material appliances for the life which
modern civilization recognizes as good. The means of
transit are fast and hideous; the population is moved and
moved continuously, since it has lost the art of being
still. The individual suffers agonies of discomfort in
the process, but this is thought to be of no importance.
The subways are much faster than the English underground, but, by comparison with their noise and overcrowding, our underground is a haven of rest and spaciousness. Every year there are fewer places to live in and
more places to herd in. Private houses and residential
quarters are torn down and replaced by offices and super-
apartment houses, incredibly expensive, fitted with every
mechanical convenience and as spacious and home-like
as rabbit warrens. The streets are jammed by high-power
cars that during work hours cannot move more than a
mile an hour. These cars, like everything in America,
have been standardized out of every semblance of individual beauty. In time even the sky-scrapers will present
an unvarying picture of unrelieved uniformity. There is
neither space nor time for the individual. Even in
material things, the appropriate medium in this civilization for individual display, the individual can no longer
express himself. Taste and beauty are standardized until
they degenerate into efficiency and regularity so completely, that the ideal seems to be the complete effacement
of the individual. Even lovely women, whose *raison d'être*
consists in being different, accept a uniformity of fashion
that is like a uniform. The men, who frankly accept their
status of beaver-ants, dress as such and all look alike.

The whole civilization is hag-ridden by the ideal of

efficiency, which means that it exhausts itself in doing the wrong things in the right way. It is too busy thinking to have time to stop and think; too busy doing to wonder whether it wants what it does. Can a highbrow, dominated by an obsolete loyalty to reason and still faintly amorous of those traditional dowagers of the spiritual world, truth, goodness and beauty, see in such a world anything but a nightmare?

But I see that my dislikes have already invaded my one poor chapter of likes. Not wishing further to pollute this chapter with the grumbling which I intend to reserve for the rest of this book, I end it here.

CHAPTER V

Dislikings—I. The Cult of Unreason

IT IS my belief that many of the developments in the post-war world which I regard with dislike are due to a particular view of human reason which modern psychology has made popular. The prevalent twentieth-century view is that human action is rarely dictated by rational considerations, and psychologists use their reasons to prove that reason is neither important nor free. I do not myself subscribe to this view. I think, on the contrary, that man can be, although he rarely is, rational in the old-fashioned sense of the word, and that reason can, although it rarely does, determine our beliefs and prescribe our conduct. I think, further, that it is in the advance of rationality, that is to say in the increasing adoption of beliefs which are held because there is reason to think that they are true, and in the increasing choice of actions which there is reason to think will be productive of good, that the chief hope of the race lies. I shall try, therefore, first, to indicate the causes which have led to the modern contempt of reason and are thought to justify it; secondly, to show why, in my view, they do not in fact justify it; and thirdly, to trace certain unattractive manifestations of modern thought and conduct to their source in this attitude. The account of these manifestations will embrace much of what I as a middle-aged

The Cult of Unreason

Edwardian find foolish or distasteful in the modern world.

Nineteenth-Century View of Reason. Our age, the fact is notorious, is one of little faith. We are lukewarm in religion, unimpressed by authority, distrustful of moral codes and impatient of moral restraints. We are also sceptical about reason. The present position of reason is, indeed, highly paradoxical. On the one hand, the last twenty years have seen the triumph of critical and militant Rationalism; on the other, the world of thought has been swept by a wave of irrationalism, which threatens to undermine the seat of reason and to abrogate her authority by exhibiting her as a mere cork floating on the waves of instinct and desire.

The nineteenth century believed on the whole that reason was free. Its deliverances might be, and no doubt in practice frequently were, biased by prejudice and distorted by desire; but the fact that reason could be deflected by these influences was, it was thought, a temporary defect due to man's incomplete evolution. It was, indeed, a basic assumption of the age that reason in theory could and in practice often did operate freely. It could arrive at an impartial 'reasoned' choice between alternative courses of action, and it could take a disinterested survey of evidence with a view to forming a 'reasoned' conclusion or belief. It was only in so far as men's reasons operated 'freely' in this way, that they could be said to act and think 'rationally'. Fortunately, however, in the view of the Victorians, they had already reached a stage of evolution at which appeals to their free reason were sometimes successful, and, under the influence of education and other enlightening forces, the degree of their 'rationality' might be expected continually to increase.

Now, this view of reason was, I suggest, fundamental in nineteenth-century thought. J. S. Mill, for example, to take a typical representative of the time, tells us of his father that 'So complete was his reliance on the influence of reason over the minds of mankind, whenever it is allowed to reach them, that he felt as if all would be gained if the whole population were taught to read, if all sorts of opinions were allowed to be addressed to them by word and in writing, and if by means of a suffrage they could nominate a legislature to give effect to their opinions.' Truth, in other words, will out, if men's minds are only given a fair chance to find it; for, being reasonable by nature, men have only to be given access to truth to recognize it. And, speaking of himself and his friends, J. S. Mill goes on to say that what they 'principally thought of was to alter people's opinions; to make them believe according to evidence . . . which, when they knew, they would, we thought, by the instrument of opinion enforce a regard to it upon one another.'

I do not think that I can better convey the change that has come over the intellectual climate of our age in regard to its attitude to reason, than by saying that both these quotations, which passed without comment in the nineteenth, would be immediately questioned in the twentieth century. Twentieth-century thought no longer assumes either that men will embrace the truth when they see it, or that they will alter their opinions because reasonable grounds are adduced for their doing so. And this assumption is no longer made, because men to-day are fundamentally sceptical of the part played by reason in determining our conduct and forming our beliefs. Reason, it is widely suggested, is a mere tool or handmaid of desire. Its function is to secure the ends which we unconsciously set ourselves, by inventing excuses for what we instinctively want to do and arguments for what we instinctively want to believe. Thus a man's reason follows his likings as the feet of a hungry dog follow his nose. There is, in fact, at bottom very little difference between reason and

The Cult of Unreason

faith; for, if faith is defined as the power of believing what we know to be untrue, reason is the power of kidding ourselves into believing that what we want to think true is true.

Now, on this issue I am inclined to side with John Stuart Mill. I am, I repeat, an unrepentant rationalist, in the sense that I believe that reason operating freely can, on occasion, both form our beliefs and motivate our actions; but I realize, as I have said, that it is considerably more difficult to take this view of reason than it was in Mill's time, and I realize also that many who regard themselves as good rationalists adopt a psychology which implicitly denies it.

Influence of Psycho-analysis. Prominent in the field of reason's adversaries is the conception of the human psyche, with which modern psychology in general and psycho-analysis in particular have familiarized us. They have sponsored a widespread tendency to regard our nature as fundamentally instinctive in character, and reason as an offshoot of instinct, whose operations are determined by instinct and whose function is limited to discovering means for satisfying instinct. The origin of man and the fact that his roots are deep down in nature are emphasized; the inference is that fundamentally he is swayed by the same kind of *natural forces* as those which determine the animals. Of these *natural forces*, it is said, we know very little, especially since we have succeeded in evolving reason, one of whose main functions is to rationalize them and so disguise from us their real character. But reason is itself an expression of these instinctive, natural forces, one of the latest and the weakest; it is a feeble shoot springing from a deep, dim foundation of unconscious trends and desires, and maintaining a precarious existence as their apologist and their handmaid.

133

Dislikings—I

That this or something like it is the conception of reason sponsored by the work of Freud, of Adler, and of Jung, few, I think, would deny; and that the conception is destructive of the spontaneity and freedom of rational processes is, I think, equally undeniable, though many would wish to deny it.

I propose, therefore, in illustration of my contention to cite a few relevant examples of the workings of psycho-analytic machinery.

For Freud, at any rate in his earlier writings, the conscious is completely determined by the unconscious; all the mental events of which we are conscious are, indeed, merely sublimated versions of the unconscious strivings of the 'libido'. Now, we do not know what is going on in the unconscious; if we did, it would not be unconscious; therefore we cannot control it; therefore we are not responsible for the nature of the material which subsequently appears in consciousness. Admittedly there is the machinery of the Freudian censor, which, stationed on the stairway between the unconscious and conscious, prevents the intrusion of undesirable elements from the former into the latter; or, if he cannot wholly prevent, he can at least change and edify, so that an unconscious desire to elope with a waitress may appear in consciousness as a sudden aversion from pickled cabbage. But this activity of the censor takes place below the threshold of consciousness; hence, the censor's success in edifying or in wholly prohibiting is something for which we are not responsible. The conclusion holds, therefore, that the strength and direction of the desires which appear in consciousness are matters outside our control. And reason? Reason is itself a form of desire imperfectly disguised, or, if it is not precisely a desire, it can function only in so far as we *desire* to employ it. Hence, when a conflict arises between reason and an unruly desire which reason seeks to suppress, the issue of the conflict will depend upon the strength of the respective desires involved. For these, as we have seen, we are not responsible; therefore we are not responsible for the issue of the conflict.

Reason and Belief. Impotent in matters of conduct, reason plays no more imposing a rôle in the formation of our beliefs. Freud's later work is largely concerned to represent the more advanced achievements of the human spirit as compensations which we have invented for the instinctual renunciations which the existence of society demands. They thus come to be regarded as the necessary conditions of society's functioning. Religion was treated in this way in *The Future of an Illusion*, being derived from our desire for a Heavenly Father and protector in place of the earthly one who fails us. The conclusion, acceptable to advanced thinkers in its bearing on religion, is apt to be disconcerting when it is extended to embrace activities which we are accustomed to regard as rational, to science, for example, to ethics and to art. Thus ethics, which we have been wont to think a product of reason, is on this view merely a barrier which man has invented to hold in check the instincts whose release would make society impossible; conscience, in fact, is society's policeman implanted in the individual. Hence our beliefs about what is right and good are determined by the nature of the instincts which society feels to be most dangerous to it. For example, the ethical demand to respect our neighbour and treat him as a person possessing equal rights with ourselves, is a precaution against our instinctive tendency to hate him. It is not a rational precept as we fondly believe; it is imposed upon us by the necessity of thwarting our instincts. As with ethics, so with science, and so too with intellectual activity in general.

This, too, is a compensation for thwarted instinctual

activity. What is more, the views we hold on apparently abstract questions are determined by the nature of the particular instincts whose substitute gratification is being found in the intellectual activity which led to their formation. Our instinctive desires, in fact, determine what we think true just as much as they determine what we think right, and the reasoning activity which proceeds to provide us with arguments for reaching the conclusions which our instincts have already determined, is a sublimation of the same instincts. To trace the origin of so-called rational activity in the instinctive need which it satisfies is to demonstrate the forces which determine both its direction and its conclusions. This is done in Freud's book *Civilization and its Discontents*.

The same conclusion is reached in Adler's psychology, although by a different route. For Adler the key to human psychology is the desire to compensate for an unconscious feeling of inferiority. This feeling takes its rise in childhood in the forced recognition of an impotence and deficiency, of which the child is made only too painfully aware by the outrageous knowledgeableness and competence of its leaders. The feeling of impotence is usually concentrated upon some particular defect, the rectification of which becomes the life object of the individual. The set of circumstances which, if realized, would rectify it is called by Adler the life goal. Thus the physical weakling unconsciously sees himself as Mussolini, the child who cannot draw as Botticelli. The life goal, once established, determines the direction of our activities throughout life. And not only of our activities, but of our beliefs; for just as we shall have only those experiences, so shall we form only those views which are compatible with its realization.

As, however, the life goal is unconscious, we shall not know this; hence we shall go through life under the delusion that our reason is operating freely in arriving at conclusions which, if Adler's psychology is correct, are

The Cult of Unreason

already predetermined for us by the nature of the inferiorities for which we are under the necessity of compensating.

I will take one more example, this time from psychology proper, afforded by McDougall's well-known theory of instinct. According to this theory (I am quoting from McDougall),

'the instincts are the prime movers of all human activity; by the conative or impulsive force of some instinct every train of thought, however cold and passionless it may seem, is borne along towards its end . . . all the complex intellectual apparatus of the most highly developed mind is but the instrument by which these impulses seek their satisfaction. . . . Take away these instinctive dispositions with their powerful mechanisms, and the organism would become incapable of activity of any kind; it would be inert and motionless like a wonderful piece of clockwork whose mainspring had been removed.'

Reason, in other words, is a mere mechanism; it is the engine of the personality, and instinct is the steam that sets it going. And, since reason can operate only under the impulsive force of instinct, it can proceed only along the path which instinct indicates to the goal which instinct dictates.

The conclusion is the same as Freud's. As regards conduct, the notion of the *rational* will—that is of a will which operates freely to discipline the passions and regulate the conduct—is a delusion. Either the will is a form of instinct, an instinct conceivably to suppress other instincts, or an instinct for the good of the whole, or it is not. If it is not, it is only instinct which can bring the will into operation. If the instinct to use the rational will to suppress an undesirable instinct is stronger than the instinct suppressed, reason is said to triumph; if not, we are said to yield to temptation. But the issue is one which is determined by the respective strengths of the conflicting instincts, and reason plays no part in its decision.

So far as thought is concerned, reason is a mere tool for reaching those conclusions to which our instincts prompt us. The beliefs we hold are not the result of an impartial survey of evidence, but are reflections of the fundamental desires and tendencies of our nature. We believe what we do upon instinct; but we have also an instinct to use our reason to find arguments in support of our beliefs. Reason, therefore, is suborned from the first; she can dance only to the tune which our instincts pipe her.

It is, of course, perfectly true that psycho-analysis itself aims at correcting delusions and restoring the patient to a condition of sanity; true, also, in many cases that it has done this with marked success. The precise definition of a condition of sanity is not clear. It is to be presumed, however, that it involves among other things the ability to take an impartial survey of objective fact, to see things, in other words, as they are. Certainly to be a victim of delusions implies that we see things as they are not. Hence the practice of psycho-analysis presumes that there is such a thing as rationality, and its methods aim at enabling those who are irrational to become rational. That rationality is possible is, in other words, a presupposition of analytic practice. But what can be meant by rationality if our reasons are the mere tools of our unconscious desires, I do not know. Perhaps the psycho-analytic definition of a rational man is one whose reason is determined by the same desires as those of psycho-analysts; in which case to be irrational would be to hold beliefs and to have desires other than those of analysts.

Influence of Behaviourism. A second type of psychological theory which expresses itself in an attitude which is hostile to reason and destroys its freedom is that which culminates in modern Behaviourism. This is, I take it, the view of psychology which is pre-supposed by most materialistic theories. The view has emerged by process of historical development from the philosophy of Descartes. The science of dynamics which was developing in Descartes' time showed that, given sufficient data, the movements of material bodies could be mathematically calculated. The atoms, in fact, blindly run. Now the human body is a material body; therefore the motions of the human body are determined by the laws of dynamics, and the human body too 'blindly runs'. This result was distasteful to philosophers who wished to think that their minds, at least, were free, and led to the introduction of a radical distinction between the mind and the body. This distinction was elaborated in the theory of parallelism. The mind and body ran on two parallel lines which never intersected; but, owing to the benevolence of God, every event in the one was accompanied by a corresponding event in the other. The pairs of events, in fact, had no causative connexion, since this would involve the interaction between mind and body which was denied, but through the agency of a divine miracle were made to synchronize like two perfectly accurate clocks striking in time.

This ingenious device was, however, unsuccessful in securing the wished independence of mind, since, as the body events were determined by the laws of physics, so those mental events which kept step with them must also be determined. Moreover, scientists were impatient of the incessantly repeated divine miracles, while rationalists were sceptical of the benevolence which was thought to have inspired them. Hence causative connexion was gradually introduced, but causative connexion operating from the side of the body. We are now in sight of the familiar mechanist view. The cosmos is a vast mechanism,

Dislikings—I

the body a cog in the machine; the mind reflects the events occurring in the body, and the problem of psychology is to discover how the reflection takes place.

This problem is solved by representing the mind as a clear wax tablet upon which copies of the events taking place in the brain are scored. Upon these events the mind has no influence; it is not even necessary that mind should be aware of them in order that they may take place; but, unless they do take place, nothing can occur in consciousness. The culmination of this view is, as I have said, to be found in Behaviourism. All human action is explained in terms of mechanical reactions to physical impressions, that is to say, in terms of reflexes and conditioned reflexes; mind or consciousness plays no part in causing these reactions and reflexes; it may or it may not register them. When it does, we are said to be conscious. But consciousness, being merely a spectator of events for which it is not responsible, may be ignored when we are seeking to discover the springs of human action.

Now, reason is conscious, or is an aspect of consciousness; what, therefore, is true of consciousness as a whole, is true of reason. Its operations, too, are determined by physical events which it neither initiates nor controls. Thus the view of human nature which is regarded as being peculiarly rational in virtue of its willingness to face hard facts instead of sentimentalizing about spirit, the view which is currently put forward by the scientifically minded who uphold reason as the chief glory and achievement of man, appears on analysis to represent reason as an irrational excrescence upon an automatic cog in a mechanical universe. Man is a mechanical microcosmos reflecting a mechanical macrocosmos; reason is the registering machine of the microcosmos. It cannot, in other words, work of itself; it can only register the conclusions which reflect cerebral states; it is the mere wag of the tail upon the mechanist dog.

The Cult of Unreason

It is a comfort that, if the conclusions of this psychology are correct, there is no reason to think them true. For the Behaviourist psychology itself is a product of reason; it is at least reasonable, even if it be mistaken. Hence, if it is to be believed, it is the result not of an impartial investigation into mental processes crystallizing in conclusions which represent evidence considered without bias, but of a series of mechanical processes in the bodies of the Behaviourists who hold it. If it is correct in what it asserts, it tells us nothing about psychology in general; it merely gives us information about the particular cerebral conformation of those psychologists whose brain processes it reflects. To ask if it is true is, on this basis, as meaningless as to ask whether their blood-pressure is true.

Influence of Marxism. The Behaviourist psychology is only one particular kind of materialism, or rather it is only one of a number of different views which spring from and imply a materialist basis. The modern world is full of people who believe that they are all body and that their minds are only reflections of their brains. Intellectual activity is for them a sort of by-product of brain activity; it is like the bright colours of an oil film on the unresting ocean of bodily processes. This view is dominant in modern Russia, and it issues in an attitude to reason no less hostile than those at which I have already glanced.

Good Marxists believe that the character of a civilization is determined by the nature of the methods by which people satisfy their material wants. The technique of production at any given moment conditions and moulds the institutions of the society that employs it; and not only its institutions but its thought, its art, its religion, in a word its culture. To feudal societies one kind of culture is appropriate; to the mercantilist societies of the sixteenth and seventeenth centuries, another; to the fully developed capitalism of the nineteenth, another; and to proletarian communism another, another culture another truth.

On this view there is no such thing as objective truth, for reason is incapable of taking an impartial view of anything; there is only the truth appropriate to a particular stage of economic production, bolstered up by the arguments of a reason which is dominated by the necessity of proving only those propositions which are economically advantageous to the holders of power. The *Outline of Psychology*, issued in England by the Plebs Text-Books Committee, is quite clear on this point; 'the intellect' it says 'is above all things an instrument of partiality'. Its function is, it is affirmed, to secure the performance of those actions which are beneficial to the individual, the species, or, we may add, to the class. Actions beneficial to one class will not coincide with those which are beneficial to another; on the contrary, they will usually be directly opposed to them. It follows that the truths appropriate to different classes will be different truths, which the practical reasons of their members will support with different arguments.

The reasons of Marxians alone, it seems, are immune from this general partiality. 'The faith of the Marxist' we read later 'differs profoundly from religious faith; the latter is based only on desire and tradition; the former is grounded on the scientific analysis of objective reality.'

But this really will not do. Either the intellect possesses the capacity to function impartially and arrive at objective conclusions as the result of a disinterested survey of the available evidence, or it does not. If it does, there seems to be no reason to suppose that the possession of the capacity is confined to the intellects of those who happen to have been born in Russia, or for some other reason to have embraced Marxism. If it does not, then

The Cult of Unreason

here is no reason to suppose that the 'truth' formulated by the Plebs text-book has any basis in objective fact. Like all other 'truths', it is merely a statement of views which are such as to be thought advantageous to those who hold them, and is believed solely for this reason. It is no doubt advantageous to Marxists to believe that the reasons of all persons except Marxists are cheats; but, if their theory is true, then there is no means of resisting the conclusion that the reasons of Marxists have cheated them into believing it. But if the belief that the reasons of all non-Marxists cheat is itself the result of dishonest reasoning, there is no reason to hold it; in which case, it ceases to be true that the reasons of all non-Marxists are cheats.

In this way the reasoning of those who throw suspicion on reason in the interests of economic determinism defeats itself, just as the reasoning of those who seek the origin of all mental processes in the body defeats itself.

Psychology of Economists. It is a far cry from modern Russia to nineteenth-century England, but the creed to which nineteenth-century economists subscribed was not psychologically different from that of twentieth-century Marxists. The orthodox economists of the last century held that acquisitiveness was the only motive of which it was necessary to take account, because by it alone were men's actions dictated. The psycho-analysts believe that the penis is the rudder of human nature; the economists held that it was the pocket. And just as Freud believes that the *libido* uses reason as an instrument to achieve sexual satisfaction or to comfort the self for not achieving it, so the economist believed that the economic motive of pecuniary advancement used the reason to plan the steps by which a man could become richer. This view is also at the basis of the Marxist philosophy which, however, substitutes the economic self-interest of a class for that of an individual as the only object of rational desire and purposive effort. This essentially Marxist attitude to reason is still dominant among magistrates and business men, whose psychology is apt to reflect that which was beginning to be abandoned about fifty years before. Magistrates, for example, express astonishment that young women should sacrifice their earnings to marry men in receipt of the dole, and marriage with a poor person whom you happen to love instead of with a rich one whom you do not is generally regarded by respectable persons as an unnatural perversion. In war-time, however, eminent people do not hesitate to abandon this psychology and expect the young voluntarily to place themselves in positions of discomfort and danger from which no pecuniary advantage may be expected, in order to increase the security of eminent people. Thus the view that reason is constrained to prescribe only that kind of conduct and to support only those beliefs which tend to the economic advantage of the individual, is not invariably maintained in practice, nor do there seem to be any better grounds for thinking it to be true, than the view that the mind is determined by the state of the brain or of the unconscious.

Apology for the Chapter. To emancipate reason from servitude to the movements of the brain, the motivations of the pocket and the urges of the *libido* is a considerable task; I have attempted it at length elsewhere and shall not undertake it here. I cannot, however, refrain from pointing out the irony of the fact that mechanism has become popular in psychology just when it is beginning to be abandoned everywhere else. Psychologists are busy demonstrating that man is a piece of matter which works like a machine, at a time when the

[1] See my *Matter, Life and Value*, and *Philosophical Aspects of Modern Science*.

physicists are showing that a 'piece of matter' is meaningless and that nothing works 'like a machine'. Thus modern science points in contrary directions, the plain man does not know what to think, and the Church says this 'only shows what comes of trusting science'. However, the matter, as I say, lies outside the scope of this book, and I return to my main theme, which at the moment is the unpleasing features of contemporary life which seem to me to spring more or less directly from the attitude to reason, which I have sketched in this chapter. Taken together they constitute what amounts to a veritable cult of unreason. In the next chapters I shall try to show how this cult of unreason is inimical to good talk, good literature and good politics. It is also the source of a certain lopsidedness of development in modern civilization, which is already a nuisance and may become a menace. The next chapters, then, will be strictly autobiographical in the sense of being a series of personal grumbles. My apology for the inclusion of this one is that it was necessary to describe what may be called the official background of the cult of unreason, in order to bring into relation with each other those expressions of it at which I am proposing to carp.

CHAPTER VI

Dislikings—II. Unreason in Talk, Politics, and the Novel

Unreason in Talk

THE BELIEF that men's views reflect their desires rather than their reasons has a number of harmful effects in practice. For example, it is destructive of good talk and inimical to fruitful discussion. Owing to the influence of psycho-analysis there prevails in modern society a refusal to discuss any view on its merits. If X expresses an opinion Y, the question discussed is not whether Y is true or at least reasonable, but the considerations which led X to believe it to be true. Objective truth being regarded as unobtainable, what alone is thought interesting are the reasons which lead people to formulate their particular brands of error.

Now it may be the case that my aversion for Wagner's music is due to my desire to elope with a waitress; it may even be the case that my convictions that war is never right and that Socialism is not only desirable but attainable are due to the interest which my nurse exhibited in my private parts at the age of five. But admitting that these things are possible, I confess that I do not find them interesting. What interests me is whether my dislike of Wagner is justified, and my views about war and Socialism are sound; and upon the question of whether they are sound or not, the considerations which initially led me to hold them seem to me to have absolutely no bearing whatever. It may be true, although I do not think it is, that none of our views are rational in origin; but that is no reason why some of them should not be true.

Now I am much more interested in what is true than in what people think true, or in why they think true what they do. I do not very much care how it was that X came to hold opinion Y. Even the Freudian demonstration that the source of the opinion can be traced to his shame at wetting his bed at the age of two, leaves me comparatively cold; but I may be passionately concerned to know whether opinion Y is true. We should, therefore, in my view, acknowledge the possibility that the origin of all our opinions may be tainted in the sense that we may hold them for reasons which are neither weighty nor creditable, and, having made our bow to this hypothesis, forget it, and consider whether on merits and in the light of the available evidence, they are sound opinions.

Decline of Discussion. The modern interest in psychoanalysis tends to substitute biography for argument. Refusing to consider, it refuses also to discuss opinions on merits. Hence the argumentative canvassing of rival views is neither so frequent nor so interesting in the modern world as before the war. Stevenson says somewhere that the only things worth discussing are Love, Freedom and Immortality. I used to discuss Love, Philosophy and Socialism. But the true modern is not interested; if by chance any of these subjects do appear on the conversational *tapis*, he inquires only how they came to be chosen as subjects for discussion.

Yet, if he is logical, he must realize that even this is not worth discussing. If it is impossible to reach objective truth on *any* question, objective truth will also be unobtainable in regard to the question why X holds opinion Y. For the views of Z on the subject will not, in fact, tell us anything about the hidden motives of X. They will merely reflect the hidden motives of Z in adopting his particular view of X's motives. The conclusion seems to be this; a discussion on, let us say, sexual relations, politics, or Utopias, purports to reflect the views of the participants on the subject in question. It may, however, reflect merely the unconscious wishes which caused the participants to hold these particular views. But any reason there may be for asserting the second alternative, is an equally good reason for holding that the assertion itself reflects merely the unconscious wishes of him who makes it. It does not, therefore, tell us anything about the motives and wishes of the participants in the discussion, and it does not, therefore, afford a reason for thinking that their views on sex, politics or religion are *merely* the reflections of their unconscious wishes. If they are not, it is at least *possible* that they are the fruit of the intellects of the persons concerned playing freely on the subjects under discussion.

Definition of Reasonable Beliefs. It seems to me to be essential to hold that we can sometimes judge things to be so because they are so, and for no other reason; to hold, in other words, that our beliefs are sometimes determined by the facts about which they are beliefs. In common matters of fact, where the truth can be ascertained, this is generally conceded. If I see a flash of lightning and believe that it will be followed by thunder, my belief would be said to be determined not by an unconscious wish for thunder, or the unconscious expectation of any advantage which the belief was designed to secure, but by the experience of thunder following lightning in the past. When the thunder occurs, my belief would be said to be verified by the fact.

In such cases, it is not, so far as I know, suggested that our opinions are determined by anything except the objective facts which they assert, and by which they are verified. A reasonable man is one whose opinions are most nearly in accord with objective facts, and are most frequently verified by them. Admittedly in discussions of such matters as communism, immortality, free will or deity, where the facts are not known, this criterion of what is reasonable cannot be applied with certainty. It is none the less applicable. If, that is to say, a reasonable belief means one thing in regard to common matters of fact on which truth is obtainable, there is no reason why it should not mean the same thing in regard to matters where the truth is unobtainable. In such matters admittedly the belief can never be known to be true; but it can be known to be probable. A probable belief is one which, taking the fullest account of all the evidence available, bases itself on such evidence. In metaphysics, religion, literature, ethics and science probable beliefs are those that it is reasonable to adopt.

I do not wish to deny that on these and on all other subjects our beliefs are frequently biased by our wishes, and that, when these are unconscious, the bias cannot be detected except by others. But I am asserting that the elimination of bias is possible, and can be achieved by a scrupulous attention to objective fact, that only when it is achieved can the belief which results said to be reasonable, and that it is in the increasing emancipation of men's minds from subjective bias, with the resultant increase in beliefs which are in accordance with the facts, that man's chief hope for the future lies. I am admitting, in short, that men are frequently unreasonable and do not know that they are; I am asserting merely that it is possible for them to be reasonable, and that they ought to try to become so more frequently.

Unreason in Politics

In the second place, the prevalent leaning towards irrationalism appears to me to be responsible for many of the more regrettable tendencies of modern politics. The methods of democratic government have, in fact, developed into an organized appeal to unreason.

The skill of the democratic politician consists in his ability to divine what people can be brought to think advantageous to themselves. Skill in forecasting those opinions which are likely to commend themselves to an electorate does not imply skill in the formation of opinions which are rational, in the sense of being such as the needs of the times dictate. Hence the art of the democratic politician depends upon his skill in presenting policies which are other than those which the exigencies of the situation require. If he does this successfully, he is returned to power on a programme of promises which have pleased a majority of the electorate, but which have no relation to the needs of the State. It is true that the promises are quickly found to be incapable of performance, with the result that the party responsible for them is thrown out of office on the ground that it has betrayed its pledges. The defaulting politicians are, however, immediately succeeded by others who have gained favour as the result of appeals which are equally irrational. Modern politics is thus characterized by an increasing disparity between the measures which governments advocate and those which the welfare of the community demands. By 'the community' I mean the collection of nations which constitute Western civilization, since it is obvious that no useful purpose is any longer to be served by thinking of national states as if they were isolated political entities. For example, it is clear that the paramount duty of a modern statesman is to prevent another war. Another war—it is obvious—will destroy our civilization. It is equally obvious that the only effective method of preventing it is to subordinate the independent sovereignties of national states to an international body to which their separate military forces are transferred, and in which their powers are vested. Yet this is a measure which no states-man dare advocate on an election platform; it would offend the patriotism of electors.

Again, it is obvious that, if the economic crisis is to be solved and subsequent crises avoided, if, in Marxian lan-guage, the contradictions inherent in capitalism are to be resolved, there must be an international control of raw materials, which would allocate to the various nations according to their needs. Yet the measures required to establish such a control are highly technical, the subject is dull and difficult to understand, and a candidate who made it a main plank of his election programme would bore his supporters.

Another essential measure is the control of population. Steps will have to be taken sooner or later to determine the *optimum* population for each state, and then to ensure that the actual output of babies is controlled in accordance with the figure reached. Yet this, again, is a subject quite unsuitable for the public platform; it would outrage the moral prejudices of electors.

These are only a few examples of measures with which the welfare of modern civilization is increasingly seen to be bound up, but which fail to secure the attention of governments, because they are not such as to appeal to electors. They are dictated by reason and can be recommended only by an appeal to the reasons of the electors. But appeals to reason are ineffective where great masses of people are concerned, since the larger the area over which an appeal must be made, the cruder and more elementary the terms in which it must be couched.

Highest Common Factor Appeal in Cinema. The decline in the art of the cinema since the arrival of the 'talkies' exemplifies the same point. The average cinema entertain-ment is, it is notorious, now such that no intelligent person can sit through it without intolerable humiliation. The reason is simple. It costs some forty thousand pounds to make even the simplest 'talkie'. Hence, if a 'talkie' is not to be a financial failure, it must be capable of being shown a large number of times to great masses of people. It must, therefore, appeal to those elements which great masses of people have in common.

Now the part of me which I share with a Hollywood 'hick' consists of my fears and my appetites; it is grounded in my genitals, flanked by my kidneys and maintained by my stomach. It is a very dull part, being very like the equivalent parts of thousands of other middle-aged men. It follows, therefore, that a film which bases itself on what is common to me and the Hollywood hick will be a dull and boring film. Whatever depends for its success on its ability to attract the attention and win the admiration of average people, cannot, it is obvious, rise above the common level of those to whom it appeals.

Now all people, however otherwise diverse, have one element in common: this is sex, the highest common denominator of all differences between individual men and women—sex and its spiritual counterpart morality, which is the sour grapes of sex. Morality, like sex, tends to be much the same among all peoples because the herd, whose special emanation it is, is always and everywhere the same. Intellect gives off fresh lights in every age because the intellectuals of one society may be fundamentally different from their predecessors and their successors. It is reason which changes; desire which remains constant, desire and morality which is the obverse of desire.

And in Politics. This casual damning of the cinemas sounds like a digression. It is, yet the digression has a bearing upon my theme. Returning to it, I observe that the transaction of the affairs of a modern community is a highly skilled task, calling in a pre-eminent degree for the exercise of those talents and faculties, courage and forethought, intelligence, determination and knowledge, originality of thought and breadth of outlook by which a few, and only a few, members of our species in each generation are distinguished. And the lesson to be learned from the 'talkies' is that it is as idle to expect these qualities to be displayed by those whose power depends upon their ability to appeal to the average voter, as it is to expect high art in a form of entertainment which appeals to the average audience. Politics, as we know it to-day, is contemptible for the same reason as the 'talkies' are contemptible. Being based upon the goodwill of the average, it must appeal to the common denominator of passion and interest which all share alike, and not to the reason in respect of which each man is different from his fellows.

It will, of course, be said that the clever man can descend to the level of the electorate, and use reason to plan the appeal to unreason. This, no doubt, is true up to a point. An Alcibiades or a Disraeli can always score a first-rate popular success with the mob, so long as he succeeds among his own kind; but as soon as he falters, his supporters turn against him and vie with each other in vilifying the man they acclaimed. The unconscious spite, which inferior persons nourish against men of superior ability or talent, forbids them to neglect any opportunity of taking it out of those who make them feel conscious of their inferiority. For this reason they will bear more readily with the failures of those who really represent them, the George III's and Gladstones of history, than with the success of those whose unsparing contempt they sense under the affable demeanour of the popular demagogue.

Even if a democracy is prepared to place its trust in a leader of intelligence, it forbids him to exercise it. Measures which arouse passion provide a better foundation in popular support than those which appeal to reason, and the skill of the politician consists, therefore, in knowing which passions can be aroused most easily. Most of the really sweeping elections of recent years have been fought on issues such as Hanging the Kaiser, Making Germany Pay, the Zinovieff Letter, and the Post Office Savings Bank Scare, which were not only destitute of the possibility of practical application or of any basis in reality, but were known to be so by those who formulated them. It is on issues of this kind that politicians thrive. Hate, fear and spite are the most potent driving-forces in large masses of people, and when they cannot be directed, as in war-time, against an external enemy, they must be turned against the members of other classes or against other politicians. Thus politicians prosper by dividing the nation into rival groups and exploiting its division into rival classes, since by this means the evocation of unreasoning passions is facilitated. Hence governments, whose powers are based upon appeals to unreason, will concentrate upon whatever measures are easy to explain and which make for rivalry and division between nations or different sections of the nation. There seems to be no reason to think that there is any identity between those measures which are salutary and those which fulfil these two conditions.

Unreason in the Novel

Thirdly, the cult of unreason seems to me to have a prejudicial effect on art and literature. It is difficult here for me to make allowance for the bias against new work arising from the virtual closing of my mind. As I have already explained, this event occurred some time in the late twenties, and I have been unable to maintain an open and receptive attitude to those forms and fashions in art and literature which have since then come to the fore.

Talk, Politics, and the Novel

The Sex Novel. Take D. H. Lawrence for instance. One of the reasons why I have never been able to give this considerable author his due arises from his preoccupation with sex. Now I do not mean that I am not concerned with sex; on the contrary, I am and hope that I shall continue to be concerned with it continually. But the concern is practical not theoretical. The theory of sex has ceased for me to be a subject, as its practice has ceased to be a problem. That literature is a substitute for life is profoundly true of the literature of sex. Speaking generally, one only wants to read books about sex when one is sexually maladjusted, and this applies not only to the crude appeal of frankly pornographic literature to the sexually starved, but to the literary and imaginative treatment of the problems of the sexually ill-adjusted. It is the distressing amount of sexual maladjustment that accounts for the vogue of the biting, scratching, cursing, hating and ferociously loving men and women of Lawrence's novels. I am not saying that all this sexual violence is not very well in its way, and as good a subject for literature as any other; but the variety of the methods by which men and women manage to consummate, or ridiculously to frustrate the consummation of their natural desires, is not a particularly interesting form of literature to one whose demands in this department are on the whole reasonably well provided for. The vogue of Lawrence and Joyce would, I imagine, only be possible among sexually starved peoples like the English and Americans. But, when all allowance is made for the bias of an Edwardian, I still think that it is possible to pick a quarrel with modern literature on the ground of its adhesion to the prevailing cult of unreason. I will take as an illustration the work of representative modern novelists, who also happen to be writers of genius, D. H. Lawrence, James Joyce, and Virginia Woolf.

In the first place, these writers take as their theme the unreasoning elements in human nature and exalt their importance. This is more particularly true of Lawrence; it is true in a lesser degree of Joyce; it is terrifyingly true of their fearsome followers. All three delight to represent the conscious, reasoning part of human beings as a mere cork to be tossed about on the waves of unconscious desire and hidden impulse. The part of a man that controls or appears to control is, it is obvious, not for them the part that matters. Now the dark elements in the background, the unconscious desires, the atavistic forces and all the rest, are those that persist from man's past; they are, therefore, those that he shares in common with the creatures from amongst whom he has lately and precariously emerged, savages in the immediate, animals in the remote past.

Now, that conscious reason and apparently controlling will are so influenced and determined, I do not wish to deny. In the scale of biological time man's savage past is still very recent. It is not surprising, therefore, that its influence should persist; that man's feet should still be clogged with traces of the primeval slime, his nostrils filled with the vapours of the pit. But, admitting the fact, I protest that it does not amuse or interest me. What interests me about human beings is not the origins from which they arose, but the heights to which they may rise. It is in virtue of their differences from, not of their likenesses to savages and animals that human beings achieve interest and distinction.

Minds versus Emotions. The more human beings develop, the more diversity they exhibit. Desiring a beefsteak, feeling interest in a young woman and dislike for an old one, boasting in liquor and cringing when hurt, I am, I imagine, experiencing emotions which are almost identical with those of my savage ancestors. My behaviour on these occasions, at any rate, is similar although more restrained. But my responses to a Bach

Talk, Politics, and the Novel

Fugue, or a philosophical argument are profoundly different; different and richer. They are also profoundly different from, although not richer than, the responses of an equally educated and intelligent adult of my own generation. In so far as I am motivated from the testicles, the stomach, or the heart, my behaviour is like that of millions of other male humans past and present; in so far as my conduct is inspired by intellectual curiosity and dominated by reason, it is profoundly different. Now it is the differences between people that are interesting, not their likenesses. The reactions of pacifist socialist (A) and militant history-teaching don (B) to the impact of war, seem to me of enthralling interest; the reactions of bank clerk (A) and insurance clerk (B) to the same rejection by the same young woman, of none at all.

In their concentration upon the dark background of passion and emotion rather than upon the lighted foreground of reason and intellect, Lawrence and his school exchange the less interesting for the more. Their movement is backward towards the darkness, not forward to the light; but the primary fact about darkness is that it is dull. Nor is dullness the only disability under which their work labours. Violence and extravagance are the instruments of those who deal in emotion. Necessarily, since it is the violent and extravagant that they describe. The only variations of which emotions are capable are variations in intensity. From the point of view of emotion, the more intense the better. Thus D. H. Lawrence's characters live in a sort of perpetual hurricane of feeling. In a hurricane one must bawl to be heard; hence, if they desire one another to pass the mustard, they must do it at the tops of their voices. But if you shout for the mustard, you can do no more than shout for a mistress. When the great moments come, they fall flat, because the possibilities of human emotion have already been exhausted on the levels. Thus Lawrence deprives himself of all power of emphasis.

by constant over-exaggeration. The violence of the utterance defeats its own ends.

The result is, I submit, inevitable. Reason is an organ with many stops; in the hands of the skilful player it lends itself to infinite harmonies of theme and discourse. Moreover, the variations on the theme of reason are infinite, if only because the possibilities of knowledge are infinite. Reason, in short, is complex as befits that which foreshadows the future. But with emotion it is not so. Emotion has the simplicity of all that belongs to man's past; its varieties are limited and its types are few, and most emotions are quickly recognizable as belonging to one type or another. This is particularly true of the emotions which men feel for women and women for men. Ultimately the only variations that are possible are those of intensity; hence, the shouts.

To shout is to appeal to the irrational part of the soul. It was because they addressed their appeal to the irrational part that Plato, although regretfully, turned the artists out of his ideal state. They played upon those elements in the soul which should be discouraged, and aroused emotions which, he considered, were better restrained. Plato has been criticized for this exclusion of the artists, and the criticism is, I dare say, in the main sound enough. But the school of Lawrence affords an admirable example of the wisdom of his provision.

The continual hurricane of emotion in which Lawrence's characters live appears to me to offend against another literary canon, that of proportion. The most purely reasonable attitude to life with which I am acquainted is contained in Aristotle's doctrine of The Mean. The good life contains all the elements of experience, but it contains them mixed in carefully selected proportions. As with the good life, so with the good book. I am not protesting against the violent treatment of violent emotions; merely that such treatment should be kept in its rightful place, which is not coterminous with the whole novel. No emotion could be deeper than the grief of Adam Bede for Hetty Sorrel, no passion more violent than the rage of Squire Beltham exposing Richmond Roy. But George Eliot and Meredith kept the emotions of their characters within bounds; they did not permit them to slop over until they inundated the whole book. Strong feeling is mixed in due order and proportion with other elements, and the humorous shrewdness of Mrs. Poyser and the uncomplaining love and patience of Dorothy Beltham provide a perspective of good sense and quietness in which outbursts of strong feeling are by contrast enhanced. Excess brings its own Nemesis in literature as in life. What really offends me in Lawrence and many moderns is their continual trespass against the virtues of order, clarity, moderation and poise, the classical virtues, the reasonable virtues.

Interest in 'Life as Such'. Another tendency which strengthens the unreasoning part of the soul is the tendency to put everything in. Joyce is the great sinner here, Joyce and Virginia Woolf. Virginia Woolf, to my mind, is a writer of genius; the tendency and effect of her work are, nevertheless, retrograde. It is animated by an avowed interest in and admiration for life, life, that is to say, of all sorts and as such. Everything that is living is interesting, and, she almost seems to say, equally interesting; everything is, therefore, grist to the novelist's mill. Mrs. Woolf finds her model in Montaigne. She quotes him with approval on the soul.

'Really she' (the soul) 'is the strangest creature in the world, far from heroic, variable as a weathercock, "bashful, insolent; chaste, lustful; prating, silent; laborious, delicate; ingenious, heavy; melancholic, pleasant; lying, true; knowing, ignorant; liberal, covetous, and prodigal" —in short, so complex, so indefinite, corresponding so

little to the version which does duty for her in public, that
a man might spend his life merely in trying to run her to
earth.'

The attempt is, admittedly, difficult. Yet it seems it
must be made. To 'record the atoms as they fall upon the
mind in the order in which they fall, tracing the pattern,
however disconnected and incoherent in appearance,
which each sight or incident scores upon the consciousness', in these terms Mrs. Woolf avows her aims.

'Examine for a moment' she goes on 'an ordinary mind
on an ordinary day. The mind receives a myriad impressions—trivial, fantastic, evanescent, or engraved with the
sharpness of steel. From all sides they come, an incessant
shower of innumerable atoms; and as they fall, as they
shape themselves into the life of Monday or Tuesday, the
accent falls differently from of old; the moment of importance came not here but there.'

'Life' she continues 'is not a series of gig lamps sym-
metrically arranged; life is a luminous halo, a semi-trans-
parent envelope surrounding us from the beginning of
consciousness to the end.'

'Is it not' she concludes 'the task of the novelist to
convey this varying, this unknown and uncircumscribed
spirit, whatever aberration or complexity it may display
with as little mixture of the alien and external as possible
We are not pleading merely for courage and sincerity; we
are suggesting that the proper stuff of fiction is a little
other than custom would have us believe it.'

Values in Life and Purpose in Literature. No writer
has practised her art, as she conceives it, with more
triumphant success than Mrs. Woolf; yet it may be
asked whether the conception is not, perhaps, mistaken
It rests upon the assumption that life as such is interesting, and valuable because it is interesting. I protest that

it is not. The records of most lives, those of the amoeba or the polyp, for example, are unprintable; even if printed they would be, I cannot help feeling, very dull. Even among humans some lives are admittedly more interesting than others, that of Socrates for example, or of Napoleon, than that of an agricultural labourer on thirty shillings a week who never leaves his native village. We must, the conclusion is inescapable, admit that there are grades of interestingness in lives. And not only of interestingness but of value.

Life itself, it is obvious, is not a good. Indiscriminate increase of population beyond a certain level is, in fact, a definite evil. Life carries with it, moreover, not only the seeds of disease and death, but also the germ of all that is vicious and hideous in human conduct. It is life that produces cruelty, torture and rape. Lives, then, it is clear, can vary in point of goodness.

But if some lives are more interesting than others and some are better, are we justified in saying that all life is of value to the novelist just because it is life? Is it not the business of the novelist to choose the more interesting, and his duty so to treat it that he may promote what is good?

I cannot divest myself of the feeling that all literature should have a purpose. Its object should be at least in part to improve and to enrich man's life. A good book is one that makes us better, better, of course, in a wide sense and on the whole. Literature, in short, should affect our lives. If a book excites thought; if it stimulates the sense of beauty, the sense of pity, the sense of sympathy; if it helps in any way towards the understanding of one's fellow-creatures; if it moves to laughter or to tears; if it increases the general vitality; if it throws light on dark problems; if it discloses the broad principles which govern the movements of humanity; if it awakens the conscience and thus directly influences personal conduct—if it accomplishes any of these things, then it has succeeded. If it does none of these things but rather the opposite of these things, then it has failed.

I am asserting, then, that literature has moral as well as æsthetic value. I should go further and assert that its æsthetic value is largely dependent on its propagandist effectiveness. Manner is merely a device for ensuring attention for matter; beauty the sugar on the pill of meaning. Great literature should aim at promoting, and, in my view, does promote the moral virtues of kindness and humanity, the rational ones of knowledge and understanding. All the greatest novelists, Tolstoy and Dickens, Dostoevsky and Fielding and Bunyan do this. Essentially they discriminate; they have values. Conscious of a world order, they are inspired by an irresistible urge to change and by changing to improve it. Compared with them the admirers of life as such, the Henry Jameses, the Flauberts, the George Moores, the literary artists are moved by nothing more than a curiosity to handle and appreciate individual things and moods, as a woman handles stuffs on a tangled and much-littered counter.

Take this sort of thing, for instance, from Mrs. Woolf's *Jacob's Room*:

'She spent tenpence on lunch. "Dear, miss, she's left her umbrella," grumbled the mottled woman in the glass box near the door at the Express Dairy Company's shop.

' "Perhaps I'll catch her," answered Milly Edwards, the waitress with the pale plaits of hair; and she dashed through the door.

' "No good," she said, coming back a moment later with Fanny's cheap umbrella. She put her hand to her plaits.

' "Oh, that door!" grumbled the cashier.

'Her hands were cased in black mittens, and the finger-tips that drew in the paper slips were swollen as sausages.

' "Pie and greens for one. Large coffee and crumpets. Eggs on toast. Two fruit cakes."

'Thus the sharp voices of the waitresses snapped. The lunchers heard their orders repeated with approval, saw the next table served with anticipation. Their own eggs on toast were at last delivered. Their eyes strayed no more.

'Damp cubes of pastry fell into mouths opened like triangular bags. . . .'

This, no doubt, is highly amusing and well and truly observed; but it is not clear why the observation should be recorded. It is a slice of life served raw, without either selection or discrimination. Nothing is added, nothing left out. But for those who do not admire life as such, it is not enough. To photograph life is merely to substitute literature for living, and to provoke the question why, if the picture is not to improve upon the original, the substitution should be made. To answer the question is of necessity to assign values, affirming that some things are intrinsically more admirable than others. It is to affirm that literature should criticize life by putting right what life leaves wrong, and clarify it by throwing into high relief the values which life muddles and overlays. The great writer, in other words, will have a strong sense of value, and employ his literary gift only in so far as he may wish to illustrate or to support it. Undeniably Mrs. Woolf has this sense; her possession of the gift is equally undoubted.

The criticism that I make of her in these purely photographic passages—and they are one of the most distinguishing features of her work—is that by writing as if one thing were intrinsically as good as or as interesting as another, she betrays her sense and misuses her gift. In so doing she assists and subscribes to the prevailing cult of unreason. The function of reason is to discriminate, to prefer, to assign values. If reason were honoured by modern novelists it would no longer be thought that incidents were important because they happened, or people because they existed.

The low estimation in which reason is held is also responsible for what may be called the headline style. Much modern literature is characterized by a lack of continuity and cohesion; it is written in jerks. Take this, for instance, from *Ulysses* :

'Solitary hotel in mountain pass. Autumn. Twilight. Fire lit. In dark corner young man seated. Young woman enters. Restless. Solitary. She sits. She goes to window. She stands. She sits. Twilight. She thinks. On solitary hotel paper she writes. She thinks. She writes. She sighs. Wheels and hoofs. She hurries out. He comes from his dark corner. He seizes solitary paper. He holds it towards fire. Twilight. He reads. Solitary.'

Or this from *Jacob's Room* :

'At this moment there shook out into the air a wavering, quavering, doleful lamentation which seemed to lack strength to unfold itself, and yet flagged on; at the sound of which doors in back streets burst sullenly open; workmen stumped forth.

'Florinda was sick.

'Mrs. Durrant, sleepless as usual, scored a mark by the side of certain lines in the *Inferno*.

'Clara slept buried in her pillows; on her dressing-table dishevelled roses and a pair of long white gloves.

'Still wearing the conical white hat of a pierrot, Florinda was sick.'

Disintegrating the Personality. Passages of this kind seem to me to be the literary expressions of the contemporary psychological doctrines which I have outlined.

Talk, Politics, and the Novel

Under the influence of psychology there is a widespread belief to-day that personality is a myth. A man is not a continuing entity; he is a series of separate psychological states. The ego, the thread upon which the states used to be strung like beads on a necklace, has disappeared. This disintegration of the *person* is bound up with the discrediting of reason, for it was reason that gave a background of cohesion and continuity to the essentially discontinuous series of moods and feelings. If reason is dismissed as unimportant, a human being becomes not a personality enduring through change, but a succession of changing moods. A man, on this view, is like a cinematographic man; that is to say, he is a series of separate momentary men, succeeding one another with such rapidity as to create the illusion of continuity. The truth about a man so conceived will be the truth about the separate states; it will be a collection of accounts of successive little pieces of him, the tiny physical acts, the fleeting psychological moods, the semi-conscious wishes, the memories half-evoked. And in order to get as close as possible to this succession of little pieces, one writes a succession of little pictures, matching the discontinuity of life with a discontinuity of style. By this means, it is thought, the essential reality of life will be captured, its essence distilled into one's pages.

To say that the psychological doctrine is false, that a man is more than the succession of his psychological states, that he is a continuing personality over and above the sum total of the feelings and moods which go to make him up, and that the truth about him is to be reached not by cataloguing the little bits but by creating a picture of the whole, which means conceiving him as a person and a character, is beside the point. If it is, in fact, the case that by leaving out connexions, stringing together series of separate statements, writing in dots and dashes, one can really convey something about the human mind which is incommunicable by any other method, then the procedure is justified.

But is it the case? Here is a recent specimen of the *genre* from Lionel Britton's *Hunger and Love*:

'Five minutes late! Seven days notice. Like drowning a kitten. "I'll take that bridge if it costs a hundred thousand men." One night of Paris. They're used to it. Crippen! Go and have a look round inside St. Paul's at the monuments.'

The author here is obviously trying to give a faithful representation of all the contents of the mind of his character, which he presents as a series of separate pictures with the connexions left out. And quite frankly I don't know what he means. Even if people do think like that, which I doubt, writers should not write like that. Even if life is inconsecutive and unreasonable, books should be consecutive and reasonable. For it is the business of literature to interpret life and to make it coherent and meaningful. This end is not to be achieved by merely recording its incoherences. If a writer cannot see more meaning in life than I can, what is the good of him to me? But to reduce the disorder of life to order, to make meaningful the apparently meaningless and supply threads through the maze, an author must use his reason. It is by the employment of reason that our civilization, such as it is, has been achieved, and human life has risen above its crude beginnings. To disown reason, as modern authors seem disposed to do in order to make feeling and impulse their theme, on the ground that human beings are composed of nothing else, is to betray the past and to despair of the future.

CHAPTER VII

Dislikings—III. Unreason in Action. Fear of Science

"We are taught to fly in the air like birds, and to swim in the sea like fishes, but how to live on the earth we do not know." [1]

THIS CHAPTER is in dispraise of our civilization. Its object is to recount some of the concrete expressions of that cult of unreason which I have diagnosed as a distinguishing feature of the age. Distinguishing and regrettable, for, whatever view may be taken of the theoretical disquisitions of the last two chapters, there can be no two opinions about the concrete horrors to be described in this chapter and the next. And if you insist that I am merely rationalizing my dislikes, I refer you to the last chapter but one, where it is shown that it is irrational to hold that reasoning is *always* rationalizing.

Scientific Wisdom and Social Folly. The reasonableness of a civilization is chiefly shown by the ends which its members set themselves; the unreasonableness of ours by the fact that, having achieved an unprecedented ability to realize our ends, we propose to ourselves those which are foolish, trivial and vulgar, and fail to give us real satisfaction. Nothing in modern civilization is more remarkable than the disparity between our mechanical skill

[1] Quotation from an Eastern Sage.

and our social wisdom, between our power over nature and the mentality which dictates its employment. Science has won for us powers fit for the gods, and we bring to their use the outlook of schoolboys. In knowledge of what constitutes the good life for the individual and of how men should live together in society, our civilization is in no way superior—in some ways it is inferior—to that of the ancient Greeks; in scientific attainment and the ability to exploit the powers of nature in our service we have immeasurably outstripped them. See that mechanic by the roadside mending the carburettor of his car! In his display of scientific knowledge and skill in its application he is behaving rather like a superman. See the same mechanic twenty minutes later, driving in a little hell of noise and dust and stench, unable to appreciate the country himself and precluding the appreciation of all who come near him! He is behaving like a congenital idiot! Compare the almost miraculous physical processes which are involved in the production of a modern 'talkie', with the imbecilities it talks; the genius which has gone to the production of wireless, with the banalities which wireless is used to transmit. It is a sobering reflection that Clerk Maxwell should have lived in order that the remoter ether might vibrate to the strains of negroid music.

The disparity is most marked where the gifts of science have been most abundant. 'We have the best radios and the dullest radio programmes in civilization; the best automobiles and the fewest parking places; the highest paid actresses and the stupidest moving pictures'; so an American, in illustrative comment on the theme of this chapter. To the march of science there is no limit; we can talk across continents and oceans, telegraph pictures, install television sets in the home, listen to Big Ben striking in Ceylon, ride above and beneath the earth and the sea. Mechanics and washerwomen own their private cars, children talk along wires, typewriters are silent, teeth-filling painless, liners have swimming-baths, crops are ripened by electricity, roads are made of rubber, X-rays are the windows through which we behold our insides, photographs speak and sing, murderers are tracked down by wireless, hair is waved by electric current, submarines go to the North and aeroplanes to the South Pole. . . . Yet we cannot, to take a simple example, in the midst of our enormous cities provide a little space where poor people may play in comfort and safety.

Physical recreation, it is agreed, is in a modern urban community one of the pre-requisites of physical and psychological health; yet with all our resources we do not think it worth while to provide facilities for those who want it. In 1929, for example, the London County Council had applications from 1,000 clubs for cricket pitches; they could supply only 350. Eighty-five hockey clubs competed for the use of twenty-six grounds. For the right to play on 676 grass courts and 139 hard ones—grass courts in England are unplayable for four-fifths of the year—65,000 tennis players strove. It is estimated that to allow each registered person to play lawn tennis for an hour on Saturday afternoons, no fewer than 2,708 courts would be needed; 815 exist. And what courts they are! I know no more depressing experience than that of playing tennis on a public court; the net is slack and refuses to remain at the right height, while as there are no facilities for making it fast in the centre, it sags and bellies in the wind. The surface is dingy and covered with a grime which gradually imparts itself to the balls, making them difficult to see and finally indistinguishable from their surroundings. The players, in braces and gym shoes, chatter interminably and move aimlessly about the court, when they are not looking for balls. You concentrate on your own game only to find yourself interrupted by somebody coming to claim your court, or by an official on whatever pretext occurs to him. . . . So much for the recreation of adults.

As for the children, at the time of writing, November 1930, Mr. Lansbury after overcoming herculean difficulties, has just succeded in opening one new playing-ground for poor children in London. . . .

Society Checkmates Science. Science, as Bertrand Russell has pointed out, does not change human desires. It merely makes it easier for human beings to give effect to their desires. If their desires are good, this added power of realizing them is a good; if they are evil, it is correspondingly an evil.

Now man is still in many respects the same primitive creature, gullible, cruel, vengeful, credulous and vain as he was in Paleolithic days. Scratch the modern man, and, as the war showed, the savage appears. Civilization, I repeat, is only *sin* deep. Now science has taken this paleolithic savage posturing as civilized man and endowed him with the powers of gods, with the result that he is within measurable distance of exterminating himself. Give a boy an air-gun and he may shoot a sparrow or break a window, but that is the extent of the damage; give him a modern Lee-Metford rifle and he becomes a public danger. The moral is obvious; it is not that mankind is worse than it was, merely that, if it is to escape destruction, it has a need to be better.

Until our social wisdom is able to cope with our mechanical skill, and we learn to live up to the challenge of our new powers, the discoveries of science will tend to our discomfiture rather than to our good. That they have done so in the past, the history of the last hundred and fifty years bears ample testimony. Again and again the benefits which each fresh advance in applied science might have bestowed have been cancelled by the circumstances attending its use.

Fear of Science

The last century, it is notorious, witnessed man's acquisition of power over natural forces. He learned to control Nature. Cotton was cheap, coal was torn from the bowels of the earth, and one man and a machine could turn out four times as many shirts and vests as a hundred men without machines formerly produced in twice the time. Yet the only way in which men could recover from the dust, the dirt, the stench, the foul air, the racket and the overcrowding which cheap cotton and coal brought in their train, was by retiring into the country where Nature was still in more or less unimpaired control over man, with the result that those who made their money out of the powers which the scientists had won, took care to live as far as possible from the places in which the money was made. As for the multiplicity of underclothing, the number of potential wearers increased almost as fast as the machines increased the number of vests and shirts for them to wear—they had to in those early days, when every child was a wage-earner from the age of five, if people were not to starve—with the result that men were very little better clad than they were before.

About the same time medical science was making great advances in the art of maintaining life in aged bodies, in consequence of which we now keep alive many old and disagreeable people whom previous civilizations had the sense to allow to die.[1] It also achieved an unprecedented skill in the art of patching up broken bodies; but chemical science was meanwhile making equal strides in the power of blowing them to pieces, so that in the last war men could be seen employing all the resources of medical science to piece together shattered bodies, in order that the resources of chemical science might be utilized for the purpose of shattering them again. Since even the best surgeon can only patch up one broken or mutilated man at a time, while the chemist has enabled the gunner to

[1] See further on this, Chapter X.

blow to pieces a score at once, the increase in man's power of destroying the body must be reckoned on balance to have outweighed any gain from his increased knowledge of how to patch and to restore it.

We have reached a new and wider understanding of the problems of insanity; mental derangement is not now considered to be a single homogeneous malady, alike in its causes and its effects, nor are lunatics any longer regarded as incurable. But this improvement in the treatment of the insane is more than offset by the rapidly increasing number of the insane. Modern science, which is undoubtedly responsible for the better treatment, is responsible no less for the conditions of turmoil and strain which calls for its increasing exercise.

A hundred and twenty years ago the man with a taste for a country life whose work lay in the city lived five miles out and walked the distance between his house and his office twice a day. To-day science has so improved means of transit that by taking a tube or a suburban electric train he finds the radius of accessibility increased from five miles to twenty. But in making a distance of twenty miles possible, science has also made it necessary; for society has showed its sense of the transit advantages which science has conferred by immediately extending its cities to the extreme limits of the radius that science has enlarged, with the result that, although a man can travel further to find the country, the country is proportionately further to find. As a consequence, the country lover must now spend as long travelling to his work as he did before; but, instead of enjoying an hour and a half of health-giving exercise, he must burrow twice daily like a mole in the earth, scowl behind his paper as an alternative to meeting the opposed scowls of those ranged in front of him, and emerge at his journey's end with heavy head and shattered nerves, blinking like an owl at the sunlight he has lost.

Thus modern science has solved the transport problem

by turning the home into a dormitory and its owner into a peripatetic mole.

By the invention and perfection of contraceptives science has taught us how to control birth. But instead of using our knowledge to improve the species by gradually eliminating the unfit and deliberately breeding from chosen stocks the type of citizen we require, we have allowed the invention to depress the level of the population by a dysgenically selective birth-rate. The idle, the feckless, the half-witted and the dull, all those who are too stupid to know how to apply birth-control devices or too careless to use their knowledge if they had it, continue to breed like rabbits, while the more responsible members of the population partially sterilize themselves by their refusal to bear more children than they can bring up in decency and comfort. Thus the better stocks fail to keep up their numbers, while society grows like a pyramid continually flattening out at the top and proliferating at the base.

Machines. Of the hundred and one ways in which our failure in social wisdom causes us to misuse and misapply the goods which scientific knowledge has bestowed, none is more striking than the use to which we put our machines. I have already noted how the population insisted upon increasing up to the limit of its machine-made shirts and vests. The illustration, it is obvious, is allegorical. It is also symbolical of our extravagant wastage of the potential goods which machines might have bestowed. Machines, I take it, were invented to be man's servants. Their justification lies in their ability to increase productivity and to diminish human toil. In so far as they produce these results, machines are beneficial; in so far as they do not, they are neither beneficial nor harmful but unnecessary. That machinery has increased production is obvious, that it has lightened human toil is, however, very far from

Dislikings—III

being the case. Men never worked so hard as in the nine-teenth century when machines first became important; they never had so little leisure as they have to-day when machines are dominant. Men's new-won ability to exploit the forces of nature might have been expected to increase their leisure, and to confer a certain spaciousness and dignity upon their lives. Yet they live at greater pressure than before, and the whole urgency of the modern world is towards speeding up, greater efficiency and more intense competition, when it ought to be towards more ease, less hurry and greater co-operation. These evil results are due not to the fact that machines exist, but to the fact that they are revered.

Besides diminishing leisure the reverence for machines is destructive of joy and hostile to beauty. Though man's working day is shorter than it was at the beginning of the machine age, it is also far duller. Machinery robs works of the interest of a varied and creative process, and sub-stitutes the unending repetition of a trivial and monotonous task. Since the advent of machinery few men see the beginning and end of the things they make, while their status is that of cogs in an organization which is itself mechanical.

I once had an affair with a young woman who had been engaged for eight hours a day for the preceding five years in a process which she believed to be incidental to the making of biscuit tins. A metal band containing holes or slots passed immediately before her; into each hole or slot as it came opposite to her she was required to insert a small peg of metal, in appearance like an elongated bullet, which the band then carried on to the next worker to be subjected to some further process. If you did not insert your stick of metal quick enough, you were apt to lose a finger; my young woman had already lost one and a half. It was only after I had known her for a couple of months, when I had occasion to interview the manager of the factory at which she worked, that I found she was, in fact, engaged in making not biscuit tins but umbrella ferrules.

From our irrational attitude to machines spring two separate dangers; the first, that we shall turn ourselves into robots in time of peace; the second, that we shall blow ourselves to pieces in time of war. In peace-time the machine threatens our souls, in war-time our bodies.

Robotization. The danger of Robotization is first hinted at in Samuel Butler's *Erewhon*. It is the function of great men to tell us not so much what they think, as what we think. They make us, in other words, articulate to ourselves. If we are not already unconsciously thinking on our own account what they have to tell us, their message evokes no response. The novel ideas of which the human mind is capable are, I imagine, strictly limited, and most of them have already been discovered several times without being noticed, until the time came when men's minds were prepared to receive them. They were then said to be discovered, when all that had happened was that their rediscovery for the first time attracted attention. This, I take it, is the explanation of my excitement on reading such a book as *Erewhon*. I shall never forget the thrill of delighted recognition, recognition of what I had unconsciously thought yet had not the wit to tell myself consciously that I thought, when I first read the chapter on the machines in that astonishing book. Since *Erewhon* appeared in the 'eighties a number of writers have essayed the same theme. The Morlocks in H. G. Wells's *Time Machine* and the Robots proper in Karel Kapek's *R.U.R.*, are only concrete embodiments of a fear that we all feel, a fear that runs like a recurring *motif* through the symphonic disharmonies of modern literature, the fear of machines. You have only to see the first half-dozen shots of the film *Metropolis* for the fear to take visible shape. And the fear, if we put it into words, is that man will become the slave of the machines, and that his nature will be cast increasingly in the likeness of his masters. The care of machines is already man's chief occupation. Already we spend more time in tending and looking after machines than in tending and looking after one another. And the service of the machines is no light one. Having been brought up to expect attendance and consideration, they make things very unpleasant if they fail to get it. If they are not given fuel and water and oil, when they expect it; if they are not cleaned and warmed and washed and given their meals regularly, they grow sulky, or angry and boil over, or burst and blow up, destroying themselves and spreading havoc and destruction all round them. And knowing this and fearing it, men become increasingly subject to them. We made machines to be our servants; but servants have a knack of achieving mastery over their masters by making their masters so dependent on them that they cannot do without them. And it is thus that the machines are learning to master us, for——the admission may as well be made——we cannot live without them. Deprive us of our machines and we should starve.

The machines determine the filling of our minds no less than that of our bellies. When some years ago the one London Labour daily paper, the *Daily Herald*, found itself in one of its recurring financial crises, it was saved by Odhams Press, which, although a capitalist concern, stepped in to the surprise of the newspaper world to put the *Herald* on its feet. That the Socialism of the *Herald* was no very serious menace to capitalist society is, no doubt, true; it may even be said to remove the stings of the dispossessed masses by drawing off their revolutionary ardour into football competitions and free insurance policies, and so to do capitalism a service. But this possibility is obviously too subtle to have occurred to business men, who still regard the British Labour move-

Fear of Science

ment as a sinister force aiming at the overthrow of society, and some other explanation must be sought for the action of Odhams. This was provided by the Chairman at the annual meeting of Odhams Press, at which he was reported to have said that the decisive factor in determining Odhams to take over and capitalize the *Herald*, was the necessity for providing work during the other six days of the week for the greatly enlarged machine plant which they had had to install for the printing of the Sunday *People*. Thus it was the necessity of providing machines with work which determined the continuance of England's one Labour daily. The *Herald* is still very mildly labour, and presumably makes some converts to the cause which it professes to support, so that we may say that the political convictions of thousands of human beings are largely determined by the necessity of giving machines occupation.

It is, indeed, a fact that we care less about what goes into our heads than into any other part of our bodies. The 'Murder and Motherhood Press' feeds our minds on a diet of sweetmeats swimming in sexual treacle and of crimes sauced by snobbery, yet, although we are ready enough to blame our food for the disorders of our stomachs, when we get moral indigestion in the shape of complexes, hysterias, neuroses, and overpowering depression, we never dream of blaming what we put into our minds. Nor, so long as we insist on paying the dentist who fills our teeth more highly than we pay the journalist who fills our heads, can we expect our intellectual health to improve.

Not only do the machines fill our stomachs and our minds, they also prescribe our pleasures. Most of us have already forgotten how to play without their aid. The modern notion of play is to step on the throttle, insert coins in metal slots, scan headlines, crowd through clicking turnstiles, rush headlong down water-chutes, or through the air in aeroplanes or swing-boats. Dependent on machines for our work and our play, owing to them our very existence, can we wonder that we should serve them, and in serving, become like unto the things we serve? For with the growth of mechanical efficiency comes a terrifying growth of uniformity. Prolonged service to mechanisms imposes something of the nature of the machines themselves—their soullessness, their regularity, their efficiency and their uniformity—upon their attendants. This tendency is already perceptible in America, where men look alike, dress alike, read the same news, eat the same food, think the same thoughts, and 'enjoy' the same amusements. If it continues unchecked, personality will become a thing of the past, and we shall develop into efficient automata devoid alike of creative power and initiative, mere emmets in the antheap of society.

Extermination. The danger of extermination in war must be put in the form of an allegory. Let me, then, take a leaf out of the book of a Martian historian writing in 10,000 P.M.I. (Post Martem Incarnatum).

'On our neighbouring planet, the earth, the age of the greater reptiles was followed by that of the vertebrate mammals. Of these the homunculi, in spite of their physical deficiencies, which included a constitution so ridiculously inadequate that it was only by covering themselves with the skins of other animals that they were able to keep warm, and a complete helplessness in their young protracted over a period of extraordinary duration, were nevertheless enabled through their possession of a low-grade cunning, which pessimistic writers have likened to our own intelligence, to establish a complete domination over the rest of the planet. This they employed for the purpose of preying upon the other inhabitants of the earth, and they would ultimately have succeeded in denuding the whole planet of life, were it not for the internecine feuds upon which their quarrelsome nature led them to

Fear of Science

embark among themselves. The domination of the homunculi was eventually terminated by their discovery of how to release the forces locked up in the atom, a discovery of which they speedily made use to exterminate themselves altogether. The destruction of this noxious species through its own innate mischievousness has always been acclaimed by Martian theologians as affording one of the strongest pieces of evidence for the Providential government of the universe.'

Want in Plenty. But the most remarkable of our misuses of machines has still to be recounted. This misuse is peculiar in that its effects are so immediately disastrous that we can no longer avoid noticing them. The intensive application of physical and chemical science to industry has in recent years enormously increased man's productive power. Men should be, in consequence, richer and their toil lighter. Nothing of the kind has occurred. Our social science lags so far behind our physical and chemical sciences, that we are increasingly unable to distribute the goods we so abundantly produce. Prices fall for want of buyers, manufacturers are ruined because they cannot dispose of their products, the world's granaries burst with unsold wheat, its quays and warehouses are stacked with rotting fish and fruit, and in all countries men are thrown out of employment because none can buy the proceeds of their labour. Thus arises the greatest paradox of modern civilization, the paradox of want in the midst of plenty.

For it is not true that human beings do not need what science enables them to produce. As I write, there comes a report that Brazil has been destroying its surplus coffee by burning it; yet men will still shiver in the European winter and crave the hot drink they cannot buy. Surplus wheat is being used in America as fuel for boilers, yet the masses of China are still half-starved, and thousands at the moment of writing are dying of starvation. The United

Dislikings—III

States Federal Board is proposing the destruction of one-third of the year's planted cotton; yet most of the women of the world still suffer from a lack of adequate under-clothes. We are, it seems, so little able to control the results of our own inventive skill, that our civilization is in danger of collapse because we produce so much of the very things we need. This is mechanism run riot with a vengeance.

When I was in Russia the walls of the factories exhibited a poster depicting this latest paradox of civilization. Picture a British miner's home in the depths of winter. The grate is empty, and a little girl in rags asks her mother why they cannot have a fire. 'Because, my dear, there is no coal.' 'Why is there no coal, mother?' 'Because Daddy is out of work and there is no money to buy coal.' 'Why is Daddy out of work?' 'Because there is too much coal.' . . .

Reflecting upon the situation a visitor from another planet might be justified in supposing that the world was entirely mad. I do not myself think that this explanation is correct. It is, however, the case that the irrational elements in man have for the present got the better of the rational elements. The world contains many reasonable men but they suffer under two disabilities. First, they have not the faintest idea of what they can do to mend matters. Secondly, even if they had, they have no means of making their reasonableness felt. If the forces of reason could be organized as determinedly as the forces of unreason, they could, I believe, control the world without difficulty. But reasonableness is an arm-chair quality. No man has ever exerted himself in favour of the probably true proposition that $7 \times 7 = 49$, nor is popular enthusiasm aroused for proposals to improve health and education by which mankind would be benefited. Intellectuals, moreover, divided against each other and consumed with mutual jealousies are inherently unorganizable. Whatever the explanation, there is no doubt of the fact; there was never a time when men of reason pulled so little weight in the world as to-day, nor, until the world has destroyed itself with unreason, are they likely to come into their own.

So far I have spoken only in general terms of that disparity between scientific skill and social wisdom which I have taken as the text of this chapter. I will conclude by illustrating the theme from an example which, coming more directly within my personal experience, has touched me more closely than any other of the consequences of endowing with the results of the work of half a dozen men of genius a population with the minds of schoolboys and the souls of typists.

The Pianola

Pianola Music. I have for the last fifteen years been a persistent player of the pianola. By dint of continual practice I have achieved a fair degree of competence in the use of the instrument, and, provided the pianola is not asked to play music written for instruments other than the piano or for orchestras, I can make it sound sufficiently like a piano to deceive any but trained musicians. I once gave a pianola recital in a London Hall, at which a pianist and myself played the alternate movements of a four-movement Beethoven sonata. The audience, from whom we were hidden by a curtain, were subsequently asked to decide which movements had been played by the pianola and which by the pianist; at least 45 per cent. of them gratified me by guessing wrong. Skill in pianola-playing consists entirely in the use of the feet, expression and phrasing being effected by variations of foot pressure on the pedals. After a time the soles of one's feet become very sensitive in respect of their capacity to register different degrees of pressure.

Dislikings—III

My time for playing the pianola is in the morning after breakfast. The music of Bach and Mozart, which I play almost exclusively, demands a fresh and alert mind, and is better discriminated by a clean musical palate unsullied by the sounds of the day. In the evenings I play Beethoven, Purcell or Handel. The Aeolian Company which in England has a practical monopoly of the supply of pianola rolls—its only competitor is the Blüthner—has recently been taken over by Harrods. You pay a subscription, join the library and receive twelve rolls as often as you care to send for them in exchange for the twelve which you already have.

At first I had little difficulty in securing rolls of merit. The Aeolian Company's catologue produced in 1914 contained a fairly respectable selection of reasonably good music. There were nótable omissions; for example, the number of rolls rendering the music of Purcell and Byrd was negligible (Purcell five rolls, Byrd only one), and Handel's piano music was practically unrepresented; but on the whole and taken as an earnest of better things to come, the catalogue was not discouraging. Better things, however, did not come. As the war proceeded the character of the rolls issued deteriorated, and since the war it has gone from bad to worse. In saying that the character of the rolls has deteriorated I do not mean that the great majority were not always bad. They were. At all times the company has been concerned in the main to reproduce the ephemeral music of the day. In 1913 it was 'Oh my beautiful Doll' or ' Alexander's Rag Time Band'; in 1931 it is 'Dancing with Tears in my Eyes' or 'What is this Thing called Love?' Such things, no doubt, are inevitable; like the poor they are with us always. But in the last fifteen years the percentage of classical music to the rest has steadily diminished.

In 1917 the company brought out a catalogue of an entirely new type which has served as a model ever since.

Fear of Science

Instead of the reasonable and comparatively scholarly arrangement hitherto adopted, by which the composers were arranged in alphabetical order, the works of the different composers being listed under their names, musical works were now arranged alphabetically under their alleged titles—as if music proper could have a title!—so that 'Saul, Dead March' (Handel) appears side by side with 'Savoy Memories arranged by H. Derry' (Sullivan), and 'Well Tempered Clavichord Prelude 24 Fugue 24 in B minor' (Bach) is but two removes from 'Wha'll be King, but Charlie? (See Songs Scottish Roll III)', a childish method of cataloguing. One of the effects of this mode of arrangement was to put a premium upon rolls that had a title, and to endow with a title those that had hitherto been content with an austere opus number. It is inconceivable that in the existing catalogue Beethoven's Sonata No. 14, Opus 27, No. 2, should be anything but 'The Moonlight'.

It Deteriorates. Simultaneously there has been a decline in the quality of the rolls catalogued. So far from issuing new rolls of important music, the Aeolian Company gradually allowed its library of classical rolls to become obsolete, and no attempt was made to renew it. In the 1914 catalogue, for example, there were thirty Handel rolls; in the 1928 catalogue only fifteen, and Handel's piano music, always scantily represented, is, except for one Gigue and one Bourrée, now not represented at all. In the 1914 catalogue there were five Mozart piano concertos; in 1928 only one was available; ninety-seven Bach rolls in 1914 had been reduced to fifty-five in 1928. Instances could be multiplied indefinitely. As a result the general quality of the music which is available to the pianola-player to-day is markedly lower than it was before the war.

It must not be supposed that this declension has been allowed to take place without protest. The popular Press is continually harping upon the improvement which in recent years has taken place in English musical taste. It is, it is said, no longer true that the English are the most unmusical people in the world. Thanks to the wireless and the recent revolution in gramophone recording, good music, it is pointed out, is now available in the home for all, and an increasing number of persons is said to take advantage of it. Nor, when allowance is made for the national wish to lay claim to a sensibility which is still in large part lacking, am I disposed to disregard this testimony. Twenty years ago it was only rarely and with great hesitation that Sir Henry Wood ventured to introduce a Bach item into the programme at the Queen's Hall Promenades. Now an all-Bach programme occurs once a fortnight, and draws as great or greater crowds than appear on any other night. During the same period immense strides have been made in the technique of gramophone playing and recording, and the gramophone has become to all intents and purposes a new instrument. With the improvement in the technique of recording has come an improvement in the quality of the music recorded. I go to hear a friend's gramophone and find that he has a reasonable collection of Mozart quartets, or that the gramophone companies between them are shortly expected to have covered all the Brandenburg Concertos.

Facts of this kind make the gradual decline in the quality of pianola music more remarkable, and have not unnaturally led to protests from pianola users. In reply to these the company have usually begun by denying the charge. When pressed with comparative statistics showing the character of the rolls now available as compared with those obtainable before the war, they have justified themselves by alleging an absence of public support for good-class rolls. At one time, indeed, they were inclined to regard themselves as performing a dual rôle of simultaneously catering for and forming the public taste for which they catered. They were prepared, they said, to issue a small proportion of commercially non-remunerative rolls in order that they might build up a library which appealed to the educated taste. 'It is' they write in 1924 'an unfortunate but true fact that by far the larger number of the rolls sold to-day are those of a light ephemeral character, and, as we are in the somewhat unfortunate position of being a commercial undertaking dealing with an art, we find it difficult to make these two ideas correspond.' They still, it will be seen, recognize that they are dealing with what had been traditionally an artistic and not a purely commercial product. There was never much substance in this plea, and of recent years it has been practically dropped. And dropped avowedly, for in 1931 I find them writing: 'We regret intensely that musical tastes appear to have degenerated since the days before the war. We believe that if it is put to Mr. Joad that businesses have to be conducted on a commercial basis, however regrettable such a thing may be, he will appreciate that it is only the public taste . . . which prevents us from adding a greater proportion of classics to our catalogue.'

The one sacrifice to art which the company has in these latter years permitted itself to make, is the issue, once every month, of the second twenty-four of Bach's fortyeight Preludes and Fugues. At the time of writing, however, they have been compelled, in spite of their avowed intention to finish the series, to suspend the undertaking half-way through, owing to 'the very considerable loss' on the rolls due to the absence of public support. It is difficult to blame the company, nor do I wish to do so. They must, it is obvious, pay their way, and if the public do not want good music, they cannot be expected to produce it at a loss.

Conclusion Means and Ends. The state of public taste

which the situation indicates, interesting enough in itself, is particularly pertinent to my main theme for two reasons. In the first place, this decrease in musical quality has been accompanied by a growth in mechanistic efficiency. The pianola has become an increasingly sensitive instrument for the rendering of music, as the music which it renders has become decreasingly worth rendering. Various devices have been introduced for bringing out salient notes; there has been an improvement in phrasing, as the result of a more intelligent cutting of the rolls; above all, the relation between the pedals and the motor has been made more direct, so that the latter is more immediately responsive to changes of pressure upon the former. Not only here is there the familiar disparity between mechanical efficiency and cultural values, there is, it seems, a definite causal relation between mechanism and beauty, as a result of which the growth of the one is accompanied by a decline of the other. The case affords, indeed, a good example of the unconscious subordination of ends to means which is characteristic of modern civilization. The means to the good life are improved and multiplied; the good life recedes.

The pianola was always an expensive instrument; you can buy a first-rate gramophone to-day for twenty-four pounds, but a pianola still costs something in the neighbourhood of one hundred and thirty. Nor of recent years has it appreciably diminished in cost. Partly as a result of the increased technical efficiency, a good instrument in 1931 costs nearly as much as it did in 1919. The consequence is—and this constitutes my second point—that to-day only the comparatively rich buy pianolas. To this fact the company itself attributes the decline in the taste of pianola users. The rich, those of them at least who buy pianolas, are not interested in music—presumably, they have been too busy violently becoming rich, or in recuperating from the strain of violently becoming rich by being equally violently amused, to have cultivated a taste for music—and the only use they have for the instrument is for the playing of dance music. The cultivated musical amateur, who at the cost of considerable deprivation might once have afforded a pianola, now buys a gramophone instead.

The conclusion seems to be not only that, as material efficiency increases appreciation of beauty declines, but that skill in living according to the demands and standards of our civilization—for it is such skill that brings men money and power—appears to be inimical to taste and destructive of beauty. To say that success according to the standards of a civilization implies failure according to the standards of which enlightened reason approves, the standards of goodness, truth and beauty, is implicitly to criticize that civilization. And it is, I think, a fact that the sense of values in modern society is weak and confused; it may even be a fact that of recent years it has become more so. This, at least, seems clear, that, if it is possible to discover and reasonable to pursue those things which are good in themselves, then our civilization fully merits the charge of irrationality which this chapter has brought against it.

CHAPTER VIII

Dislikings—IV. The Horrors of the Countryside

*T*he England Myth. It is generally believed that the English countryside is very beautiful. The Home Counties in particular are held to exhibit in a most marked degree those characteristics in which its attractiveness resides and which confer upon it its peculiar charm. These include farm-houses, country lanes, village streets, thatched cottages, babbling brooks, water meadows, wayside flowers, coppices in spring, woods in autumn, and a general mildness of atmosphere, softness of outline and haziness of view attributable to the wetness of the weather and to the gentle contours of the land. These things combine to invest the south of England with a tranquil charm which is generally regarded as unique; those whose privilege it is to dwell among them are noted for a certain sweetness of character and serene dignity of living, while in the heart of the exile they live on as a memory of quiet loveliness, from which he should never have been parted and to which with wistful longing his thoughts inevitably return. Such briefly is the tradition of the English countryside, a tradition which is embellished by a long line of essayists and enshrined in some of the greatest poetry in any language. Not being a poet or a literary essayist I have refrained from embellishment, and set it forth as prosaically as possible.

The Horrors of the Countryside

A journey to the Coast. (1) *The Suburbs.* Filled with the emotions which a reading of this great literature engenders, you decide to make a journey through these same home counties; we will suppose it a train journey through Surrey and Sussex from London to Worthing. The first twenty miles is continuous London. You pass through the southern suburbs, protracting themselves interminably like the lengths of a pulled-out telescope. They are drab and squalid, meanly conceived and meanly executed, an abiding testimony to a passion for cheapness and an indifference to beauty. They culminate in a climax of ugliness at Croydon. Croydon, it is obvious, was built in the Victorian Age. It is large and straggling, and falls into two parts: its centre is the same tangle of mean streets, undistinguished shops and radiating tram-lines, that you have already witnessed in Balham, Brixton, Tooting and Streatham. But unlike the nearer suburbs it is surrounded by a fringe of large detached residences, which bear witness to the premonitory stirrings in the Victorian soul of what was subsequently to become the twentieth-century stampede to the country. Built solidly of yellow bricks they are imposing and very ugly. They are approached each by its own carriage-drive wandering circuitously, in order to make it seem as long as possible, through a shrubbery of laurels, rhododendrons and other evergreens, behind which coyly lurks the house. Sheltered and screened, retired and reserved, discreet, pretentious and respectable, keeping themselves impeccably to themselves, as dull as they are ugly and as ugly as they are dull, these residences are an abiding expression of the civilization that produced them. They serve to carry us on from Croydon to Purley, where the twentieth century begins.

The twentieth century joins hands with the nineteenth somewhere about Purley Oaks. Its predominant architectural colour is pink, and its predominant architectural

note sprightliness. In rows of cheerful villas and bungalows the dormitories of contemporary stockbrokers sprawl
over the Surrey hills; the city man approaches, and the
earth breaks out in an angry red rash, for all the world as
if it had caught measles. Like their Victorian parents the
stockbrokers are still imbued with the importance of keeping themselves to themselves, and as a consequence their
houses are placed as far away from one another as their
means allow. But not being so rich as the preceding
generation of Croydonites, they cannot afford such large
distances from their neighbours. Moreover, they do not
find it necessary to hide their residences behind a merciful
veil of evergreens. On the contrary they are blatantly
exposed. Seen from the railway they greet you with a
shout; it is harsh and metallic, albeit cheerful, and it
continues until you are well past Redhill.

Redhill itself, now continuous with Earlswood, stretches
southward for half a dozen miles, Victorian at the core,
red rash at the outskirts, but after Earlswood you run
into something like country, which extends until you
are well past Three Bridges. It is rolling country, well-
wooded, fertile and intricate as is all the Weald, a fair
sample, I suppose, of what all this South Surrey–North
Sussex countryside must once have been. But it has been
whittled away on both sides, until there is now no more
than a thinnish belt, a bare score of miles across, to show
what was the English countryside. And the belt grows
narrower every year. Some twenty-five miles from London, London ends; some forty-odd miles from London,
Brighton begins. Its influence first makes itself felt at
Haywards Heath where the red rash breaks out again
in a scurf of villas and bungalows, and from there to
Brighton the bungalows are with us more or less all the
way, increasing in numbers and virulence as one approaches the coast. Before the coast is reached grass-
covered chalk ridges begin to appear. They run in long

lines, and they are of all shapes and sizes; but whatever the shape or size they are uniformly lovely, and make one of the most beautiful skylines in the world, or did, until the builder descended on them. For to-day the lines are broken and the clean, sharp edges serrated with teeth of angry red brick, the residences of city men. These staring great houses might seem to have been dropped there by chance, so devoid are they of any orderly or coherent arrangement, were it not for the fact that each one has been planned with a view to being seen over as large an area of the Downs as possible. You can see them, you cannot help seeing them, from any point within a radius of six miles, and seeing you realize that the thin belt of country, such as it was, is definitely at an end. You are, it is clear, already within striking distance of the coast.

(2) *The Coast and its Towns.* The South Coast has now become one more or less continuous town. Brighton stretches out to meet Shoreham, Shoreham to Worthing, Worthing to Littlehampton. Locked together in a continuing embrace these dreadful places spawn horribly over the countryside. Ugly in themselves, they have put forth growths which are even uglier. Big towns surround themselves with a ring of municipal dustbins, prisons and asylums, workhouses and cemeteries, where refuse souls and bodies are corrected, maintained and buried by the community. These in their turn are girt by rows upon rows of small houses, stretching out interminably into the countryside, fringed with allotments and threaded by motor roads. To the walker who does not choose to be chivvied along the straight broad roads where the motors are, the business of getting out of one of these towns is fraught with immense difficulty. He will have to make his way along dingy side-streets, through back gardens, over refuse heaps and across allotments. He will have to climb barbed-wire fences, cross ditches, negotiate poultry runs,

face the jeers of small boys and the curses of infuriated owners. Escaping he will find his way barred by a golf course. By the time he has negotiated all these obstacles and emerged at last onto the Downs, he will be in a state of nervous exhaustion, unfit for some hours to come to appreciate such beauty as remains to him.

Should he turn to the coast he will fare no better. Along the whole length of seaboard from Brighton to Little-hampton the sea-board is polluted, and this pollution has infected practically the whole stretch of the coasts of Sussex and Kent. For example, take Camber Beach. Camber Beach near Rye in old days was a glorious stretch of sand flanked by low dunes with their coarse grass. To-day before and behind the dunes a bungaloid growth has sprung up of quite unspeakable ugliness and vulgarity. Shacks and old tramcars have appeared on the beach. A dozen shabby stalls, built apparently from sugar-boxes or petrol-tins, press tea, sweets and aerated waters on your unwilling attention. The dunes, where formerly you could picnic or bathe at will, are now for the most part shut off by barbed-wire entanglements. On a summer's day gramophones and portable wireless sets compete against each other in a horrid cacophony. And all round the coast the same destruction of the elementary amenities of privacy and beauty is going on. Consider Shoreham, for instance, or Peacehaven!

(3) *A Seaside 'Resort'*. But to return to your journey. Having threaded its way through some dozen miles of this sort of thing, your train brings you at last to Worthing. Worthing (and Worthing might stand for Eastbourne, Littlehampton, Margate, Bognor, Folkestone, Ramsgate, Ilfracombe, Blackpool, Yarmouth) is totally abominable. I have never been able to take our seaside resorts for granted; like London, they have always seemed to me to stand in need of explanation, apology or excuse.

The Horrors of the Countryside

Yet coming upon Worthing as I did recently in the middle of a hot day in July, I was struck anew by its purulent beastliness, its utter horror. The place was so much worse than I could have believed possible. Bad enough in itself compared with what it might have been, compared with what it was before it became a pleasure resort it was nothing short of a calamity. Along the length of its front there ran a hard, unyielding stone pavement, the promenade. On one side of it there was the glory of sea and sky; gulls wheeled, sails glittered in the sun, and in the distance were shining cliffs and a bold promontory jutting into the sea. On the other side, the side which has been laid out for 'pleasure', eating-houses and stalls and shop-windows; shops with buckets and spades, with ghastly imitation jewellery, with unusable pottery, dusty, archaic purses, pincushions made of shells, and ornamental pipes which no self-respecting smoker could ever have brought himself to put into his mouth: nothing real and everything pretending to be something else. Tawdry finery, sticky sweets, fly-blown cakes, and a general air of hot dustiness were the predominant features of the Worthing front. Over everything was the careless, squalid disorder of trivial profit-making. Even the beach had broken out into a rash of dirty side-shows. Dirt, heat and discomfort were, indeed, the main features of the beach. The very pebbles were greasy, their surfaces covered with a film of dust.

Upon these pebbles people sat or reclined in attitudes of varied discomfort. They were mainly family parties, the men bored, the women nagging and disagreeable, the children noisy and perpetually being forbidden to do things. Most of these families were eating something, and from time to time one was accosted by people soliciting one to buy more eatables, sweets or chocolates or ice-cream, or shell fish in little saucers. Gramophones played, children cried and shouted, and the voices of boatmen inviting one to go for a row or a sail rose in rivalry. From a distance came the sounds of the jazz implements of a party of entertainers mingling the hoots and wails of negroid music with the general clamour. Upon this scene the sun beat with great violence. Beaches are by their nature shadeless, and people wilted visibly in the heat. Seeking shelter under the unlovely pier which, supported on iron pillars, spanned the beach, I found the place unaccountably cold and draughty. It was too hot in the sun, too cold in the shade; there was nothing left but to try the sea. The sea is after all what seaside places are for, and the ability to immerse oneself in it the one compensation for the horrors they engender.

Luckily I had a bathing-suit and towel in my rucksack, and finding a sheltered place behind one of the iron pillars, I began to undress. I had taken off a coat, a boot and a sock when an official descended upon me and told me that it was forbidden to undress upon the beach. I did not understand this, and asked him how one was to enter the sea without undressing. He replied that 'undressing' was permissible, but that it must not be done on the beach. The Corporation, he said, had provided huts and machines for bathers, and, if I liked to go and stand in the queue, I would doubtless, when my turn came, be allotted one. And taking me to the other side of the pier he pointed out a long line of people extending from the promenade nearly to the edge of the sea with towels over their arms. The head of the queue was at a small shed, a sort of office, from which a young woman dispensed tickets and costumes on payment of a sum of money. But the queue moved very slowly—owing to the heat, it seemed, the pressure on the accommodation was very great—and during the few minutes that I watched I only saw three persons pass the office. At that rate the people at the back of the queue would not enter the sea until nearly dinner-time.

For the privilege of entering the sea at the seaside, it

The Horrors of the Countryside

seems, you must wait and pay. And the south coast of England is increasingly becoming one continuous seaside.

Incomprehensible habits of those visiting resorts. It is an astonishing thing, when one reflects upon it, that people should go to such places. Yet it is, I suppose, a fact that for the vast majority of civilized adults in this country a day at a seaside resort constitutes at once an ideal of happiness, a source of rest and refreshment, and a vision of beauty. On such rare occasions as they are released for a few hours from the necessity of obtaining the means to make life possible, and have leisure to live, a visit to the seaside presents itself inevitably to their imaginations as the one way of living that really *is* living. A day on the beach at X— embodies and exhausts their conception of the good life. I once went to Southend to observe and participate in the enjoyments which the most advanced civilization that the world has seen offers to the bulk of its members. Getting out of the train I at once found myself a member of a great crowd which, streaming out of the station, moved slowly forward in a surging mass until we reached the sea-front. There with one accord we turned to the left and settled ourselves in the half-mile between a pier and some gasometers. This was one of the most unsavoury spots that could be well imagined, squalid and dingy, swarming with noisy beach photographers, winkle-sellers, vendors of rock and postcards. Why we stayed there none of us knew; every other part of the beach, either in the direction of Thorpe Bay and Shoeburyness or Westcliff and Leigh, was quieter and pleasanter and prettier, but we settled ourselves down in a solid mass in this one half-mile, leaving it only to patronize one of the dreary 'amusement palaces' with which Southend is studded.

Why these places, which contain most of the duller features of a Bank Holiday Fair, attract people on their

Dislikings—IV

one and only holiday of the year I do not know; at least,
I think I do, but to pursue the question would take me
far beyond the scope of this chapter. Crowd psychology is,
I daresay, involved in the answer. But crowd psychology
is an ambiguous phrase. I take it to mean that, whereas,
if you stand a sheep on its hind legs, you do not turn it
into a human being, if you stand a flock of sheep on their
hind legs you do turn them into something passably like
a political meeting, or a retreating army, or a crowd of
holiday-makers.

Machinery is, however, the real villain of the piece. If
you pass your days in tending machines, feeding them and
cleaning them and warming them and giving them the
wherewithal to eat and drink, they will come, as masters
always do, to impose something of their own nature upon
the servants who tend them.

Thus men become uniform even as machines are uniform, and soulless even as machines are soulless. In
America where the application of machinery to life has
proceeded furthest, the lack of individuality is most
marked. Americans dress alike, look alike, talk alike and
think alike. It is appropriate that Behaviourism should
be the special philosophy of Americans, for it is to Americans that it is specially appropriate. So dependent are
they upon the machines in whose likeness they grow, that
they cannot conceive of the good life except in terms of
them. And the good life must be pursued in concert;
it must be enjoyed in crowds. Hence when we come to
the amusements of British robots, we find that they are
modelled on the same pattern. They are partaken of in
crowds with the aid of machinery.

But I seem to be allowing myself to be drawn insensibly
into the digression I feared. My excuse must be that the
phenomenon of the British population enjoying itself is so
remarkable that it is not humanly possible just to mention its pursuits and leave it at that. It clamours for com-

ment, and a word of explanation must be attempted in passing, even if it is both digressive and inadequate. Moreover, it is not to be expected that a population so trained and so employed can do other than pollute the country, when it descends upon it—you cannot expect people whose sense of fitness has been dulled by inhabiting Leyton or Rawtenstall, to come to terms easily with beauty, even if they could recognize it—and the horrors of the countryside are my theme.

But so far I have concerned myself only with the comparatively poor. In company with them we have travelled down from London by train, and looked at Worthing and Southend. What of the middle-classes? The middle-classes are busy enjoying the country; they are on the roads. What does on the roads mean?

The Motoring Classes spend a summer evening in the Country. It is a summer evening and all day I have been walking. I have had cold beef and pickled onions, bread and beer for lunch, and at six o'clock I am making for the nearest station to catch a train back to town. I have been walking across country, part of the time on the downs, and since three o'clock in the afternoon have seen only one shepherd and a country woman sunning herself at the door of a gamekeeper's cottage. It is a perfect evening, still and mild; the air is a benediction, the slight breeze a caress. The sunlight lies level in lances of gold across the fields; faintly from the distance comes the sound of church bells.

Suddenly I become aware of a noise; it is an irritable noise like the buzzing of a swarm of angry bees, but more explosive and less regular, as though a regiment of soldiers had begun to suffer simultaneously from flatulence or a herd of swine to belch in ragged unison. The noise is accompanied by a smell, a smell of oil and petrol, and then, as I top a rise, I come into full view of a main road. The road is covered with cars. Bonnet to tail they stretch continuously in an unending procession. From time to time the cars break wind irritably in one another's faces. The procession moves, now faster now slower, and every now and then two cars in it change places; but always it goes on. Above it there hangs a murky, blue haze. The faces of the motorists are strained and angry; upon them there is an air of tense expectancy, and in the intervals between their spasmodic bursts of activity they glower at one another. From the country they are completely cut off; they cannot see its sights, hear its sounds, smell its smells, or enjoy its silence. They are hemmed in by other motorists and, even if they were alone, they are in no frame of mind for æsthetic enjoyment. The pool cannot reflect the sky when it is troubled, and these motorists are very troubled, for they are trying to pass each other. Growing interested in the sight, I sat down on a fallen tree on the top of a rise overlooking the road, and began to count. From this eminence the main road presented exactly the appearance of an ant-run, and as it was now towards evening, nearly all the ants were facing the same way. The motors, I found, were passing at the rate of 600 an hour in an almost continuous line. Above the tremendous din of their passage could be distinguished a screeching of electrical horns, mixed with the high-pitched hooters of motor-cycles. Just ahead there was a crossing where the main road was cut diagonally by a smaller one, and every now and then the motors would be held up to let the cross traffic pass. When this happened there was a great bellowing and hooting on the part of cars trying to get the advantage of each other; and directly they were released, they all began with one accord to bellow and shriek and scream at one another, like a pack of fiends released from the nethermost pit. The noise of all this was appalling; it spread for nearly a mile on each side of the road. And wherever there is a main road in England to-day, there over an area two miles wide along the whole length of the road the peace of the countryside is shattered.

That is how the motoring classes enjoy a summer's evening in the country. And the habits of the motoring classes constitute an ideal of 'enjoyment' for nine Englishmen out of ten.

The Two Countries. There are in England to-day two countries existing side by side. There is the country as it was, the country through which I had been walking that summer's day; and there is the country as it is becoming and as it will increasingly become. The first is quiet and peaceful, and the people who live in it are dull and a little stupid. Their status is prescribed by a well-defined hierarchy. There are the squire and the parson, the farmer, the yeoman, and the agricultural labourers. These last form the bulk of the country population; they go to church on Sunday and foregather of an evening in the pub. They know their place and their betters; but, although they are respectful, they are rarely servile, and about them there is a quiet dignity. It is still possible to find even in the counties bordering on London villagers who know no more of the metropolis than did their ancestors in the days when pack-horses performed the office of railways and motor-lorries. When it is invaded, this country does not change; it disappears often with startling rapidity and is replaced by country number two.

Country number two is the country which surrounds the towns and adjoins the main roads. Its characteristic features are petrol pumps and garages, tea places usually 'Old English', tin shanties, bungalows and innumerable notice-boards. It has few native inhabitants, but it is a dormitory for town workers and a corridor for motorists. Maiden ladies retire into it and keep poultry farms. Those of the original working-folk who remain in it abandon their traditional occupations and become parasites on the motorists and suburbanites; they keep wireless sets, buy gramophones and tea cakes in frilled papers, batten on the Sunday Press and grow basely rich. Their country pubs are replaced by motoring hotels in the hinder parts of which they drink in dingy obscurity. Country number one had a life of its own; country number two derives its life from the towns. To pass from country number one into country number two, is to pass from one age into another and from one civilization into another; it is to exchange silence, dignity and beauty for noise, vulgarity and ugliness. And country number two encroaches continually on country number one. A few years ago it comprised only the main roads, the suburbs, the coastal towns and a few 'picturesque' villages and 'beauty spots'; but it spreads like a blight and every year the diseased area extends further. London in particular is a centre of infection. According to the Report of the Greater London Regional Town Planning Committee published in 1930, the population of Greater London is expanding at the rate of over 1,000 a week, and building is going on at the rate of four solid square miles of houses a year. That is the explanation of the red rash of Purley which we saw on the way to Worthing, and of the ribbon development that now extends practically from London to the coast.

The New Industrial Revolution. We are, in fact, witnessing a new phase of the industrial revolution. The nineteenth century saw the influx from the country to the towns; the twentieth witnesses an efflux from the towns to the country. Not that the original influx has ceased; on the contrary, the countryside, countryside number one that is, is being drained faster than ever, and the old life of the country is rapidly disappearing, to be replaced by a new. And the new is the life of the towns artificially introduced into the country.

The Horrors of the Countryside

At the approach of the new-comers the country disappears. It is, indeed, a most pathetic thing to see how the exodus of those who find life in the modern town no longer tolerable destroys these very rural amenities which they go forth to seek. Pathetic but inevitable, for you cannot take the kingdom of beauty by storm, nor acquire the life of the country by simply dumping yourself on the countryside.

We must, I think, concede that it is some obscure desire for the country that accounts for the Purley rash. Young people in particular returning from a life of open-air hardship endured during the war, resolved not to go back to the cramping rows of suburban houses from which they had emerged. At the same time the suburban lines were electrified and access to the towns was cheap and quick. One went, then, and lived in the country. What could be more obvious? Thus the return to the country was in many cases the outcome of a definite need, the expression of the desire for a new way of life. Yet how inadequately is the need fulfilled!

Ribbon Development. Take, for example, the phenomenon of ribbon development. I had occasion recently to motor along one of the new arterial roads, the one running from London to Southend. For the greater part of the way it was flanked by houses, so that one had the sensation of motoring through a continuous loosely strung-out town. A few of the houses were semi-detached, but the great majority were separated by nicely calculated intervals of half a dozen or a dozen yards. At the back of each house was a narrow strip of garden, at the far end of which there were cabbages; barbed-wire fence separated the cabbages from the flat Essex country which, inflamed by occasional blobs of angry pink, stretched mournfully away into the distance.

Here were no satisfying lines or harmonious colours

upon which the eye could rest and be at peace, no suggestion of country quiet. On the contrary, there was continuous noise caused by the motors which passed at the rate of a
dozen or so a minute, hooting violently at each other. For
to every house there was attached a garage; advisedly, since
the neighbourhood, threaded by its main arterial road,
provided admirable facilities for escape in the car. Apart
from this it was difficult to see what could be said for it.
There were no signs of civic life, no churches, chapels or
meeting-houses; but equally there were no signs of rustic
pursuits, no farms, no ricks, no animals. Except for their
cultivation of cabbages, which could have been undertaken equally well at Ilford or Barking, there was no positive characteristic to distinguish the lives of these dwellers
in the 'country' from those of their brethren in the towns.
They did not till the soil, pasture animals, shoot, fish or
ride; they did not even go for walks. Nobody could walk
along the arterial road, and for miles on end no roads led
away from it. Possessing none of the advantages which
town dwellers lacked, they nevertheless lacked most of
those which town dwellers possessed. They could not go
to theatres or cinemas; they could not call upon their
friends, for all kept themselves rigidly to themselves, and
no man knew his neighbours; they enjoyed neither private
peace nor public excitement, and they could not lose
themselves in a crowd. But on Saturday afternoons and
Sundays they took advantage of their admirable opportunities for escape, and went for a drive along their arterial
road to Southend, I suppose, or to London. Cut off from
the life of the spirit, outcasts from the great herds of their
kind, without part in a community or roots in the soil,
they continue to keep themselves to themselves and to go
out in the car on Saturdays.

Why are they there? Again I can only answer because
of some obscure impulse which causes them to feel dissatisfaction with life in towns without fitting them for life

in the country. They have no knowledge of country things, neither skill in country pursuits nor love for country sights and sounds, and no capacity for solitude. Yet something impels them to dump themselves upon the countryside, and they spread like locusts over the land.

The Motorist in Quest of Beauty. It is the same impulse to leave 'the beaten track' that is taking motorists in increasing numbers off the main roads. There was a time when no motorist left a main road of his own accord; he had two aims, to travel as fast and as smoothly as possible, and the unparagoned brutality of an environment composed as it was of hoardings, advertisements, garages, petrol pumps, villas, motor-coaches, and other cars, gave him no temptation to linger. To-day people are at last discovering that motoring for pleasure is no pleasure at all, and are beginning to ask more of their cars than that they should merely convey them rapidly through space. They have been led to understand that somewhere behind the noise and the hurry there is a place of peace and refreshment known as the country; and they are beginning dimly to recognize that they know no more of this than before they owned their cars. And so motorists are met with in increasing numbers on by-roads, trying, as far as the virus that is in their veins will permit, to drive slowly, pretending to enjoy the scenery, stopping to look at views, discovering country villages, picnicking cheerlessly by the roadside. They even drive their accursed mechanisms on to the downs. Have I not with my own hand pulled a man off a motor-bicycle on the top of Blackdown?

But no more than the dwellers in the villas and bungalows do they find what they seek. The motorist straying off the main roads is driven by the need to escape from modern civilization. He is a man seeking to withdraw himself; he is in quest, though he may not know it, of a retreat, a retreat bathed in an atmosphere, the fragrance, that is distilled by old and traditional things. He finds it, but only for a moment, for in the act of finding, he transforms it into something other than what he sought. It is a lane, say, leading to a village; yet scarcely has he passed that way, when others follow in his wake. Gradually the lane is widened to accommodate him. Each year the banks are cut back, the hedges trimmed, the edges tidied. Presently the native surface which reproduced the colour and characteristics of the soil, disappears beneath a coat of tar, and the transformation from a lane into a road is complete. Another weal left by the whiplash of civilization seams the face of the land. There is a country lane that runs past my cottage; or rather, it was a country lane. To-day it is thick with motorists trying anxiously to escape from other motorists.

The Beauty Spot. And what of the village at the end of it? As the motorists reach it, it is miraculously and pitifully transformed. The country pub becomes a second-rate motoring hotel, the village street a roaring thoroughfare, the village shop an emporium for picture postcards. Garages and teashops spring up like mushrooms, and on every side the country breaks out into the familiar red rash. The village has changed its character. It *was* beautiful; it has become a 'beauty spot'. It will be said of this generation that it found England a land of beauty and left it a land of 'beauty spots'. And the motorist who has transformed it is the modern 'Midas'; whatever he touches turns to tin and brass.

In this and a hundred ways the country recedes at the motorist's approach, and in this and a hundred ways country number two encroaches and grows at the expense of country number one. Already it is a rare experience to come upon a landscape in southern England that is not flawed by at least one modern bungalow, planted, as bungalows almost invariably are, so as to command and in commanding to ruin the maximum possible area. You may have been walking for an hour in a secluded valley and quietly happy or exuberantly exhilarated, you feel at peace with a world which, in becoming remote, becomes innocuous. You top a rise and immediately there breaks upon the view some shouting pink horror to remind you that the remoteness was an illusion. Civilization, it seems, in the south of England, is always just round the corner.

Sounds of the Country. And this which is true of the sights of Southern England is still truer of its sounds. Silence, the peace of the country, is becoming yearly a rarer thing, and as it grows rarer it grows more precious. Our civilization which boasts of hygiene and despises the men of the Middle Ages because they had no drains, has made a more serious assault upon the senses than the bad smells for which it reprobates its ancestors. The world may not smell to-day except of petrol, but never assuredly was it so noisy. Modern civilization, in fact, has saved its nose at the expense of its ears. I sat one evening last summer in a garden in Hampshire of such peace and beauty as only English gardens know. It was in the heart of the country, an undulating country of fields and woods and streams, far from any main road, farther still from a town. A mile away was the nearest village, a hamlet of a few thatched cottages in the shadows of the downs. As I watched the sun setting slowly into a haze of ruddy gold, my ears were suddenly assailed by the noise of a loud speaker, more powerful than a company of many men, bawling through its brazen snout the incomprehensible words and disjointed rhythms of some American negro song. The sound smote the horrified air, but only for a space; for presently along the little lane outside the garden came the noise of a motor-cycle. With a succession of shattering explosions like a machine gun or an electric drill, it approached, passed and hurled itself away into the distance. For five minutes the sound of it was audible, and then came another. For in the little hamlet a mile away there were half a dozen of these machines. This murder of solitude is now universal in the south of England. Noise is taken so for granted that nobody complains; but we pay in ill-temper, shattered nerves and loss of the ability either to concentrate or to meditate for this invasion of our peace, this thwarting of our need for solitude and silence. And yet, I repeat the point, it is largely to the growing dissatisfaction with modern civilization, to a distaste for its sights and its sounds, a dislike of its hustle and turbulence, that this continual encroachment upon the country is primarily due. Paradoxically it is those who are most dissatisfied with country number two who are chiefly responsible for the disappearance of country number one. It is the newly discovered sense of beauty in the motorist which is responsible for the destruction of beauty. We are entangled, whether we like it or no, with the apparatus of our civilization, and eventually we destroy what we invade.

The Misers of the Country. And knowing this we grow miserly and secretive about the country. We make discoveries of inns and villages, of hills and lakes and coves and valleys, and we are jealous to keep them to ourselves.

I have been engaged for some years past in collaborating with three other men in the compilation of a list of places, inns, farms, cottages and so forth, to stay at in the country. To be included a place must possess the following qualifications: it must be in unspoiled country; it must be comfortable; the food may be simple but must be good; it must be cheap, and motorists must not know it. (These last two qualifications are, in fact, the same qualification.) Provided that the conditions are satisfied, it is immaterial whether the place is an inn, an hotel, a

The Horrors of the Countryside

boarding-house, a farm-house, or just 'digs'. The list, of course, is for private circulation and is jealously guarded. A considerable number of the entries are addresses in the north of England; there are a few from the Midlands, a very few from Devon and Cornwall. Dorset, Wiltshire and the Cotswolds are well represented, and East Anglia has several mentions. Hampshire too appears, though there have been many deletions from this county in recent years, as it has been increasingly overrun. But the Home Counties are practically unrepresented; whatever entries there were have, with one or two exceptions, been removed. In Surrey and Sussex, Kent and Bucks there is practically no place left that possesses the required qualifications (I say practically because, as I say, there are still one or two exceptions which wild horses would not drag from me).

Walking on the Road. And now that by a devious route I have returned to the Home Counties, I want to ask the question which has prompted the writing of this chapter. What, under modern conditions, is the country walker to do? He cannot, it is clear, walk on the roads. Apart from the perpetual noise and stench and harrying of the cars, the unyielding tarred surface, there is the unparagoned brutality of their scenery. The new arterial roads to-day are practically hedgeless and treeless. They are lined not by living things but by iron or wooden fences interspersed at intervals with villas planted singly or clustering in pink blocks. There are also pumps and garages and boards covered with paper notices. These last are to be found in amazing numbers. They are mainly advertisement hoardings; but there are also sign-posts, A.A. notices, builders' boards and estate-agents' announcements that such and such tracts of country are to be developed and offer eligible building sites. When the surrounding country can be seen it is raw and mutilated. Nobody, it is obvious, can walk here.

Dislikings—IV

There are, of course, the side roads and the traditional country lanes. But even these, as I have already pointed out, are invaded and invaded increasingly by cars escaping from other cars. To walk on them is to invite constant harrying from the drivers of these cars. The motorist assumes automatically that it is the business of everybody and everything to give way to him. Bearing down on you suddenly from round the corner of some winding lane, he demands insistently that you should stand aside and let him pass. And, if you do not get out of his way soon enough to please him, he will play a perfect devil's tattoo on his horn and make a pretence of driving over you. Certainly, if you refuse to budge, he will consent to slow down. I have even when in a desperate mood made him stop altogether; but the flurry of nerves engendered by this defiance destroys all the benefits which are supposed to attend country walking, and leaves one as exasperated and ill-tempered as the motorist himself. No, assuredly the walker cannot walk on the roads.

Hence all that literature of walking and walking tours in which the English language is so rich, of which the essays of Hazlitt and Stevenson and Richard Jefferies are luminous examples, is hopelessly out of date. For it is mainly a literature of road walking: 'Give me the clear blue sky above my head and the green turf beneath my feet, a winding road before me, and a three hours' march to dinner,' cries Hazlitt, and goes on to speak of 'thinking', 'running', 'leaping' and 'singing for joy', all apparently on that same 'winding road'. He writes, it is obvious, about a country in which motors were unknown and the roads were walkable. But that country is no more. Even that fine essay entitled *Walking*, written in the early years of this century by Sir G. M. Trevelyan, is grossly inapplicable to modern conditions.

Walking Across Country. But, if you cannot walk on the

The Horrors of the Countryside

roads, where can you walk? Across country? But the south of England is all enclosed. Apart from the farmers, traditionally hostile to those who 'trespass' on their land and particularly fierce in the Home Counties, it is owned by stockbrokers who breed pheasants and maiden ladies who breed poultry. Both are given to fencing, and the country is accordingly criss-crossed with barbed wire as if it were a disputed sector on the Western Front. Where the roads are teeming with cars and the country is barred and fenced, where all the woods are private and all the fields farmed and trespassers will everywhere be prosecuted, what is the walker to do? There are footpaths, of course; but a footpath, pleasant as it is, is limited, and every year sees more of them closed to the public, while many of those that remain are fenced or walled on either side to prevent the feet of walkers straying on to the sacred properties through which they run. What, then, I repeat, is the walker to do? What, indeed, but to go across country, climb the fences, negotiate the hedges, cross woods and fields, brave the notice-boards and trespass?

Personally I have always preferred cross-country walking to any other kind, and should still to a large extent go across country, even if the roads were tolerable and it were not forbidden. You get more varied walking that way than any other; to go across a field and over a hedge, through a copse, and then over another hedge into an orchard, and so through a gate into a farmyard with barking dogs, to be followed by a quarter of a mile down a lane and then up a bank and over another hedge and so into the fields again is for me the ideal type of normal walking; it is what a walk should be. In a mile of it you see more country sights and hear more country sounds, you come across more flowers, you get more glimpses of bird and beast, and you have more peace to your soul than in a week of road walking or a month of motor tours. You know nature, and the knowledge brings peace to your soul. And if you have no desire to witness the small incidents of natural life and your soul is already at peace, or troubled past appeasing, there is always the exhilaration produced by manifold physical exercise and the excitement of coping with farmers and keepers. For, the country being private and not free, these latter are a constant menace.

The Timidities of 'Hikers'. Now I find people's attitude to these pests of the countryside rather puzzling. There has been—it is notorious—a great revival in country walking these last few years. Fired by the example of the *Wandervogel* and eager to escape from the civilization which their parents have made, young men and women scour the country at week-ends in increasing numbers. They go in twos and threes, in groups of ten or a dozen, and in organized parties of twenty or more with a guide or leader. There are walking clubs, rambling clubs, and 'hiking' clubs. For it is not customary to call these activities walking, but tramping, rambling and (especially in the north) 'hiking'. 'Hiking' is more energetic than rambling, and ardent hikers will do their twenty-four or even thirty miles a day—along roads of course. Now these young people subscribe in theory to the views expressed in this chapter. They profess a love for the countryside, lament its ruin and regard motorists as their natural enemies. Most of them, moreover, belong to the Labour Party and profess Socialist opinions, including an objection to the private ownership of land and a contempt for keepers as a parasitic class, base minions of the rich. As for farmers, they consider them to be gross reactionaries who embrace diehard politics as an excuse for underpaying their labourers, and automatically oppose all movements for social betterment. Holding these views, it is not to be expected that the young people of to-day who

The Horrors of the Countryside

walk through the countryside on Saturdays and Sundays,
should entertain an exaggerated respect for the rights of
landowners. Nor, indeed, in theory, do they; they affect
to ignore the injunctions of notice-boards, despise the
menaces of keepers, and cheerfully profess their willingness, nay their eagerness, to trespass. In practice, however, I find them as law-abiding as the most jealous farmer
could wish. They keep to the paths, observe the boun-
daries of hedge and fence, dutifully obey the injunctions
of notice-boards, and, on the rare occasions on which they
can be tempted to defy them, go in terror of keepers and
apologize abjectly whenever they are caught.

An 'Outing' with 'The Walking Fellowship'. I was recently asked to lead an all-day 'ramble' for a body
which I will hide from its shame under the pseudonym
of 'The Walking Fellowship', an organization for inducing people to enjoy out-of-door activities communally.
I arranged to meet the party at Newlands Corner at
eleven o'clock one Sunday morning, the time being
fixed to allow them thirty-five minutes to walk the two
miles from Clandon Station. At about a quarter-past
eleven the advance guard of the party appeared. They
were aggressively dressed for walking with woollen stockings, bare knees and hob-nailed boots or shoes; some of
the women wore breeches; every back had its rucksack
and many carried iron-shod sticks or staves. In spite of
this tramping apparatus the party did not impress me very
favourably. They contrived, I thought, to look less like
walkers than like mannequins displaying costumes for
walkers. Accordingly by way of experiment I made a few
remarks on country walking. Did they, I asked, mind
negotiating fences, climbing over gates, crossing streams,
getting their feet wet and their boots muddy? They
answered that they did not; they were, they said, used
to these things, so much so, that a walk which omitted

them, would be no walk at all. Did they, I concluded, mind trespassing? Of course they didn't, there was nothing they liked better. They were quite unanimous about this, and seemed surprised that the question should have been asked.

I took them along the ridge of the North Downs to a point opposite St. Martha's, and then ran down the slope to the valley. At the bottom there was a ploughed field; it had not yet been sown, or, if it had, nothing as yet showed above ground. I went across it at a fair pace; at the far side I found that I was alone. I turned round and saw to my surprise the ramblers straggling slowly and hesitatingly across the field, the hindmost a good quarter of a mile behind. When they came up they began to remonstrate with me. Was it not wrong to cross ploughed fields? Did I not know that it was one of their rules to do no damage to property? I pointed out that it was impossible to walk without walking over private property—the farmers and stockbrokers were everywhere—and impossible to walk on private property without doing a certain amount of theoretical damage. If they were to leave the roads, then it was necessary that they should in theory do damage. Or, I asked, did they think one ought never to cross fields? Apparently when it came to the point, they did; they always kept to the footpath. And then why did I go so fast; they were not accustomed to running. 'Not even down hill?' 'Not even down hill.'

St. Martha's is covered on the north side with woods which are strictly private. As I went through them, I heard sounds of altercation. The hinder members of the party had, it seemed, become embroiled with a keeper. How they dealt with him I do not know, but when some twenty minutes later they reached the top, they reported that they had been trespassing on private property, and that they had been caught. I shall never forget the look of shocked horror with which they told me this; they looked as if they had been guilty of some unforgiveable offence, of the nature of sacrilege or blasphemy, for which they deserved and expected instant and condign punishment. And so it was all through the day. On the south-east side of St. Martha's there is a steep drop of a couple of hundred feet or more through a wood to a lake. I ran down this as fast as I could, revelling in the steep descent. There were only two with me at the bottom, two who had begun to enjoy this novel method of rambling and ran as I did. The rest climbed painfully down with torn legs and stockings, muddy shoes, wet feet and woebegone appearance, and they were still straggling in twenty minutes later. Two never turned up at all.

On the far side of Blackheath there was another encounter with a keeper. I was ahead and passed by before he was fully arrived on the scene, and so did those with me. But the bulk of the party was deeply embroiled. For ten minutes or more they stood arguing, provoking the keeper by alternate displays of truculence and humility, and in the end solemnly giving their names and addresses in order that they might the better be summoned. By the time lunch was taken, a lunch eaten miserably in the open air and an east wind with a great display of wholemeal bread and health-giving cheese and green stuffs, the party had diminished by a further five; at tea only half the original number were present, and only nine of the original thirty caught the eight o'clock train with me at Clandon. And yet you would have thought that these people were walkers; they dressed like walkers, talked like walkers—at least they talked interminably about walking—and belonged to an association formed for the purpose of getting young people into the open air. Also they were acutely conscious of what they considered to be their right of access as citizens to the countryside, and vocally defiant of those who sought to deny them the free exercise of their right.

Dislikings—IV

Coping with Keepers. This talk of rights reminds me to say a word about keepers. There is a definite technique for dealing with keepers, a technique which includes several different methods adapted to variations of need and mood and the exigencies of time and place. At the best method I have already hinted; it is always to be in the front of and, if possible, leading a party. Persons so placed who meet a keeper can afford to ignore him and to proceed as if he were not there. For the keeper confronted with this situation will be torn different ways; on the one hand, he will wish to pursue you and curse you for your impertinence; on the other, he will see a considerable *posse* of people bearing down upon him from behind and will be moved to stay where he is and remonstrate with them. In my experience nine times out of ten he will do the latter. Thus the rearguard of the party draws the keeper's fire, while you in front pass serenely out of the infected area. But the rearguard cannot stay long, since they dare not run the risk of losing you, and with you their way. Consequently, however great their fear of the keeper, they are obliged to defy him and to continue on their way, being impelled by a greater fear. They find you waiting for them some three fields ahead. You greet them with a look of amused surprise that they should have thought it worth while to bandy words with a keeper.

But this method, admirable so far as it goes, can only be followed when you have a large party behind you. For walkers caught alone a number of different methods of keeper-discomfiting are available, all of which I have on occasion employed with success. There is, for example, the polite method. On sighting the keeper you approach him, making, if possible, signs of surprise and pleasure, explain to him that you have unfortunately missed your way and ask to be directed to the nearest road. To pursue this method successfully it is necessary to speak in a governing-class voice and with a cultivated accent. In the

The Horrors of the Countryside

course of your remarks you may mention that from the appearance of the woods and the length of time you have wandered without coming upon a road, you have begun to suspect that you must be on private property; if this is, in fact, the case, you are exceedingly sorry and would like to be directed out of it as soon as possible. A variant of this method is the cringing. You voluntarily admit the fact of trespassing, apologize humbly for it, say you will not do it again, and explain that it was only great pressure of time that induced you to take what you imagined to be a short cut over somebody else's property. You know, you say, that you have no business there, and hope that, if you withdraw as rapidly as possible, no harm will come of it. This is the method most usually adopted by persons caught trespassing; but I do not really recommend it. It is apt to infuriate the keeper and encourages him to domineer. If, however, for reasons of constitutional weakness, timidity or some other defect this method is adopted, it is essential that the trespasser should take the initiative. He should always himself challenge and beard the keeper; never wait to be challenged and bearded.

At the other end of the scale there is the blustering method. You take your courage in both hands and brazen the thing out. You say that you *did* know that it was private property, but that the fact does not really interest you. Presumably the land belongs to somebody—after all most land does—but you didn't know to whom, and you do not care. If the keeper likes, he can summon you, for which purpose you are prepared to furnish him with the necessary particulars. And drawing his attention to the board informing all and sundry that trespassers will be prosecuted, you ask him to make good its undertaking, say that you are willing and ready to be prosecuted and bid him act accordingly. And taking out your pocket-book you give him a false name and address and proceed. If you are a big man and the keeper is small, or, if you are in condition and a good runner, all this is, of course, unnecessary. You simply tell the keeper to go to hell, and go on your way.

Or there is the ironical method. You remark humorously that you did not know that this was private property; that, had you known it, nothing of course would have induced you to trespass on it; that your respect for property is, in fact, immense; and here, you add, is a sixpence to cover the cost of any damage you may have done to blades of grass, twigs, branches or the feelings of pheasants.

I myself am partial to this method, and often adopt it if in good spirits. But it requires practically incessant talking—the whole point of the method is that the keeper should be dazed and bemused by your verbal dexterity—and those inapt in words should not attempt it.

Or there is the heroic method. Affecting an indignant resentment at being stopped, you say as dramatically as you can: 'I fought for this land for four years in the Great War. I fought, or so I was told, to keep it free, free, that is, for the enjoyment of us all. By God, then, I am going to enjoy it, and neither you nor anybody else shall stop me.' The surprise occasioned by this announcement often leaves the keeper temporarily speechless, and taking advantage of his discomfiture you turn on your heel and walk with dignity away.

I have often found it useful when found trespassing in a park or the grounds of some large country house, to say merely that I have been to call on the inmates, and am making my way out. (I should say that I make it a practice, whenever I find myself near a country house, to walk openly on the paths or carriage-drive in order to lend countenance to this suggestion.) The objection to this method, at any rate for me, arises in the difficulty of determining which should be the inmates upon whom one may most appropriately represent oneself as calling. I look, or at any rate dress, like one of the lower middle- or working-classes, but I talk like a gentleman. Hence the difficulty of determining the status of the inmate whom I might plausibly visit. Generally I give a name like Miss Smith, hoping thereby to be taken as indicating a house-keeper or one of the servants, but, if I know the name of the owner, I assume my governing-class voice and give it. Indeed I have on occasion engaged in long conversations with keepers about the present circumstances, past history and personal peculiarities, which I have invented for their employers.

Disgust for Keeper-baiting. Yet, when all is said and done, what a sorry business it is. This skill that I have acquired enables me to trespass with comparative im-punity; yet it is a horrid accomplishment and I would sooner be without it. I do not play the game of keeper-baiting and keeper-deluding for fun; on the contrary, I dislike it more as I play it better. For even when I win it, as I almost invariably do, and retire with honours from the field, the sharpening of wits, the gathering of energies, the marshalling of forces for the contest, still more the contest itself, disturb and excite and leave me in a state of mind (or nerves) which effectively precludes the enjoy-ment of the country. Conflict and excitement—it is obvious—are inimical to æsthetic appreciation. One does not after all go into the country to wrangle with keepers. Yet, as I asked above, what is the walker to do? The area of free walkable country in the south of England, country which is neither privately owned nor infested by cars, nor rashed by bungalows, is very small and yearly grows less; the deserted places where a man may wander at will and be at peace are rapidly vanishing, and in a few years they will be no more.

Lament over a lost piece of Country. Take, for instance, a part of Surrey celebrated among walkers which I happen to have known well over a period of some fifteen years, the Dorking–Guildford district. In 1916 I lived for a time in a cottage near Boxhill; the country was delightful and owing to the war not, except on Sundays, over-visited. By 1919, however, it was already infested. Cars passed across Burford Bridge at the rate of forty a minute, and were drawn up in serried masses in front of the hotel. Hordes of people descended weekly, and in the summer daily, from charabancs, to uproot flowers and plants, and scatter ginger-beer bottles, paper and sandwiches far and wide. The roads were strewn with primroses and bluebells trodden underfoot, carelessly plucked and carelessly thrown away to perish in the dust. The hill itself became a centre for every kind of hateful activity. On its summit were swings and cocoanut-shies and overworked donkeys forced to give rides to children. Its sides were covered with a scurf of litter, the refuse of innumerable picnics. For miles around the country was wired and fenced against its invaders. I moved further afield to the Gomshall and Shere district which, protected by the quite remarkable inefficiency of the Southern railway system, preserved some rural characteristics for a few years longer. But only for a few. By 1924 Gomshall, too, was developed; bungalows sprawled, garages spawned, pseudo-peasant industries sprang up, the local pubs turned into second-rate pretentious hotels, and the motors came in ever-growing numbers. I retreated again southward to the Leith Hill country and made the heather wastes to the north and west of Leith Hill my main walking ground. But there, too, the flowing tide caught me up and threatened to engulf me. The Wootton Hatch hotel quickly came to rival that at Burford Bridge in the number and vulgarity of its clientèle. Friday Street became one continuous picnic, and the slopes of Leith Hill were littered with the débris of walking parties. (There is some country to the south of Leith Hill by the way, of which I could still tell a different story, but for obvious reasons refrain.) Again I retreated, this time to the west and with Pitch Hill for my centre walked and stayed in the country to the north and west of it. Here is the Great Hurt Wood, a great tract of woodland and moor, part of the primeval forest of the Weald. It is wild, gloomy and roadless, and except for gipsies and jays practically uninhabited. I am not over fond of it, but at least a man can be alone there, or could.

To approach it from the north was for me to enter a realm of silence and of mystery. Farley Green, the hamlet to the north, was only a handful of scattered cottages, and leaving it one felt, or with a stretch of imagination could make oneself feel, that one was leaving the human world of civilized men behind and entering an unknown land, unknown and forbidding. At the south end of the wood was a windmill overlooking the Weald. This windmill came to take on for me—mind, I am not excusing my imaginative follies, merely describing them—a symbolic significance. Seen from the depth of the wood it became an outpost of the world of men, assuring me that it existed still, and that, could I reach it, I was safe. This, no doubt, was playing at mystery—the wood itself cannot be more than three or four miles across—nevertheless there was a something, there still is a something of eeriness there. But the area of eeriness grows yearly more restricted and the eeriness, such as it is, more attenuated. For even here the tide creeps on. Peaslake is an outpost of suburbia; to the south and west an advance guard of bright new houses is being pushed up from Cranleigh and Smithwood Common, while the wood itself is now fringed on its northern side with pseudo-antique houses in the Tudor style.

Clearly I must retreat again, and to that country to the south at which I have so indiscreetly hinted. But here I shall be too far from London for daily access, and the Saturday walk, so cleansing to the spirit, will be impracticable. Here nothing short of a week-end will serve. And so one comes reluctantly to the conclusion, a conclusion which may as well be stated here as elsewhere, that there is no really good walking country, no solitary country that is, where one may be assured of quiet and that refreshment of the spirit that quiet brings, within a day's reach of London.

The Wild Places. I have confined these lamentations mainly to the Home Counties, where the processes of vulgarization and urbanization have proceeded furthest. But the same thing is happening in a greater or less degree all over the country. Dorset and Wiltshire are comparatively untouched—the cars hurtle through them on their way to Devon and Cornwall—but Devon and Cornwall themselves are badly infected. Their coasts are infested with resorts; their villages have become thoroughfares for charabancs; even their wild places are invaded. I have seen a stream of cars a mile long on the road by Dartmeet. Nor are cars the only enemy in the field. Such few wild places as are left are, it seems, a standing temptation to large industrial towns, who exploit them for their needs. In particular they have a *penchant* for ravishing them with waterworks. Rivers are harnessed and mountain waters collected into reservoirs. A lake in the Welsh hills is used to give electricity to Manchester, a road is threatened over the Stye Head Pass, the Lulworth cliffs are raped by the War Office, Dartmoor is affronted by china-clay works, and so on and so on.

Moreover, even upon wild places there is the blight of keepers. I have climbed Kinder Scout and been harried by persons appointed to preserve grouse for the guns of stockbrokers. I led one of them a dance for miles over that scarred plateau. All over the North Derbyshire moors the hand of the sportsman lies heavy, as it will continue to do, so long as society thinks it more important that rich business men should have opportunities for the unhampered slaughter of wild birds, than that those who made them rich should wander freely in the waste places where wild birds make their home; more important that birds should be killed, than that work-worn men and women should regain spiritual health. There is a large class of persons in this country for whom the good life consists in the practice of depriving other creatures of life, and as this conception tends to be bred of riches, there are many moorlands and open spaces in England to which only those who are prepared to kill may have access. As for Scotland, its moors and mountains have been delivered wholesale to Americans, who sit concealed in shelters and employ what remains of the native population to drive frightened birds over their heads, in the vain endeavour to give themselves social distinction by indulging in what they mistakenly believe to have been the main pursuit of the aristocracy they have replaced.

The Army. And there is always the army. To walk across the northern half of Dartmoor is to traverse a land seamed and scarred by high explosives, pitted with shell-holes and littered with the fragments of burst or exploded shells. If the army scouts catch sight of you, they forbid you access to the moor, while, even if you evade them, you yet must cross it at hazard of life. Thus many square miles of some of the loveliest wild country in the south of England are denied to the country walker, in order that the British army may perfect itself in the art of killing men from a distance. Other wild places are similarly infested. I have been compelled to make a detour of many miles in the neighbourhood of Trawsfynnydd in the Welsh mountains because great tracts of country had been permanently commandeered by the army for rifle and cannon practice.

Nor is this virtual closing of the moors the worst of the

evil. The army, it is well known, defiles and pollutes everything that it touches. It puts up ugly buildings, it lays down ugly paths, it destroys trees and flowers, dirties streams, obliterates meadows and turns them into grass-less wastes. Everywhere it erects barriers; the country is stiff with fences and bristles with barbed wire. To descend into Okehampton from the heights of Dartmoor is to pass through one of the most grievous scenes in England. As you come down from the hills, you see the country below defaced by line after line of tin-roofed huts, staring brick buildings, and by what appears to be a vast scarlet house. Presently your path becomes an asphalt road lined on each side with yellow stones which runs for over a mile through corrugated iron sheds, barbed-wire enclosures, allotments, patches of kitchen gardens with clothes drying on lines, notice-boards and latrines. These latter are strictly graded according to the army hierarchy. There is, for example, a latrine labelled 'Sergeants only'. . . .

Of course all this seems more unutterably beastly than it might otherwise do by comparison with the moors one has left. 'Sergeants only' after the view from Hamish Down is inevitably distressing, and it may be unfair to tax the British army with the contrast. Nevertheless when all allowances are made, the fact remains that next to poultry soldiers create more uglification, create it more quickly and create it over a wider area than any other form of living organism.

The Future. But this complaint has gone on long enough, and I had better stop. There exist many societies in England to-day for the preservation of the countryside, and they advocate many salutary measures. Local author-ities are to be pressed to make bye-laws dealing with bun-galoid growths, motorists confined to certain scheduled main roads, and prohibited from driving through gates or

The Horrors of the Countryside

on to downs; it is to be made a penal offence to leave litter. There is to be country as well as town planning, and unregulated building is to be prohibited. A jealous eye is to be kept on the foreshore and jazz bands, niggers, cinemas and merry-go-rounds concentrated at fixed spots. Walkers are to be given access to moorland and mountain irrespective of the needs of 'sportsmen', and large tracts of country set aside as national parks. These provisions no doubt are excellent, and, should they become effective, would perceptibly mitigate our present horrors. But in the present state of public opinion it is extremely unlikely that they will become effective, or that they would do more than delay a process which there is only too much reason to think inevitable. Short of a change in public opinion nothing, as I conceive, can prevent the destruction of the English countryside. To demand such a change is to demand nothing less than that we should become civilized, a contingency which, to say the least of it, seems unlikely. Hence, beyond the pleasure it has given me in the writing, this complaint can serve no useful purpose.

It is always pleasant to grumble, but in this case I would prefer to have no occasion for my pleasure. It is probable that my children will see none. My generation is a survivor from a world rapidly becoming obsolete, a generation which, having known the beauty that was England's, cries out to see it pass. But our children growing up in a world of garages and bungaloids, nourished on concrete and surrounded by the monuments of the men of tin and brass, not knowing what they have lost, will not miss what they have never known.

I recently read a book written exactly a hundred years ago, the memoirs of a Mr. James Robinson, a gentleman of independent means. Mr. Robinson was a great lover of the countryside and a great walker in it. In the course of his book there is scarcely a county of England that he does not visit, and he has a number of judicious remarks to make about the distinctive feels and smells and sights of the different types of country as he goes from one county to another. But throughout his book there runs a continuous murmur of complaint, which towards the end swells to so great a volume of protest that it dominates everything else. The railways are Mr. Robinson's bugbear. Great iron bonds laid over the countryside to bind and to fetter it, inhuman monsters of iron belching smoke and flames to blacken and besmirch it, clankings and grindings and shriekings and puffings to disturb its peace. This, in Mr. Robinson's view, is what the railways meant to England, and, as he inveighs against them in season and out, he concludes that the beauty of England will be irretrievably destroyed unless this defilement is stopped.

Now I rather like railways; I cannot imagine the countryside without them, and I should not like it to be without them. And what I feel for railways my grandchildren will, no doubt, feel for all the horrors I have enumerated in this chapter.

Where Unreason comes in. It may be asked what bearing the horrors of the countryside have upon the theme of 'irrationality' which has run like a thread through the last three chapters. The connexion is not far to seek.

The situation I have described, distressing as it is, is ludicrous as well as distressing. It is true that we are destroying the country as no previous generation has destroyed it; it is also true that we probably care for the country more keenly, and that more of us care for it, than any previous generation.

Of all civilized peoples the English like most to get away from their fellows. We go about looking for 'unspoiled places'; we make a cult of 'escaping from the crowd'; we love to see things in their 'natural surroundings'. In May 1931 when the new Zoo at Whipsnade was first opened to the public the crowd was so great that at four o'clock in the afternoon all traffic from London in the direction of Whipsnade was stopped. The original car-park which contained provision for 500 cars was quickly filled, and an emergency park with space for 2,000 extra cars was jammed with cars by eleven o'clock. Thousands of people who had taken the train to Luton found themselves waiting for buses in queues half a mile long.

Why this unprecedented rush? The animals were the same as those which the people could have seen at any time, and had in fact seen many times in the London Zoo. Only a small proportion of civilization's prisoners had been moved and these, from the point of view of human interest, not the most exciting. The only difference was that in the words of the press reporters, the animals were to be seen 'roving amid natural surroundings'. The phrase acted like magic upon a generation starved of nature, lusting for nature, awakening at long last to the fact that nature in England is slipping through its fingers and will shortly be gone past recall. Yet it is precisely this generation which is responsible for the gradual destruction of the nature it venerates. Is not this irrational that we, who of all people most value 'natural surroundings', of all people do most to destroy what we value?

CHAPTER IX

Dislikings—V. Music, its Interpreters and its Listeners

THE TASK of listening to music of the highest order is one of considerable difficulty. I do not mean by this that it is not an enjoyable task, but I do mean that it requires effort and concentration, that it demands a fresh mind and quiet nerves, and that it should not be attended by discomfort or exposed to distraction. Above all, no factors extraneous to the music should be allowed to intrude.

Importance of Comfort. It follows that the person listening to music should be in a condition of secure physical comfort. Ideally he should be at rest in an arm-chair, with facilities for crossing his legs and putting his feet up; he should be able to smoke, to drink, and, if he feels so inclined, to expectorate, and he should be perfectly easy in the matter of his clothing. Such conditions are, I dare say, impossible of realization in a modern concert hall. In Germany, however, where they understand these things, there is a sufficient approximation to them to satisfy reasonable men. You sit in a café, you drink your beer, you remove your coat in hot weather and take your ease in your shirt-sleeves; you smoke, you chuckle—for chuckling is appropriate to the hearing of some music, a bassoon concerto, for example—you take out your collar-stud, if the collar feels tight round the neck, and there is a spittoon. The players, moreover, are accessible, and in due course will drink with you.

Consider now the conditions at the ordinary London concert hall. Rows of straight-backed, red-plush seats strike a note of strict formality, and discourage any suggestion of ease. The fact that you have paid exorbitantly for your seat suggests that music is an expensive luxury, a suggestion which the appearance of the perfectly groomed person who shows you to your seat confirms. The general tone of the place is markedly high; the appointments are refined, the lighting subdued; it is a place in which nobody could possible swear, and, even if you could smoke, which you cannot, it would not be a pipe. You are, moreover, uncomfortably dressed, since, if you do not look more or less like other people, they stare at you, producing a feeling of embarrassment which is inimical to the enjoyment of masterpieces. If it is evening, evening dress is the rule. The general effect is to put music in its place as an embellishment of the elegant life, an adjunct of the drawing-room.

In spite, however, of the elevation of the social tone you are thoroughly uncomfortable. Your chair is straight-backed and too narrow; there is nowhere to put your hat and stick, and very little room for your legs. You may not smoke, drink or eat; you may not spit, put your feet on the seats in front of you, stretch, yawn or laugh. You feel very much as if you were attending a social function —a church parade is not dissimilar—and the anxiety displayed by members of the audience during the quite unnecessarily long intervals to be seen by other members of the audience, suggests that they are under the same impression.

Unimportance of Performer. Next to the importance of physical ease in the listener is the assignment of a proper unimportance to the interpreter. All first-rate music is pattern music. It announces a theme and then proceeds to work it out; the working out is analogous to a process of embroidering, but it takes place in accordance with certain rules of ordered development which in retrospect are seen to be as inevitable as the deduction of the conclusion from the premises of a syllogism. The interest of music lies not in the way in which it sounds so much as in the way in which it is arranged. Its affinity is with mathematics and with chess rather than with literature or even with art, as art is commonly understood, and its most satisfactory interpreters are not romantic personalities with long hair and irregular lives, but competent craftsmen with cool heads, sure hands and no souls at all. They should possess the virtues of the clerk rather than the temperament of the artist. What is important is that as little as possible should intervene between the composer and his audience. I am interested in the patterns of Bach's music, not in the idiosyncrasies of the temperamental Miss who undertakes to interpret it for me. Hence the less 'personality' in the performer the better.

I do not wish to suggest that the rôle of the interpreter is negligible. It is obviously essential that he, or she, should be a competent performer, possessing a degree of skill adequate to the task of rendering all the intricacies of the music with ease and assurance. But this is a question of manual acrobatics, of mere digital dexterity, and, provided the interpreter can render a satisfactory account of himself on this score, the less he has of 'temperament' the better. He is, after all, but a medium through which the music reaches us, a stage in a continuous process which beginning with the impact of hammers on wires, terminates with an agitation of the fluid in the cochlea of the inner ear. The excellence of a medium consists in being as clear and as transparent as possible, and any infusion of murkiness due to what is called the 'temperament' of the artist can only serve to distort and obscure the message of the composer he is seeking to interpret. The best Bach player I know is a classical schoolmaster, a little wizened man, formal and precise, with a soul that has dried up within him and rattles like a pea in a pod.

These views are shared neither by those who promote concerts nor by the artistes who perform at them, nor, apparently, by the audiences who attend them. Advertisements of forthcoming concerts in London are eager to inform us that Miss X Y will give a recital; but with regard to the music she proposes to recite they remain silent. It is in the same vein that friends blazing in the lustre of new gramophones ask me if I would like to hear Madame So and So sing. If I ask 'What?', as often as not they do not know. The question, it is clear, is thought irrelevant, if not actually impertinent. And when presently some intolerable female voice begins to squawk, their faces assume a rapt air and they ask reverently if Madame X is not wonderful.

The Audience. The preliminary notice on the walls of the underground railways strikes the key in which the whole performance is pitched. Suppose that you have taken the trouble to pay an advance visit to, let us say, the W—— Hall, obtained one of those leaflets from which alone the items on Miss X Y's programme are to be ascertained, and found something to your taste. You decide to attend the concert, and punctually at 8 p.m. you are in your uncomfortable and expensive seat. The audience is composed largely of women in evening dress; most of them seem to know one another; they are delighted to see their acquaintances and hail them loudly across the hall, with the result that the scene suggests nothing so much as a reunion of old-girls.

The spectacle of a crowd of women always inclines me

to a naturalistic interpretation of human psychology. I am reminded that biologically the human race is a species of animal, that behaviouristically it is a species of automaton. Viewing women in bulk one is led irresistibly to interpret their activities in terms of stimulus and response. Apply the stimulus and you can predict the inevitable response. On these occasions the stimulus is not so much the music as the presence of other members of the sex, well dressed like oneself, and, therefore competitors and rivals. They are there to see and be seen. On the whole the music bores them. It is an unnecessary interruption of social amenities. While it is in progress they whisper, fidget with their feet and rustle their programmes. Directly it is over they burst into chatter like a cloud of magpies. A few only seem to care for the music. On their faces is a look of dreamy rapture; they are being reminded that they have souls. The rest assume a similar expression as often as they remember. It was, I believe, after observing the behaviour of women at a concert that Schopenhauer wrote his famous essay on women.

The interchange of social amenities enables the audience to tolerate with equanimity the lateness of the performer who, after discreetly waiting until the audience has been keyed up to a proper pitch of expectation, finally puts in an appearance for an eight o'clock concert about eight-fifteen. She is greeted with tumultuous applause, which is redoubled after the performance of each item, and again after the numerous encores. Also, she is overloaded with bouquets. Most of the audience, one gathers, is in a state of adoration, and the schoolgirls are ecstatic with hero-worship. Treated as though she were a *prima donna* or a cinema star of modified lustre, the performer fills the limelight and dominates the music. The latter has become an incidental accompaniment to the triumph of Miss X Y. It is not a performance of works by Bach, Mozart and Beethoven that you are attending, but a public exhibition of the musical prowess of a modern young lady, a display of skill not dissimilar in kind and in the manner of its reception—witness the anxiety of the audience to obtain positions from which they can see the pianist's hands—from that of troupes of acrobats and jugglers at an old-fashioned music-hall.

The glorification of the interpreter being the *raison d'être* of the concert, it follows that only that type of music is chosen which tends to subserve that end. Chopin, between whose lines what a world of wistful meaning may be read, and Debussy, with his challenge to the stresses and pathos of the pianist, are obvious choices. So is Bax, or, indeed, any composer whose modernity gives scope for a highly personal interpretation untrammelled by tradition, while showy pieces with bravura passages are naturally popular.

Bach, of course, is a thankless job; it is not to be believed that so much hard practising should have gone to the production of so little apparent effect, and would-be stars are right to avoid him. I wish, though, that on those occasions on which, having rendered a piece of Bach, they meet with an encore, they would not so readily relapse into the moderns. Nobody encores Bach in order to hear Ravel; and the pianist is wrong in thinking that the encore is provoked *entirely* by her playing.

Chamber music is less popular than solo performances. It demands team-work, and playing so carefully dovetailed that no one instrument should dominate, even when it may be distinguished from the rest. It holds, therefore, little attraction for the celebrity and sensation-seeking audience, still less for the star player, who, by the way, is usually a shocking performer of trios and quartets. Hence the tradition of the public performance of chamber music in this country is chiefly kept up by the enthusiastic amateur, who, innocent alike of a reputation to enhance and an ambition to acquire one, can afford to dispense both with stunts and 'starring' and to be merely workman-like; he plays, that is to say, exactly what was written in a manner not wholly at variance with what may be presumed to have been the composer's intention, and in so doing is content. But such fare is too insipid for audiences who desire above all things what is called 'the personal touch', and who are led to demand fireworks from a soloist for much the same reason as they have come to prefer tennis as a spectacle to cricket.

Confession of Musical Faith. To the unduly inflated importance of the interpreter, the 'artiste', in the modern concert-room, I owe my most miserable musical moments. In order that what follows may be understood, I should remind the reader that I regard music as practically the most important thing in the world; I derive more pleasure from listening to it than from any other single pursuit, and I hold it to be more worth while, more significant (in a sense which it would be necessary for me to write a book of metaphysics to explain)[1] than any other activity of the human spirit. It also happens that I hold the strongest possible views about the comparative merits of composers, so strong, indeed, that prejudiced persons would be justified in calling them prejudices. I consider Bach to be the greatest of the composers; his supremacy in music is, in my view, unparalleled in any other art, and I regard him, therefore, as the most important human being, or, if you prefer it, the greatest man who ever lived. Next to Bach I honour Mozart (why, by the way, is it so difficult to hear his operas in England? The Old Vic might at least do for him what they have done for Shakespeare. As it is, they dole us out a beggarly allowance of about one Mozart opera every month, embedded in a great welter of Aidas, Rigolettos, Cavallerias, Trovatores, Traviatas

---

[1] I have done so, by the way. See my *Matter, Life and Value*, Part II. Oxford University Press, 18s.

and I know not what Italian romanticizings), and after Mozart come Handel, Haydn, Purcell, and at a considerable distance Schubert. I ought to have said Beethoven, but my position in regard to Beethoven is equivocal. I used to think him a god, praised him intemperately and between the ages of twenty and thirty used to irritate men of judgment by saying about him the sort of things I now say about Bach. I can still on occasion recapture something of those early thrills, but the occasions grow rarer and the thrills fainter. After the twentieth repetition I have begun to find most of the sonatas boring and, though the seventh still holds me, I have to report the same of the symphonies. There still remains the Beethoven of the last period. The last four sonatas, the ninth symphony and the posthumous quartets seem to me to be unlike anything else in music, conveying an impression of unearthly tranquillity which to my mind can only receive adequate interpretation on mystical lines. There is another world, it seems, static, permanent and perfect, in a sense in which ours is fluctuating, transitory and faulty, of which we may catch fleeting intimations in this last-period music. Beethoven's later music is a window clouded and misty, but clearing every now and then into patches of comparative transparency, through which we may obtain a glimpse of the real world, the world of the mystics and seers, the home of the spirit and the goal of life's pilgrimage which is yet unaffected by and indifferent to the process of life's evolution towards it. Into this world Beethoven, one feels, has for occasional moments of ecstatic contemplation penetrated. To get there he has —it is obvious—'been through it'; but he really has in these moments, and for so long as they last, 'got there'. So much we may grant. But how much better to have got there without 'going through it', to have been in a sense *there* all the time. This is the happy position of Bach and in a lesser degree of Mozart.

Dislikings—V

Bach. Bach's music is faultlessly perfect from the
beginning. It means nothing—at least it has no meaning
which can be interpreted in terms of this world; it belongs
altogether to another. It is, in fact, sheerly beautiful. Bach
himself was obviously a very ordinary man. He had the solid
qualities of the good bourgeois. Marrying two wives and
begetting a great variety of children, he lived a humdrum
life of propriety and comfort, quarrelling a good deal with
his patrons and the ministers of the churches at which he
was organist, putting in periodical requests for a rise in
salary, sensitive to the point of touchiness over his reputation as a choirmaster, and completely ignorant of the fact
that he was inspired. Never did a great man set less store
by his own work. Bathing the children he would remember that he had still to write his cantata for next Sunday's
service, and drying a baby with one hand, he would write
the cantata with the other. It was a masterpiece, of course,
but Bach knew nothing of that, and more likely than not,
having served its purpose, it would be consigned to the
waste-paper basket or put to even baser uses by the Bach
household. Yet, while the man was of the earth earthy
and led a life of humdrum cares, honourable employ-
ments and small ambitions, the life of the good bourgeois
all the world over, there was a part of him, the part that
found expression in his music, that quite obviously lived
in heaven.

And it was there from the first. There is no development in Bach's music, no passage through turmoil and
strife to tranquillity. Perfect from the beginning, it remains perfect to the end. The last of the forty-eight
preludes and fugues is neither better nor worse, neither
more mature nor less, than the first. In listening to this
music I am moved, and regularly, by an intense emotion
of a kind which no other experience excites in me. The
theme, a bare phrase or two, is announced. It is a lovely
theme, pure and perfect, and, as I hear it, the goose-flesh

rises all the length of my spine! But the theme has to be developed. Lovely in itself it is, it seems, but a matrix pregnant with significance, from which are evolved complex patterns of sound. It is inverted, reversed, turned upside-down, inside out, varied, embroidered, tossed from key to key, from instrument to instrument. But never for a moment is it lost; like a thread of gold it runs through all the complex tapestries of sound that are woven around and at the same time spring from it. The movement is as remarkable for its economy as for its consistency. No extraneous matter is introduced to impair the coherence of the whole; throughout the original materials suffice. As the development takes place, the excitement grows, an excitement which is of the whole being. Borne along by the resistless impetus of logical necessity, intellect and emotion fuse in an ecstasy of delighted absorption. Suddenly your breath is taken away by a development which is as unexpected as it is inevitable. 'This man' you say to yourself 'cannot possibly go one more'; and then he does 'go one more' and leaves you gasping, until at last the movement comes to its profoundly satisfying close. Bach alone among musicians knows when to stop, and how to stop.

There follows the slow movement; the composer, it is obvious, is speaking straight from heaven. This, one says to oneself, is the way cherubs talk. And then . . . But this is meant to be a paper in criticism of interpreters and listeners, not in praise of musicians, and I must not let enthusiasm run away with the pen of just indignation. But, of course, there is Mozart. If Bach shows us the way cherubs talk and sing, Mozart shows us the way they laugh; but not so often, and there is more dross with the gold.

Dislike of the Moderns. Now it is not possible to feel with this degree of intensity for certain kinds of music, without being exposed to a number of serious inconveniences. Among them is modern music. Now I dislike modern music almost as much as I venerate that of Bach and Mozart. Modern music does not merely bore me; I find it positively distasteful; repulsive is not too strong a word. It irritates, disturbs, startles and depresses. The musical expression of frayed nerves, it frays the nerves of its auditors. The abolition of all music—with the exception of a little Schubert, less Schumann and some occasional César Franck—written since 1827, when Beethoven died, would give me almost as much satisfaction as the abolition of motor-cars. The subject—it is obvious—is one upon which I feel with all the strength of gross prejudice.

Let me try to rationalize my prejudice. The great composers of the past had one aim, to create something that was beautiful. In order to achieve beauty, they paid considerable attention to form. Their music is coherent; it has a structure, a sound vertebra, from which the subsidiary themes branch and to which they return. It is expressive music, admittedly, in the sense that it expresses the personality of the composer; but it is more than expressive, it is beautiful, and the composer's object is not to express himself but to achieve beauty. For this reason first-rate music of the great epoch is strangely devoid of associative qualities; it does not, that is to say, remind you of anything. Hearing it, you are not led to wistful brooding over your broken-hearted past, or to project the castles of a roseate imagination into a triumphant future. The music means nothing, calls up nothing, refers to nothing: it does not even prompt you to speculate on the personality or the intentions of the composer. Listening to it, you are aware of nothing but the music.

The aim of modern composers is different. They do not seek to merge the individual in the universal; indeed they are not concerned with the universal at all, still less with that aspect of it which is beauty. Their object is self-expression; they desire to give musical expression to their individualities. Hence their music is intensely personal and individual. It has the effect of some one engaged in an intimate and painful process of self-revelation, speaking to you privately for *their*, rather than for *your* good. Again it is like those invalids who, bound up in their illnesses, are never tired of discussing them with others; nor will they consent to let them off a single one of the details, however repulsive. And, because the personality expressed is very much like your own, you find that, instead of losing yourself in something greater than yourself, you are merely reminded of yourself; you are introduced not to beauty but to your own psychology, and voyaging in a sea of sound, re-live the scenes and emotions of your past.

As a substitute for beauty these musical expressions of the psychologies of composers are very poor fare. Considered as a medium of expression, music is merely an inadequate substitute for words. Certain emotions can be conveyed by music in a vague sort of way, but without force or precision. The effectiveness of music as a medium of expression may be gauged by the fact that what is called programme music is so little able to convey the intentions of the composer, that a tone poem entitled 'Night in the Woods' might, and in my experience has been called 'Morning by the Fountain' without any feeling of inappropriateness on the part of the audience. Some hold that the object of modern music is to communicate emotion, rather than to express it. But to estimate the value of music by its success in communicating emotion is to make it at least in part dependent upon the perceptiveness of the audience. In order that emotion may be communicated successfully, two parties are required, the communicator and the recipient. But the absurdity of rating Bach's music as dull merely because an audience of schoolgirls or shopkeepers is incapable of responding to it, would be too patent to be worth pointing out, were it not for the fact that many people still subscribe to the subjectivist fallacy of supposing that the merit of a work of art depends upon its effects.

Disliking modern music as I do, I seek to rationalize my dislike by the hypothesis of poverty of creative ability on the part of modern composers. Who, I am tempted to ask, that has enjoyed a revelation of beauty and possesses the creative capacity to convey his vision in music, can think it important to express himself? It is only when beauty has refused to appear, that we are offered the composer's personality as a substitute; psychology only intrudes when inspiration flags. To the same cause I am accustomed to attribute the modern composer's love of discord. Unable to hold your attention by beauty of form, he seeks to startle it by surprise of sound. Modern music has a horror of saying the expected thing. The diminished sevenths and calculated discords, the perverted structure of ill-mated notes and unfinished phrases, flitting in sheer caprice from one end of the keyboard to the other that go to the making of a modern composition, are so many conjurer's tricks, musical sleights of hand to disguise the fundamental poverty of the composer's imagination. After a time one becomes accustomed to the surprises, one expects the unexpected, and the device defeats its own ends. One is first startled, and then bored, and thinking of the corpus of lovely music that exists, one wonders why one should be so wasting one's time.

Presumption of Artistes. Why indeed? It may well be asked, why, holding these views, I should listen to modern music at all? After all there is no compulsion! I don't, if I can help it. I sedulously avoid concerts at which any music is to be played of a later date than the death of Beethoven. But I am not always successful in my endeavours. There are misadventures; one gets

let in. There is, for example, the unfortunate resemblance between the names of Bach and Bax. There
are in London numbers of small social music-circles
and clubs which give more or less informal concerts,
the items to be played being announced on hand-
written programmes circulated in advance. More than
once, misled by bad handwriting, have I attended such
concerts and, expecting to enjoy the music of Bach, been
regaled instead by that of Bax. Indeed, for one reason or
another, it is constantly happening to me to hear Bax,
when I am expecting to hear somebody else, which brings
me back to the point from which I began this digression,
the inflated importance of the interpreter in the modern
concert-room.

The interpreter, the artiste, being the pampered darling
of the concert-going public, he, or more usually she, is
licensed to indulge all her fancies in the matter of re-
arranging the order of items on the programme, or
even of substituting other pieces for those which she is
scheduled to play. Artistes are supposed to be very temperamental people, sensitive to delicate *nuances*, percep-
tive of the finer shades; yet it never seems to occur to
them that to the comparatively insensitive concert-goer
the difference between Bach and Bax may be all the
difference in the world, so that it may be a delight to hear
the one, a torture to hear the other. Such a consideration
could not, I say, occur; if it did, the irresponsible levity
with which they transpose the order of their items would
be inexplicable. No hostess would serve the meat before
the *hors d'œuvres*, or offer claret with the sweet. The
musical palate is, it is generally conceded, more sensitive
and more delicate than the palate for food; certainly it is
capable of more exquisitely pleasurable sensations. Very
well, then. It should be respected; it should get what it
expects in the order in which it expects it. And so it
would and does, except when it is catered for by star

artistes. An orchestra never dreams of transposing its items, but I suppose that to the professional artiste all music comes in time to sound pretty much alike!

However this may be, the casualness of artistes in this matter is intolerable; it is responsible, as I have said, for some of the most miserable musical moments I have known, and it is incidentally responsible for most of my knowledge, such as it is, of modern music.

An Evening at Crowndale Road. Let me take a recent example. There is a concert society in North London, which gives chamber concerts every Sunday at six-thirty at the Working Men's College in Crowndale Road. The concerts are free, except that there is a silver collection at half-time, the audience intelligent, keen and exceptionally well behaved; the music played is of the highest class, and the performers, eminent in their profession, give their services for a very small remuneration. No praise can be too high for these concerts. They and the famous South Place concerts, on which they are modelled, are the best things of their kind in England, and the Working Men's College is one of the very few places where for the sum of sixpence good music can be heard competently rendered without snobbery and without fuss. It is solely because of their manifest and numerous excellences that I am emboldened to make my complaint. How comes it, one wonders, that a management, otherwise remarkable for its judgment, good sense, and a just appreciation of relative values in music, should allow its artistes to monkey with its programme?

The first half of the programme for the opening night of the ——— season was, from my point of view, admirable. There was a Haydn Quartet, a group of old English songs by Purcell, Arne and others, and three preludes and fugues from the Well Tempered Clavichord. The second half was almost equally objectionable, consisting of a group of Brahms songs, followed by a Bax quartet. I arranged accordingly to leave at half-time and to return to Hampstead in time to play my usual Sunday evening game of Bridge. Two members of the Bridge four were also attending the concert and were to be collected at half-time; the fourth was to go direct to my Hampstead flat. I estimated that the first half of the programme would take about an hour, and accordingly told him to be at the flat at about eight-thirty, thus giving myself and the others ample time to get to Hampstead and have a scratch meal before he arrived.

The quartet was admirable. As I have said, I never hear Haydn without surprise that he should be so good, and blame myself for the perpetual injustice I do him by underrating him when I am not hearing him. Haydn like Trollope can be commonplace without being dull and he is always better than one had remembered. The Haydn over, my troubles began. The singer appeared and announced that he had decided to take the Brahms songs first. No reason was given and no apologies offered. Before singing them, however, he thought it necessary to tell us what they were about, since they were to be sung in German. There followed a résumé of the themes of the songs, which occupied a full ten minutes. As if it mattered what songs are about!

Brahms is not in my opinion vicious, he is merely dull. I tried to like the songs, but could not concentrate my attention. Besides, I was irritated at the thought of missing Arne and Purcell. The songs concluded, the programme secretary appeared, made the usual speech about the concerts that ought on the opening night of the season to have been made in the interval, and then calmly informed us that the Bax quartet would be taken next. No reasons, no apologies!

What was I to do? I could not go, because there was the arrangement to meet two of my Bridge four at half-time, and half-time had not yet arrived. At the same time I suspected that the Bax quartet would take considerably longer than the three preludes and fugues from the Well Tempered Clavichord, and that half-time would be later than I had bargained for. How much later, I was as yet happily ignorant. Should I go out and wait? On the whole I thought not. I had, I knew, a gross prejudice against modern musicians, and frequently condemned their music without hearing it. Here was a chance to hear it and rebut the charge of prejudice. Bax, I knew, was an eminent representative of modern composers. Very well, then, I would give them in the person of Bax another chance. With some misgivings I prepared myself for the impact of the quartet. Half a dozen bars had not been played before I realized that it far exceeded my worst forebodings. Never in my gloomiest moments had I believed that music could be so dismal, so ugly, so utterly incoherent. The movement was, so far as I could see, completely destitute of either form or design. There seemed to me to be no reason why any instrument should begin to utter or why, having begun, it should ever stop. Baffled in my search for unity, seeking in vain for a connecting thread, I endeavoured to discern significance in the sounds themselves. There might, I thought, be beauty or at least strangeness in the quality of the individual chords. Strangeness there was in plenty, but I could find no beauty. On the contrary, the noises emitted by the different instruments seemed to me monstrously ugly. And I could not get away from them. Vainly I tried to lose myself in day-dreams, to wrap myself in thought or to remember my engagements for next week. But concentration was impossible. Relentlessly the music broke in, administering a series of shocks to my nervous system, which left me irritated, miserable and depressed. The effect was similar to that produced by a spell of the dentist's drill. And the thing went on and on. Half a dozen times at least the music came to a complete pause, and I thought it was done. But no! Scarcely had I congratulated myself that the first movement at least was over, than one of the instruments would break out again, squirting out a little jet of bad-tempered sound like a bad smell, for all the world as if it had been pricked shamefully behind. The movement lasted half an hour before it was finally appeased. I could bear no more, and during the second movement walked dismally about the empty corridors of the place. I liked the corridors as little as I liked the music, and for the third movement I went back, hoping for some gleam of interest, even perhaps of beauty, to relieve the boredom of waiting for half-time. Again I was disappointed. The third movement seemed to me exactly like the first, and, except that it did not exasperate me by stopping and then beginning all over again, was as incoherent, as ugly and as irritating. It was well after eight o'clock before the quartet was finished and half-time was announced. Hurriedly I collected my two guests and made for home. We did not reach Hampstead until a quarter of an hour after the time appointed for the arrival of our fourth. He had been, knocked, found nobody at home and gone away. I had missed Bach, Arne, Purcell and Bridge, and been miserably bored and irritated for well over an hour into the bargain. These things do I owe to the temperamental vagaries of artistes; my only consolation is that I can no longer be charged with criticizing modern music without hearing it.

Women and Music. I hinted above that women do not for the most part really care for music. I was wrong. I ought to have qualified my generalization by the admission that they seem to approve of modern music. They go into raptures over Strauss, and adore Stravinsky. Ravel too, especially when played in the twilight, moves them, and Debussy, whose music is not so much heard as overheard, gives them the pleasant sensation of listening in to a conversation meant for the ears of somebody else. Women do not want to be made to concentrate on music; they want to lose themselves in it, to ride away on the crests of swelling harmonies into a rose-coloured world of day-dream, or to melt into a wistful melancholy over the poetic tenderness of tone poems. I once saw a woman dissolve altogether over a nocturne of Chopin.

Hence, while women flock to the fashionable concert halls to chatter, to rhapsodize, to melt and to watch the hands of the fashionable pianist of the moment, they rarely go of their own volition to places where serious music is interpreted in a workmanlike way. Take, for example, the Queen's Hall Proms. Here is to be seen the largest and most democratic audience in the country. Night after night the house is full. In the promenade people are packed so tight that they cannot move except to faint, which several do every evening. This promenade audience is composed almost entirely of young men and women, mainly clerks and typists, belonging to the lower middle class. They are one of the best-behaved audiences in the world, and their stillness and concentration in most uncomfortable conditions would put the ordinary fashionable concert-going audience to shame. Many of them are in small groups or pairs—a noticeable feature is the number of lovers—but the young men considerably outnumber the young women. This is because, while there are many unaccompanied young men, there are practically no unaccompanied young women. This disparity in numbers is not, I think, due to any reluctance on the part of young women to attend public concerts alone; such an interpretation, appropriate in the Victorian Age, has ceased almost entirely to be applicable, and in no stratum of society is the independence and self-reliance of young women more marked than among the young, urban, clerical workers who attend the Queen's Hall Proms.

Music and its Interpreters

I can only suppose that women, except when instigated by the wish to secure the approbation of men, have very little desire for serious music. There is not in them the sort of drive which there is in many men, which makes them insist on having good music at any cost, just as they would insist on having food or clothes. And so, while they flock multitudinously to the cinemas alone or in pairs, when left to their own devices they rarely make a spontaneous move in the direction of a classical concert. It is a corollary of this generalization that women seen at the Queen's Hall Proms should be considerably above the average in the matter of good looks, just as most of the women to be found in church are below it; and, as a matter of fact, they are. Music, in fact, unlike the Almighty, gets the sort of women men want. This is not to say that, when they are taken to concerts by men, women do not like the music, that, in short, they are hypocritical and only praise to please men; on the contrary, they enjoy it immensely. But it remains a fact, nevertheless, that women do not seem to miss music when they do not get it, and do not go out of their way to seek it. That this, or something like it, is the explanation of the smaller numbers of women at cheap popular concerts of first-rate music, is borne out by my own personal experience. At various times I have known fairly intimately a number of women. As I have already explained, I have a passion for music of a certain kind, and what more natural than that I should go with them to the Queen's Hall? Hence over a number of years during which I have regularly attended the Proms, I have been accompanied at different periods by three or four different women, and all of them have seemed to enjoy themselves as much as I did. They went into ecstasies over Bach, talked learnedly of harmony and counterpoint, criticized intelligently the playing of the orchestra, and compared in an experienced manner the conducting of Sir Henry Wood with that of other well-known conductors. In God's good time these intimacies ceased, and in each case the attendance at the Queen's Hall of the woman concerned ceased too, ceased, mind you, not only for that year, but indefinitely. No longer associated with a male who cared for music, she seemed driven by no initiative of her own to insist on having what she had seemed so much to enjoy.

The Temple Gardens. I will conclude with another instance. In the Temple Gardens on the Embankment in the summer-time brass bands give short concerts during the luncheon hour. You pay 2*d.* for a seat, eat your lunch out of a bag, and listen to the music; and very pleasant it is. The music is not of the highest class, consisting mainly of selections from grand operas and Gilbert and Sullivan, and popular overtures such as Zampa, Masaniello, Tancrêdi, Semiramide and so forth; but it is not bad, and the audience enjoys it immensely. Now for every fifty men that listen to these concerts there is an average of just over one woman—I got interested in the matter one day and counted them—and, while most of the men will sit or stand for half an hour or more, the one woman halts casually for a minute or two and passes on.

Consider the significance of this. Here is a crowded city area, in which there are nearly as many women working as there are men. Everybody in the city takes lunch at about the same time. How do they employ their luncheon hour? A small proportion of the men go to the Temple Gardens in order to hear music; but of the women none at all. Note that this is one of the few cases in which there is and can be absolutely no reason for one's presence except one's desire for music. One does not go to the Temple Gardens at lunch-time as one may go, for example, in the evening to the Park, to flit mothlike round the bandstand in quest of amorous adventure. Here there is no picking up; the hour is too prosaic; men's thoughts are on business; the time for women, if it is to come at all, comes later. One does not go in the hope of acquiring social reputation by being seen at a fashionable function; most of those present are in humble positions; clothes are strictly utilitarian, and a lovely dress will be ignored. No, there is absolutely no reason for one's presence except a desire to hear the music; and the audience is accordingly almost exclusively male.

CHAPTER X

Dislikings—VI.   The Wickedness of the Body and of the Old

Bathing at Hampstead.   In the summer I often go to the open-air bathing-pools on Hampstead Heath. On the Hampstead side there is only one in which bathing is permitted, but it is a very lovely pool, fringed with rushes and flowering shrubs, and in springtime gay with lilac, laburnum and May blossom. Men and women are not permitted to bathe there on the same day, four days a week being set apart for the men and two for the women. Apparently it is thought to be wicked at Hampstead for men and women to see the outlines of one another's bodies even when veiled by regulation costumes. It is not thought wicked, however, a few miles to the eastward at Hornsey, where mixed bathing is permitted. I find these variations in the moral codes of different London suburbs puzzling. We are accustomed to the notion that morality is largely topographical, that what is right in China is wrong in Peru, that the eating of human flesh which was regarded on occasion as a sacred duty among the Aztecs is a loathsome offence among the Nordics, and that to take human life, which is a crime in 1913, may be an obligation in 1914.

But that what is wicked in Hampstead should at the same time be observed as a respectable, social function a few miles away at Hornsey is surprising, and throws an interesting light on the moral foibles of borough (or should it be county?) councillors. I asked the attendant at the Hampstead ponds why mixed bathing was not permitted, and quoted the Hornsey precedent. He said that mixed bathing might be all very well at Hornsey, but that it wouldn't do at Hampstead because of the riff-raff. The riff-raff presumably are the poor, from which I infer that opportunities for the observation of the outlines of one another's bodies permitted to men and women whose incomes rise above a certain figure, are considered improper for those whose incomes fall below it. Apparently the attendant belongs economically to the permitted class, for he is on duty every day irrespective of the sex of the bathers. And why not? Personally I envy him his observational privileges; so, no doubt, does the reader. Men and women like to see and to show those parts of the body which are usually covered; but whereas men like seeing best, women are fondest of showing. Ever since civilization began, it has only been with the greatest difficulty that women have been restrained from exhibiting large areas of their persons to the public gaze, in the belief, usually though not always justified, that they are making themselves attractive. Those who have achieved a social position which renders them comparatively immune from public criticism, bare their necks, arms and bosoms every evening at dinner; they take advantage of tennis to bare their legs, and of a heat wave to bare their backs. I read in the paper (June 1929) that 'Police-Commissioner Grover-Whalen, who is satirically known as the "Mussolini of New York", has been thundering anathemas against "unseemly dresses". With the new frocks go backless bathing-dresses, and beach pyjamas even more "scanty". Some of the authorities at sea-side resorts near here are welcoming these styles, but Coney Island (New York's popular pleasure beach) is standing out for more clothes'. The wearers are said to claim that backless frocks are essential to health, just as it is claimed that stockingless legs are essential to tennis.

Seeing and Being Seen. It is, of course, possible that these contentions may be true. Possible, but not probable, for women appear to have been healthy before the summer of 1929, and I seem to remember that Lenglen wore stockings. For my part, I ascribe these phenomena to women's natural and laudable desire to be seen—seen as much and over as large an area as possible—a desire which I regard as a fundamental characteristic of feminine nature, and liable, if thwarted, to proceed to any lengths. Hence I applaud the recent decision of an American society leader to have her baby daughter vaccinated on the sole of a foot, so that she may be quite sure that the fashions of the future will reveal no disfigurement.

Owing to the fact that they are allowed to make public avowal of their possession of knees, it is said that the present generation of females is exceptionally shameless in this matter of body revelation. People get considerable pleasure from the belief in the wickedness of their own times, and this belief is accordingly widespread. It is nevertheless a delusion. Fashions may change and the precise area of the body open to inspection may vary from generation to generation, but women's tendency to exhibit parts of their persons to the public gaze is more or less constant.

Take, for example, the Victorians. Now the Victorians are supposed to have been very proper, that is to say, they regarded very large areas of the body as improper, and Victorian women in particular are usually conceived as given to wrapping themselves up in a sort of frenzy of decency. And, no doubt, they were immoderately covered. But not always. I have in my possession my grandmother's

wedding bodice: it is exactly 3½ inches deep. I am told
that no modest young bride of to-day would expose herself in such a bodice. On the principle that you could not
have too much of a good thing, Victorian women fattened
themselves up, and then curtailed their bodices beyond
the low-water mark of wise abbreviation. We have grown
prudish over a bust now; we shudder at portraits of
protruding ladies of the Stuart period; we are not intrigued
by the fat nudes in portraiture over which our grand-
parents glowed. But our women make a brave show with
their legs.

I conclude that people have at all times tried, and will
on the whole continue to try, to observe as much of one
another's bodies as they can, and will evade, as far as they
are able, the attempts of borough and county councillors
and other respectable persons to prevent them. Yet the
borough and county councillors and other respectable
persons are themselves men and women, and presumably
share the tastes of their fellows. (This may even be true
of Police-Commissioner Grover-Whalen.) Why, then,
should they forbid in their public capacity what they would
enjoy in their private? I do not know. It is one of the puzzles
about morality, which largely consists of the rules voluntarily made by people in one capacity to prevent themselves
from doing what they would like to do in another.

The Body's Zones of Wickedness. The regulations which
govern Hampstead bathing also raise interesting questions
as to the wickedness of the body. Where precisely
does the body begin to be wicked? At Hampstead
bathing-suits or costumes must be worn and slips [1] are
regarded with disfavour, from which it looks as if the
body begins to be wicked at the thorax and becomes
virtuous somewhere above the knees. At other swimming

[1] Little slips of material round the loins, the chest, abdomen and legs
being left bare.

places, however, drawers are permitted, which suggests
that the wickedness of the body begins lower down
and ends higher up, and at others again slips, which
would seem to imply a still larger area of decency. The
body is, however, always wicked somewhere, and the
wicked part must be covered up. In many places where
mixed bathing is permitted the men have to wear slips
under their costumes, from which it is to be inferred that
the body gets wickedest at the hips. That there is a zone
of special wickedness round the hips is, I think, in the
light of the available evidence fairly well established, at
least as regards men's bodies. Women's bodies, however,
seem to be generally wicker, and wicker over a larger
area, than those of men, and more of them must, accordingly, be covered. At Hampstead for example, women
are not allowed to see one another undressing, and whereas
men may sunbathe in slips, women must wear costumes,
even when there are only other women to see them.

Another interesting point is that the body is considered
to be more wicked when gradually and progressively
revealed, than when its nakedness is allowed to burst upon
the eye all at once. For this reason, in many places where
bathing in public is permitted, undressing in public is
forbidden, even though the area of flesh revealed in the
process of undressing is smaller than that exhibited during
the actual process of bathing. Hence governing bodies
of sea-side resorts make stringent regulations against
undressing on the beach, thereby inflicting discomfort and
deprivation upon hundreds of respectable citizens. In
order that the peculiar iniquity of these regulations may
be understood, it is necessary that I should say a few words
about the general conditions governing the entrance of
English people into the sea.

The Wickedness of the Body at the Sea-side. In the first
place, it should be premised that most of the sea that

surrounds the coast of England is not free, in the sense
that it may not be entered without payment. Most
of England's coast line is now ringed with 'resorts' or
with the extensions of 'resorts'. Where there are 'resorts'
there are promenades; there are also beaches. Now to
enter the sea you must, it is obvious, undress. Where are
you to undress? On the beach, one would have supposed.
But it is not so. To undress on the beach is at a sea-side
resort regarded as a serious offence; you can be imprisoned
for it. Presumably it is thought to be important from the
point of view of morals to guard against the possibility of
public glimpses of those parts of the body which even the
most furtive undresser cannot help momentarily exposing.
Legs, for example, are seen, and, as shirts are removed,
there are fleeting glimpses of white skin. Since you
cannot undress on the beach, your only course is to take
advantage of the facilities afforded by the authorities, and
for these you must pay. Hence, I repeat my assertion, the
sea is not free.

At many sea-side resorts the only facilities for dressing
and undressing are those afforded by antiquated bathing-
machines of the Victorian era; occasionally there are more
modern huts and tents. During a hot spell there are not
enough of these to go round, and visitors have to queue up.
This did not matter in the days before the war when people
were content with a ten-minutes' dip, or did not matter
much. But now a bathe is a lengthy and altogether more
elaborate affair; it is not one bathe but many. Women in
particular like to go in and out and in again, and in the
intervals between the immersions to sun-bathe on the sands.
A bathe so prolonged may well last the greater part of the
day. Meanwhile, what is happening to the people in the
queue? They have either rioted or gone away in disgust.

How is the new situation to be met? One can, of course,
curtail the period of the bathe and therefore of the use
of tent or machine; thus, in many places the limit of a

bathe is fixed at half an hour. But this annoys the bather, and the town may lose his custom. Or one might let people undress otherwise than in tents and machines; on the beach, for example. But the beach, for reasons already given, would not do at all. It is too exposed! But why not in their cars? People motor in hundreds to the sea-side and draw their cars up in rows on the front. Why may they not use them for dressing and undressing?

It is not clear. Yet almost unanimously the governing bodies of our sea-side resorts prohibit the practice. It is possible that they are actuated by the thought that undressing in cars might take money out of the pockets of the Town Council; there would be fewer people to use the machines. Morality is not always what it seems; indeed, if we are to believe Marx, it is but a cloak for economic interest. Thus Pope Pius XV at the time of the great crusade against the religious persecutions of the Bolsheviks happened to promulgate one of his numerous edicts forbidding women with bare arms to enter Catholic churches, or to wear skirts which exposed their knees. This admittedly looked like marked morality on the part of the Pope, but the Soviet organ *Pravda* said that the edict was due to his large holding of shares in a Milanese textile firm!

But to return to the resorts, the loss of money occasioned by motor-car undressing would not, one would have thought, have been a serious matter, seeing that the machines are notoriously unable to provide for all who wish to use them. The real reason, I suspect, is an objection to the gradual revelation by undressing of the normally covered parts of human bodies upon the esplanades of sea-side towns, even when such undressing is decently veiled in the privacy of closed cars. Again, there might be those tantalizing and corrupting glimpses of white flesh. This too must be the real reason why 'mackintosh bathing' is regarded with disfavour, and Eastbourne has achieved an ignoble celebrity. Hence, because of the foibles of Town Councillors, people bathe less often and for shorter periods than they might do, or are prevented from bathing altogether.

And on Sundays. The body also appears to get wickeder on Sundays. I recently had occasion to attend a week-end Conference in the summer in a large industrial town. It was very hot and the narrow, squalid streets lined with rows of ugly houses all looking alike were unendurable. On the outskirts of the town there was an open-air swimming-bath set in a large and spacious public park, the gift to the town of Mr. X, a prominent local capitalist. It was a splendid bath, elaborate and commodious, and the young people of the town went there in great numbers, sunning themselves after bathing on the strip of grass with which the water was bordered, and on Saturday afternoons making tea and listening to gramophones. I regretted the gramophones, but otherwise thought the place as pleasant a thing as I had seen in industrial England. The surroundings were ugly enough, and the bodies reclining on the grass were many of them twisted and deformed by the conditions of their owners' lives and work; but there was an air of gaiety about the place which scenes of more pretentious sun-bathing, the Venice Lido for example, lack. The people, one felt, really were enjoying themselves. I bathed once on the Friday and twice on the Saturday, and had much pleasure and refreshment therefrom. The Sunday was hotter than ever. Escaping from the Conference I took a bus to the baths. They were closed. Why? 'Mr. X' I was told 'doesn't like people bathing on Sundays. He is very religious.'

This seemed and still seems to me intolerable. The people of the town, many of whom Mr. X employs, have little or no time to go to the baths during the week; they are working too hard making money for Mr. X. Sunday comes round. Having spent all the week acquiring the means to make life possible, they may at last begin to live. It is a hot day! Why not bathe? 'Not at all,' says Mr. X. 'Bathing is wrong on Sunday. You ought to go to church.' They don't go to church; they swelter in their homes, or parade the streets cursing Mr. X; at least, I hope they do. Mr. X is probably some dyspeptic and hypocritical old Puritan, whom chance and the capitalist system have endowed with power over the lives and happiness of hundreds, possibly thousands, of his fellow-beings. And not only over their work but, it seems, over their play. For not only can he give them the sack; he can prevent them from immersing their bodies on Sunday.

Capitalism having given him his power, it is religion and morality which dictate his use of it. For why does he use it like this? The prohibition is, no doubt, in part merely conventional. People have always been prevented from doing things on Sundays; Sunday is naturally and notoriously a day of boredom and inaction; one closes things automatically and, as it were, without thinking. In part, perhaps, the prohibitor is actuated by unconscious envy. It is improbable that Mr. X was ever a bather, improbable that he can swim, and in any event his body is now no longer in a condition suitable for immersion, still less for public exposure. He dislikes the thought that young people derive so much satisfaction from the pleasures in which he cannot share. On week-days he has no plausible reason for forbidding them, but on Sundays religion provides him with an excellent excuse. 'I cannot myself partake of this pleasure; why, then,' he reasons, 'should these young people enjoy themselves, when God, possibly, and the Church certainly, agree with me in disapproving of such enjoyment on Sundays?' Probably, however, the fact that it is a Sunday is a sufficient reason in itself. The public display of the body, at all times dubious, becomes definitely indecent on the Lord's Day. 'All this flesh lying about the place!' thinks Mr. X, looking interestedly about him. 'I never did much like the idea of it! But after all, I suppose people must bathe—at least they always have done so—and they say this sun-bathing is good for one. So in a general sort of way I dare say it may be all right, strictly regulated, of course, and with plenty of attendants about. But on Sundays! That's another matter! There is a decorum, a dignity appropriate to Sundays. Things may not be proper, they may even be improper on the Lord's Day, which are all very well on a weekday. The body, for example! God, it is well known, never did like the body much. And to exhibit it, and so much of it, on the day set apart for His worship. It's disrespectful! It's more; it's irreverent. Close the baths!'

The Power of the Old. And so hundreds of young men and women are deprived of their pleasure because of the religious fancies, sublimations of God knows what lusts and envies and uncharitablenesses of some dyspeptic old manufacturer, whom the chances of an inequitable economic system, coupled with a certain *flair* for exploiting his betters, have placed in a position of authority. The power of the old in modern society is, indeed, very great and ought to be diminished. Young people are in the main noticeably kinder, more modest, more generous, humane and tolerant, not to speak of being better-tempered than old ones, and their rule, on the few occasions on which they are allowed to exercise authority, is milder and juster. Young men lack the pride of old ones. Having no dignity to maintain, they are not touchy, which means that they do not so easily take offence, or look so anxiously for causes of offence. Were the Chancelleries and Foreign Offices of Europe staffed exclusively by men under thirty-five, there would be no wars. They are not, and the offended dignities of elderly diplomats play no small part in engendering that atmosphere of hostility and suspicion which generates wars as surely as a heat wave generates thunderstorms.

The veneration with which the old are regarded in England is as surprising as it is unwarranted; surprising, because it is unwarranted. Men whom nobody would dream of employing as clerks, gardeners, butlers or doctors, are cheerfully entrusted with the management of the affairs of the country. In fact, the more manifest their decrepitude, the more unhesitating the trust; a man who is only a politician at forty becomes a statesman at sixty, and at seventy he is thought to be ripe for supreme power. No doubt, judging by results, it requires little ability to rule a nation, but it is always open to question whether, were the ability greater, the results might not be better. Why the young let themselves be governed by the old to the extent they do, always puzzles me. I suppose the old have rubbed into the young for so many years how wise they are, that the young cannot help but believe them; provided, of course, that they are young enough. When they get a little older, they are already looking forward to the time when they will wish to practise instead of being taken in by the deception, and so refrain from blowing the gaff.

Monopolies of the Old. One of the greatest objections to placing power in the hands of the old is their tendency to use it in such a way as to diminish the pleasures of the young. For instance, most of the desirable places on the earth's surface are owned by old people, who monopolize them for their own uses, or rather their own neglect. You see a lovely country house, Queen Anne or Early Georgian, poised on a spacious stone-flagged terrace, the centre of a park of a couple of hundred acres. The house is large as well as beautiful, containing, no doubt, a room or several excellent rooms admirably

adapted for purposes of dancing or ping-pong. On that
level stretch of velvety turf at least four tennis courts
might be laid down. The park was made to be galloped
over, and that lake on the western side will do admirably
for boating in summer and skating in winter. Moreover,
it is probably well stocked with fish. Now it is nine
chances out of ten that this exceedingly desirable place
is owned and occupied by a couple of old ladies upon
whom all its opportunities are wasted. They do not dance,
they do not play ping-pong or tennis; they never gallop,
they do not wander romantically through the park witnessing sunsets, and they neither boat, skate nor fish. Yet
because of them, all the chances of happiness which the
house and park offer, chances for the lack of which the
lives of young people are stunted and starved, are wasted.
For within a few miles of the park gates is a large industrial town, teeming with young eager life denied its appropriate forms of expression. Without space and the
opportunity for occasional solitude which space gives, it
can neither find vent for its energies, nor display its bodily
skill, nor cultivate its soul. Perhaps there are a few badly
kept tennis courts in the public parks (bookable for an
hour at a time) with half-obliterated lines and torn and
sagging nets, whose uneven and polluted surface blackens
the balls after ten minutes' use; perhaps an indoor
swimming-bath; but there are no facilities for boating and
fishing, and horse-riding has never been heard of. There
is nowhere to play cricket and football, and, when the
frost comes, there is nowhere to slide or skate. For this
and similar anomalies the old are largely responsible. The
old are like the British Empire; having staked out their
claim on most of the desirable parts of the earth's surface,
they naturally enough will have no squatting on such
valuable property, and maintain themselves sullenly
against all comers. The two old ladies monopolizing the
park which they cannot use, are exactly like the English

monopolizing Australia which they cannot populate. I use the term 'earth's surface' advisedly, for the old possess not only its lands but its waters, a circumstance which combined with the mention of sliding and skating brings me to the case of Miss P.

The Case of Miss P. On those rare occasions in England when there is a hard and prolonged frost, London is the most difficult place in the country in which to come by any skating. So far as the inner waters are concerned, the lakes in Regent's Park, the Hampstead and Highgate Ponds or the Serpentine, the authorities demand a positively phenomenal degree of thickness of ice before permitting it to be used. Their reason for this excessive demand is that it is impracticable in London to permit a few people to use the ice; if some are allowed, there is no ground for excluding any, and the ice is at once thickly crowded. To bear the burden of a London crowd it must be phenomenally strong, so strong indeed, that in England it practically never attains the requisite degree of thickness before the inevitable thaw comes and there is no skating after all. And the authorities are quite right; on the rare occasions when skating is possible in London, the crowds are enormous, so enormous, indeed, that it is impossible to hazard an edge much less a figure, for fear of knocking somebody over, even if the condition of the ice, littered as it is with matches, cigarette-ends, empty cigarette packets, stones and dirt from people's boots, did not in any event render figure skating impracticable. As for the outer waters, those at Hampton Park, for example, Keston Common or Ruislip reservoir, they are troublesome to reach, there is no sure method of discovering whether the ice upon them bears or not—the papers by the way, which are usually so beforehand with the news that they often announce events before they have happened, are for some reason

always a day or two behind time with their skating
announcements—and one is naturally averse from taking
the risk at the end of an hour's journey through the
suburbs of finding that there is no skating after all. No!
The skating facilities for people living in London are not
good.

So much the more, therefore, did we appreciate the
generous action of one of the governors of a well-known
public school in throwing open the lake in his private
grounds for the use of masters, boys and their friends.
The offer came at a time when after a week's continuous
use the ice on all the waters in or near London was so
rough and broken as to be practically unskateable. The
lake was a large one, the ice virgin, and it was with the
happiest anticipations that in the capacity of 'boys' friends'
we went to the London suburb, where the good governor
lived. Expecting an eager thronging of the grounds, I
was surprised to see nobody in the neighbourhood. There
was, I could not help thinking, a singular absence of boys,
masters and 'boys' friends' going in at the gate. With
some anxiety we approached; on the gate was a notice to
say that Miss P., the owner's sister, had died that morning
at Brighton aged seventy-eight, and that in view of this
sad event Mr. P. thought it undesirable that the private
grounds should be used. The permission to skate on the
lake was, therefore, cancelled. Mr. P. added that he felt
sure the masters and boys of the school would sympathize
with his feelings, and appreciate the motives which had
led him to close the grounds.

I cannot, of course, speak for the masters and boys of
the school, but, so far as I was concerned, Mr. P. had
counted on a measure of agreement which was undoubtedly lacking. Who was this Miss P.? Probably, I
reflected, some rancorous old harridan who for the last
fifty years had used the power which her money gave her
to make herself a nuisance to young people. She had been

waited on and tended by pretty young maids, driven slowly and boringly about by bold young chauffeurs, been propitiated by indigent young nephews and nieces. For fifty years, idle and useless herself, she had commanded the services and wasted the time of her youngers and betters. In a thousand ways she had tried their tempers, repressed their natural ebullience of spirits, and, in the interests of safety or decorum, put an irksome restraint upon the expression of their energies. She had died at last, and, it might have been thought, would be a nuisance no more. But it was not so! Still, though dead, Miss P. was tyrannizing over the young, interfering with their pleasures, and preventing them from the enjoyments which she herself was incapable of sharing. Nobody, so far as I am aware, has or had denounced skating as wicked. The limbs of skaters are well covered, and even the most sensitive Puritan has not, so far as I know, been able to detect anything sinful in the spectacle of bodies moving over an ice surface on steel blades. Somebody may have done so, of course—there are people who never call a pleasure a pleasure, if they can call it a sin—but, if the feat has been achieved, I have not heard of it.

No! It was not because skating was wicked that it was forbidden, but because it would have been wanting in respect to the memory of Miss P. It was instinctively recognized that she would not have liked it. She would, it was felt, have disapproved; also and unaccountably, that, because of the prohibition, her memory would be the more honoured, and the name of Miss P. smell the sweeter in the nostrils of the thwarted skaters. There was one pair of nostrils at any rate in which it stank, and I was moved to the uncharitable reflections here set down.

Tyranny of the Old. For the case, though extreme, is not untypical. The power which modern civilized society gives to the old is as widespread as it is disastrous. This power is exercised with lamentable effects over the lives of the young. All over the country old and disagreeable people tyrannize over young and agreeable ones. Old men are naturally more vindictive, bad-tempered, malevolent, and narrow-minded than young ones. They are easily provoked to disapproval, and dislike more things than they like. Having for the most part lived their own lives, they have nothing left to do but to interfere in the lives of others. They form the governments, misrepresent the people whom they oppress, preach to the people whom they exploit, and teach the people whom they deceive. They mete out rewards and punishments, sentence criminals to death, direct businesses, make laws which they have no temptation to disobey and wars in which they do not propose to fight. I said above that governments of men under thirty-five would not make wars, but I am sometimes tempted to believe that, if everybody over that age were forbidden to interfere in public affairs on pain of being sent to the lethal chamber, the world would be not only more peaceable but in many ways a happier and a better place. And I am forty. . . . Unfortunately the young men are too busy trying to make a living in the subordinate positions to which the old men grudgingly admit them to have the time or energy to interfere with other people. Besides, being young, they wish to live, a process for which the regulation of the lives of others is a poor substitute.

And, finally, the old object to bathing on Sundays. They probably object to bathing at any time, but have not the face to say so. The exhibition of bare bodies offends them. 'The body was made to be covered not to be looked at. We cannot understand all this indecent exposure.' So think the old; not unnaturally, considering the state of their own bodies. Nobody, after all, wants to look at them.

CHAPTER XI

Morals and my lack of them

The Victorian conscience. The Victorians used to believe in the existence of a faculty called the conscience. Conscience was the barmaid of the Victorian soul. Recognizing that human beings were fallible and that their failings, though regrettable, must be humoured, conscience would permit, rather ungraciously perhaps, the indulgence of a number of carefully selected desires. For a time and up to a point; but not beyond it. Once the appointed limit was reached, conscience would rap on the bar of the soul. 'Time's up, gentlemen,' she would say, 'we close at ten-thirty.' If gentlemen continued to drink after closing hours, they got into trouble with the law; their consciences in other words gave them a bad time. The process of being nagged by conscience was known as suffering remorse.

Conscience also figured as a protagonist in moral struggles. Quick to detect the signs of evil, she would wrestle with it for the salvation of the individual's soul. Owing to the Fall we all of us have wicked desires; knowing what is right, we nevertheless wish to do what is wrong. Conscience not only tells us what our duty is, but intimidates us into doing it; for remembering what a bad time we had on the last occasion when she nagged, we are anxious to avoid further nagging in the future.

Now the Victorians were not peculiar in possessing consciences, nor was it only in the nineteenth century that

264

human beings were battle-grounds of moral conflict. The Victorian conscience certainly was more sensitive than that of most civilized adults; it disapproved of more things, and as a consequence the moral conflicts of the Victorians were more frightful and more frequent. But the prepotent conscience of the nineteenth century should not lead us into the error of supposing that conscience itself was a Victorian invention. On the contrary, throughout the literature of our countrymen one finds references to conscience. The references, it is true, are usually abusive. 'Conscience is a pair of breeches' said Swift 'which though a cover for lewdness as well as nastiness, is easily slipt down—for the service of both.' Or again, 'Conscience is a cur that does not stop us from passing, but that we cannot prevent from barking as we pass.' But these impolite references are in a sense a compliment, testifying to the strength of conscience as a source of potent discomfort to the wrong-doer.

The Victorians seem to have differed from their predecessors in welcoming this discomfort as a sign of grace. Conscience is for them the voice of God. Hearkening to it they are saved; disobeying it they tread the path to perdition. Their lives, indeed, bear witness to a constant struggle between the forces of good and evil; their souls are a battlefield whereon conscience strives for victory with the devil. Even the emancipated Victorians subscribed to this dramatic view of human psychology. Discarding the dogmas of the Christian religion, they yet retained the Christian conception of moral conflict. Take, for example, the following passage from Mark Rutherford, a sceptic and a rebel, a harbinger of the Shaws and Wellses who were to come, whose energies seem to have been mainly devoted to a not altogether successful attempt to free himself from the preconceptions of the narrow and gloomy creed in which he had been brought up.

Morals and my lack of them

'Do not those of us, who have been mercifully prevented from damning ourselves before the whole world, who have succeeded and triumphed—do we not know, know as we know hardly anything else, that our success and our triumph were due to superiority in strength by just a grain, no more, of our better self over the raging rebellion beneath it? It was just a tremble of the tongue of the balance: it might have gone this way, or it might have gone the other, but by God's grace it was this way settled—God's grace, as surely, in some form of words, everybody must acknowledge it to have been.'

The passage is from *Catherine Furze* and records the moral triumph of the heroine in abstaining from making love to a married clergyman. A little later on there is a sermon about a Roman sculptor who is later converted to Christianity. He is an artist and a pagan, so naturally he has affairs with loose women; but, although he is only a pagan artist, the wheels of his moral machinery are made to rotate as effectively and as uncomfortably as if he were a Christian clergyman. Having succumbed to a temptation, he is so overcome with remorse that he is unable to make statues. 'Thus it came to pass that after a fall, when he went back to his work, it was so unreal to him, such a mockery, that days often elapsed before he could do anything.' The passages are typical; they might have occurred in any serious Victorian novel; and equally, I think, they could not occur in a serious twentieth-century novel. For the point of view that they represent seems to me to have passed utterly from the world, the processes described to be wholly alien from the modern man.

Contemporary Freedom from Conscience. In myself, for instance, I cannot discover anything of the kind. Whether I have a conscience or not, I do not know, but certainly the traditional processes of moral conflict, the experiencing of temptation, the struggling against it, the succumbing to it and the subsequent remorse, or the overcoming it and the subsequent gain in moral kudos, do not occur. Now I may be an unusual man; in some ways I dare say I am; but in this respect I cannot find that I am singular. For most of my generation seem to me to know no more of moral conflict than I do. They do not struggle against temptation—most of them do not even know what it is—their consciences do not fight for their souls against their passions, and they do not feel remorse. The whole apparatus of Victorian moral machinery seems to be missing from their make-up; so much so, that they are inclined to dismiss morality as they are inclined to dismiss religion as one of the many variants of nineteenth-century hypocrisy.

In the nineteenth century one of the first things one knew about a man was his religious denomination. Did he attend church or chapel, and was he lukewarm or devout? If he attended neither, or was an avowed sceptic, there was a great fuss. And just as one knew about a nineteenth-century gentleman whether and to what extent he was a religious man, so one knew immediately and almost instinctively, as it were, whether he was a moral man. One knew it when one met him in the nineteenth-century flesh, and one knows it still in the twentieth when one reads about him in nineteenth-century fiction.

The nineteenth-century world was divided into moral men and immoral; the former resist, the latter are swayed by their passions. But the twentieth-century world knows neither. Our morality, in so far as we have one, is positive rather than negative. I consider it my duty to try to be a certain sort of person and to try to do certain things; but I cannot say that I think much about it one way or the other, and if on a given occasion I do not behave quite like the sort of person I would like to be, I do not think of myself as failing in my duty or betraying my ideal, and I certainly do not suffer remorse. For example, I recognize a certain obligation to keep my faculties tuned up to concert pitch. I wish to make the best use of such talents as I possess, to develop my powers to the full and to keep myself generally at the highest pitch of efficiency of which I am capable. I want, in a word, to realize all that I have it in me to be. Accordingly, I regard it as my business to achieve and maintain as high a standard of mental and bodily health as I can compass without serious discomfort.

The Temptation of Food. In my efforts to carry out this programme my body gives me the most trouble. I am a middle-aged man with a tendency to grow fat, and the obligation to keep my body in such a condition that it does not dull my faculties or impede my activities, requires continuous attention and involves me in some attempt at self-discipline and self-denial. In the matter of food, for example! Continually I do not eat as much as I should like, nor what I should like. Yet, even so, I know that I eat more than is good for me, and it is gluttony, the sheer love of good food for its own sake, that makes me do it. Life, I am assured, can be adequately maintained on a few handfuls of rice a day; the practice of the Indian and the Chinaman confirms the fact. And on the rare occasions when poverty or circumstance have compelled me to live frugally and to eat simply, I have been sensible of a definite increase of energy and efficiency. But, as I have already pointed out, I am exceedingly fond of good food; I like my diet to be rich and varied, and I am inordinately fond of French cooking. French cooks—I have already praised them once, but I cannot forbear to praise them again—French cooks, it is obvious, are beneficent magicians. You arrive at midday, an unexpected guest in a remote country place. Lamenting that there is nothing in the house fit for Monsieur to eat, your hostess will go despondently into a palpably empty larder. An incantation is uttered, a rite performed, and in ten minutes there appears the first of a long line of appetizing dishes, whose preparation is a work of art, and whose cooking is perfection. Before such fare I am helpless; my defences are down, and for a solid hour I gourmandize my way through the delicious intricacies of the meal. As a result I expend so much of my available energy on an unnecessarily elaborate process of digestion, that I want to go to sleep. If I can do this, things are not so bad, but if circumstance makes sleep impossible, I am gloomy, stupid, dull and, in extreme cases, irritable and morose. The afternoon, in any event, is not suitable for mental effort or social intercourse. There is a time, about three o'clock, when it is just too late to be after lunch and just too early to be before tea, when all sensible people keep to themselves. At this hour there is a pause in the flow of events; the flame of life burns low. If it is a fine day, the world shows itself sharp and hard in the sunlight; there is no sparkle or freshness in the air, but a glare upon things which strikes the eye with a hint of menace; the birds are silent, nothing stirs; it is almost as if some evil spirit walked abroad. At such times, as I say, wise men withdraw themselves; by four the day has taken a new lease of life, and they emerge refreshed for the bustle and activity of the tea-table.

No! The afternoon is, in any event, an unfortunate time; embittered by indigestion it becomes intolerable. And so, if I eat a reasonably large lunch, I find it wiser to sleep it off. Now I regret this necessity. I can ill spare this time subtracted from the business of reading and thinking and doing. I am not likely to exist for such a length of time that I can afford to be wasteful with a life which on the whole I enjoy, and anyway I sleep a good eight hours every night. And so I wrestle with the flesh and try not to eat too much, because it makes me stupid and sleepy.

It is reported that the philosopher Kant also suffered

from the temptations of the stomach. He was, as everybody knows, a stern moralist who wrote in a formidable manner on the subject of duty, affirming that the only things of real value in the world are the moral will of the good man and the actions in which it issues. Yet Kant was practically destitute of moral experience, finding apparently in the question of the number of sweet cakes he should permit himself to eat at tea—he always, it seems, wanted more than he considered to be good for him—the only moral issue that afforded him perplexity; an exiguous foundation, one would have thought, upon which to rear the terrific edifice of the Kantian moral philosophy.

In spite of Kant, I insist that my temptation to gluttonize is not an ethical matter at all. The agitations it occasions are not moral, but deliberative; I am perpetually seeking to make an accurate but purely hedonic calculus of comparative pleasures and pains, and the question is how to strike a balance between the pleasures of good living and those of high thinking. Not that indigestion is the only evil that waits on gluttony. The middle-aged gourmet suffers from chronic constipation; his body is poisoned with an overflow of waste products and his mind darkened with gloom and exacerbated with spleen. He grows irritable and uncharitable, a nuisance to himself and a tyrant to the underlings, the unfortunate employees, children and so forth, over whom society permits him to exercise power. If he gourmandizes for a sufficient number of years, a cancer as often as not makes its appearance, and he dies a long, painful and disgusting death.

Spiritual Efficiency. But it is not only in the interests of *bodily* efficiency that I feel bound to restrain my appetite for food. It is, I conceive, my duty to keep myself fit and my faculties at cutting edge. But the injunction to achieve such bodily and mental excellence

as I can, does not take me very far. Why keep myself
fit, if I do not know for what my fitness is required?
Why tune up my faculties, if I do not play upon them?
Only a Puritan embitters his life with preparation for a
race that is never run. And so, in order that I may
enjoy the best that life can offer me, I recognize an
obligation to try to cultivate certain states of mind. A
sensibility to beauty in art brings æsthetic pleasure,
and the ability to understand or perform a difficult process of reasoning in mathematics or philosophy, intellectual enjoyment. Both are precluded by over-eating. If
the mind is to work properly, the body must not be stuffed
with food. When the senses are dulled, the world revealed
to them in perception is a less interesting world.

The converse is equally true. To sharpened senses a
richer and more varied world appears. We are all familiar
with the fact that an increase in the temperature of the
body may increase the sensibility of our perceiving apparatus. The temperature has only to rise a couple of degrees,
for sights and sounds, tastes and smells to acquire a new
significance. Above all, the world we touch, or rather
that touches us, is radically changed; it is richer, more
insistent, and more varied. Yet because a man's temperature is temporarily above normal, nobody would say that
his sensations are not really felt, or that the world they
reveal to him has not as much right to be called real as
that which is experienced by bodies with temperatures at
98·4 Fahrenheit. It would, indeed, be a feat of parochial-
ism to which even common sense should be unequal to
maintain that only that kind of world which is perceived
by the sense organs of human bodies heated to a temperature of 98·4 is real.

What is not so generally realized is that a lowering of
the temperature of the body may also have the effect of
revealing a new world; a new world and a stranger. It is
for this reason that men have turned ascetic. Ascetic

practices are methods for inducing artificially a certain kind of psychological and physiological condition. The condition modifies the perceiving apparatus, and the ascetic's universe is accordingly changed. Changed, and, it may be, deepened, widened and enriched. For men have found that the particular kind of abnormality that asceticism induces is one that enables them to perceive not only a quantitatively larger, but a qualitatively richer world. It is to them a more exciting world because of the things it contains. Goodness, for example, beauty, and it may be, God. Hence they seek to retain and continually to enjoy it.

Mysticism may be regarded as the systematic cultivation of a certain state of mind by observing certain rules of mental and physical health. The bodily instrument, refined by fasting and tuned by quietude, is found to be capable of harmonies of experience which are outside the range of the ordinary sensual man. That those who live in a state of mental agitation are incapable of the higher creative and intellectual processes is admitted. It is at least possible that they miss the most exquisite pleasure of which human beings are capable, the pleasure which, if we are to trust the mystics, comes from contemplation of a subtler and a richer reality.

The mystics' explanation of their delights is admittedly controversial; yet it affords the most plausible interpretation of certain moments of serenity, which are also moments of ecstatic happiness, that occur at times in the experience of most of us. Such moments may be regarded in the light of intimations, fleeting and uncertain, of the kind of experience which the mystic enjoys fully and more or less continuously. And reflecting upon the conditions of their occurrence, we realize that they came to us only at times of complete mental and bodily health, when the mind was unvexed, the spirit untroubled, and the intestines not overloaded with waste products.

Morals and my lack of them

I do not wish to imply that I endeavour to refrain from
overeating in order to become a mystic. I am seeking
merely for an illustration of what is implied, or may be,
by my assertion, that it is our duty to keep our faculties
at cutting edge. The illustration admittedly is an ideal
development of the thesis. Yet the contention that the
best life demands the employment of the most-developed
faculties we possess, would not, I think, be seriously
questioned.

Reason and Happiness. And not only the best but the
happiest. In the *Nicomachæan Ethics* Aristotle inquires
what the true function of man may be, arguing that his
happiness will be found in the efficient performance of
the specific function which distinguishes him. Now the
specific function of man cannot be merely to live—plants
do no less—nor even to experience physical sensations,
a privilege which man shares with the animals. Hence,
Aristotle concludes that it is in the exercise of the intelligence, or, as he puts it, in the faculties of the soul,
that the specific excellence or virtue of man lies. Living
according to reason he will perform his function and
achieve happiness. But to do so, he must be in command
of his nature. Man's specific function cannot be per-
formed, the excellence of the soul cannot be cultivated,
if the emotions are stirred. The exercise of the higher
faculties demands a certain mental tranquillity. Passion
and struggle dull the rarer faculties, while intensifying
the common ones. They raise the mud of the soul by
stirring. It is the delusion of romanticism to believe
itself to be at the well spring of man's nature, when it
is only stirring the muddy shallows. Affirming the
fact, I affirm also a defence of the literary tastes and
limitations which I described in Chapter IV. It is precisely because moral conflict harasses the spirit and diverts
the energies from the pursuit of what is worth while that

I object to it. Even when the victory goes to what the Victorians would have called the right side, it is achieved at the expense of mental poise. The Victorians, while remarkable for moral fervour, did not observe the doctrine of The Mean. They knew little or nothing of the contemplative life, and, except in their poetry, were strangers to beauty. Recognizing the duty to develop my higher at the expense of my lower self, I nevertheless maintain that the nineteenth-century conception of moral conflict is ludicrously inappropriate to my intermittent but honest endeavours to perform it.

Indolence and Fear. The obligation to keep myself at as high a level of efficiency as, without too much hardship, I can decently manage, imposes upon me other endeavours and abstentions. I am involved, for example, in a perpetual struggle against slackness; I am in constant fear of taking life too easily. Given two alternative courses of action, I react automatically against my natural preference for the safer or less troublesome, and consider it my duty to choose the one which involves the greater risk or effort. I conceive it to be due to my self-respect not to take the line of least resistance.

In walking, for example, I never go round by the road, but always across country. Going across country usually involves walls, hedges, streams and ditches, and the possibility of encounters with farmers or gamekeepers. Except when I am tired, I rather like the hedges and ditches, but, as I have said before, I object intensely to rows with farmers. Yet I should regard it as a form of shirking, if I refrained from trespassing when private property lay in my path. If this is a moral feeling, it operates in a contrary sense to that of the Victorians who, respecting private property, considered it to be wrong to trespass. Similarly, if the direct route lies over a mountain, I go over the mountain, or feel ashamed of myself if I don't.

Morals and my lack of them

An expression of the same attitude to life is my feeling of moral obligation to react against fear. Not, of course, when the fear is justified. I am a nervous little man anxious for a quiet life, and I should never dream of actually courting danger. But I like the sense of effort which I cultivate as a specific against slackness to be sharpened by the merest suggestion of danger. The suggestion is like a dressing to the salad. Thus, when I swim, I never go too far from shore; but I go just a little bit further than is compatible with a feeling of perfect security. I do not, you understand, take risks; but I think it as well that there should be just a moment when I can wonder fearfully whether I am not taking risks, even if I am able to assure myself a moment later that I am not.

It is the same fear of slackness, the dread of getting old and easy, that causes me in London to walk instead of taking a taxi, to dispense with an overcoat on cold days and to change and play hockey instead of going to sleep in a chair on Sunday afternoons in winter. It also drives me to write.

Why Men Write. Writing is the most arduous occupation I know. There is, in the first place, the manual labour involved. I am an abominable writer; my best and slowest writing is large, ugly and laborious, and, when I write at anything like a reasonable speed, there are only two people alive who can decipher the marks that result. My fingers were not made to hold a pen, and after two or three pages of foolscap they tire badly; after a prolonged spell of writing a lump appears in the middle finger owing to the pressure of the wrongly held pen. Moreover, I cannot write a page without covering my hand with ink.

But the manual labour is as nothing to the mental labour involved, nor can the discomfort of the body be compared with that of the mind. The question is often debated whether writers ought to depend for their liveli-

hood upon their earnings as writers. Cogent arguments
can be brought forward on both sides. It is said that the
only literary work worth doing is that which a man takes
pleasure in doing, and that a man who writes because he
must and not because he likes never writes what he likes.
It is said, again, that great literature is the fruit of inspiration or of passionate conviction. A man's best work is
that which has, so to speak, taken him up by the scruff
of his literary neck and insisted upon his doing it, whether
he would or no. Inspiration cannot be turned on like a
tap, nor can we feel passionate conviction to order, while
brains which are cudgelled for ideas become incapable of
producing them spontaneously.

This is, no doubt, very largely true; the doctrine is well
supported by tradition—there are, for instance, some pertinent remarks of Juvenal to the effect that Horace was
full when he wrote his best odes, and that, had Virgil been
poor, his Medusa's head would have lacked its snakes—
and it is good common sense. Nevertheless, it is remarkable how much first-rate work has been turned out to keep
the pot boiling. *Black Arrow*, for example, which is the
best of Stevenson's romantic novels, was 'another Butcher
Boy' written to pay the housekeeping bills.

A more important argument on the same side is that
writing to live one must produce a saleable article. Now,
unless one's reputation is very high indeed, a saleable
article may be defined as the sort of article an editor is
prepared to buy. What an editor is prepared to buy is
what will sell his paper; it is, that is to say, if he is a good
editor, what the public wants, and the more he thinks the
public wants it, the higher the price he will be willing to
pay for it. But, if a man is a good writer, what the public
wants to read is not what he wants to write; inevitably,
since his value as a writer consists in his ability to advance
and not merely to interpret the thought of his times.
People like to see their prejudices reflected in print, and

naturally resent those who challenge or flout them. Hence the ideas of the great writer are rarely acceptable to the man in the street, and, if he writes for money, he must tone down the uncompromising rigour of his original thought to the nearest approach to a saleable article he can manage. There is for this reason an element of prostitution in all writing for profit, and the great writer, who wishes to be a selling writer, must always to some extent compromise with his conscience. The mention of conscience reminds me that I have been straying badly from my original theme, and must get back to it as best I can. Luckily there is a short cut.

When all is said that can be said in favour of the view that a man should not write for his livelihood, there is, I think, one fatal objection to it. If writing were not practised as a profession, most of the world's literature, good as well as bad, would never have existed; for, if men wrote only when they pleased, most of them would never write at all. And this is not because writers are abnormally lazy, but because writing is such desperately hard work. It is desperately hard because it is always in some measure, however small, creative, and creative work takes more out of a man than anything else.

Toils of Writing. Writing is not one kind of work, but two. There is the business of thinking of what to say, and there is the business of saying it in the most appropriate way. And both are immensely difficult. It is difficult to think at all, difficult to make one's thoughts clear to oneself, more difficult still to make them clear to other people. Of most work it is true to say that once finished it is done with; but writing is never done with, for the writer can never feel without gross complacency that he might not have done it better, and to feel that is to start tinkering in the hope of making it better. Most work, again, may be regarded in the light of a more or less complicated series of responses to stimuli. The responses are, admittedly, active not automatic; they are forms of reaction nevertheless. Whether it is letters that have to be answered, examination papers to be corrected, notes to be arranged, briefs to be prepared, cases to be diagnosed, problems to be solved, there is a concrete external something to set the organism going. This something is in the nature of an irritant, and stimulates the organism to remove the cause of irritation. But with writing it is not so. The writer must be his own stimulus, and evolve from within himself not only the energy and the effort but the subject-matter upon which they are to be expended. There are times, it is true, when something, it may be a book, a vivid experience, a sense of public outrage or private wrong demands to be written about so insistently that it takes the place of, if, indeed, it does not become, a response-conditioning stimulus. But normally this insistent call to write is absent, and the writer, sitting down to his desk, must undertake the double task of conception and execution and fill the rôles of creator and craftsman in his own person. For this reason, I repeat, writing is the most arduous form of occupation I know. In my time I have been an examiner, a clerk, a teacher and a lecturer, but I would sooner mark papers for four hours, dictate letters for three or lecture for two, than write for one. I would sooner minute papers for six hours in an office than do an hour's creative writing at home.

As for other professions, the diagnosing of the diseases of the sick, the selling of goods to reluctant customers, the supervizing of organizations or managing of businesses, the pleading of cases in court or of sermons in the pulpit, all these are child's play compared with writing. They are so much more sociable and amusing. Thus—and here my short cut has brought me back—writing constitutes for me the supreme instance of moral endeavour. It is only by adopting a series of devices that I ever get it done at all.

Dodges to Overcome Them. For example, I set myself to write for a definite time. 'Only half an hour!' I say to myself. 'You needn't write for more than half an hour', and, however tired I may be, however bankrupt of ideas, I feel pretty sure of my ability to keep going for half an hour. If at the end of the half-hour I find that I can still go on, I go on. I don't forbid myself more than the specified time; I only guarantee that I will work for not less. Usually I do manage more; custom and practice make it fairly easy to go on, once one has started. Very occasionally, and by God's grace, one may even go on because one wants to. But even so, it is very rarely that I write for more than an hour at a stretch.

Or I limit myself in point of space. 'Two foolscap pages you must do,' I say, 'and then you can stop.' And I do them. Often in a rush of enthusiasm and a glow of self-approval I exceed them. That is as it may be, but I should lose heavily in point of morale, if I did not cover my allotted two. And I am so afraid of this, that fear alone usually suffices to carry me through. When they are done, I enjoy a state of mind which may, I think, be not unreasonably compared with what the Victorians called 'virtuousness'. Writing is so burdensome in itself that the mere act of ceasing to write brings pleasure. In this respect it resembles the immersion of the body in cold water. Many people, I am convinced, bathe in the winter solely in order to enjoy the pleasure of having 'got it over'.

Or I set myself a definite job of work, as if I were attempting to answer a question in an examination paper, and contract with myself to see it through before doing something that I want to do. Much of my writing has been on philosophy and psychology, in which the discussion and criticism of other people's views play a large part. Accordingly I say to myself, 'Between tea and dinner you will summarize what Mr. X says about "reflexes". Between nine-fifteen and ten'—this with slightly greater relish—'you will begin to dispose of what Mr. X says, making points A and B'. Criticisms C and D are reserved for a train journey in the morning and a preliminary statement of my own view for half an hour in a wood on a walk the following day. And that is how I get it done.

Writing in this fashion it is obvious that I do not consider myself an artist. No nonsense about inspiration for me! I am too humble, at least so I tell myself, to imagine that the winds of the creative spirit will ever blow through me, or that what I write at one time is likely to be much better, or, indeed, much worse, than what I write at another. And I don't suppose that it is.

'But this business of writing at all times, whether one wants to or not, must it not involve doing, when one is tired or stale, work which, had one waited, one could have done better?' Probably it does! Yet, I protest, it is only on condition that I make a moral duty of it that I can get any writing done at all.

And, if I am doing to order what at its best can only be done when the spirit moves, Trollope did the same. We may be very fine fellows nowadays, but few of us can write like Trollope, and what was good enough for him should be more than good enough for me. Besides, what right have I to suppose when I am flat and dull that I shall ever be any better? 'Anyway, if I don't do it now', I say, 'I might never do it at all. I know myself . . . and it is better not to take the risk.' Is this mock humility, or laziness, or impatience? Perhaps a little of all three. But it is time I returned to the moral sense.

Virtuousness over Animals. In spite of what I have said to the contrary, I find on reflection that there is, after all, one set of circumstances in which I do experience

moral conflict. I experience temptation, fight against
it, suffer remorse if I succumb to it, and give way to
complacency if I overcome it. But the circumstances are
not those traditionally associated with moral endeavour.
I have a horror of cruelty to animals. The feeling, no
doubt, is virtuous and does me credit, but it is violent and
irrational in its expression, and on the whole I am ashamed
of it, or at least of my inability to control it. Freud, I dare
say, would let fall a number of unpleasant observations as to
its origin. . . . Still it is there, and I have to make the best
of it. 'Mr. ———, fish porter of ———, Bethnal Green, was
fined £2 5s. yesterday before the ——— magistrate with
the alternative of a week's imprisonment, for blinding a
linnet with hot needles. Mr. ——— said in his defence that
it was a custom to put out the eyes of the birds, as this
increased the volume and sweetness of their singing.'
When I read this sort of thing in the papers—and it
appears often enough—I see red. My heart-beat gets
faster, I hear the blood pulsing in my ears, I begin to
sweat and I cannot sit still. I have an overpowering impulse to go and do something about it, and, as there is
obviously nothing to do, I fidget aimlessly round the
room. I cannot bear to go to the Zoo and I cannot endure
the spectacle of performing animals. The existence of the
Zoo seems to me to be an outrage in a civilized society.
An eagle in a cage is a terrible sight, and the life-long
imprisonment of lions and tigers equally degrading to
prisoners and jailers. The Roman lions did at least have
a Christian breakfast; the prisoners of the Zoo have only
the myriad, merciless eyes of their secure captors, gazing,
gazing, gazing until the flesh rots and the heart breaks in
the respectable prison.

The practice of causing animals to do tricks in public
is a device for making human beings behave like beasts,
in order that they may induce beasts to behave like imbe-
ciles. When Pavlov's famous experiments on conditioned

reflexes were first widely discussed, it was pointed out that the principle which he claimed to have discovered had been practised for years by those engaged in training performing animals. Bears, for instance, whom it is proposed to teach to dance, are placed in a large copper beneath which a fire is lit. When the bottom of the copper becomes unbearably hot the bear can no longer stand still, and hops first on one foot and then on another, never standing on more than two feet at a time. This is called dancing. While the bear is 'dancing' a tune is played on a fiddle. The process is repeated on a number of occasions, until one day the fiddle is played without the hot copper. The bear dances as before, the conditioned reflex having been established.

The Burgundian Dog. When I read of such things I am horrified, shocked, furiously indignant, but not yet are the peculiar moral feelings which the Victorians knew. These occur when I am confronted in person with a case of cruel treatment of animals, or an indifference to their feelings. I am staying in a village in Burgundy and outside the butcher's there is a dog. He is a young dog, not much more than a puppy, and he is on a chain. I have never seen him off this chain. It is summer and the sun which is pretty hot beats down for eight or nine hours every day upon the square. The dog is unprovided with a kennel and has no protection from its rays. Also he has no water. A small block of wood is set against the wall upon which there is just room for the dog's four legs, and there for the most part he sits perched, jumping off the block when anybody approaches and beseeching them to infuse a little interest into the intolerable boredom of his life by taking notice of him. I would not say that he asks to be let off his chain; he has had too little experience of freedom to warrant his supposing that such joys are possible. Being off his chain is probably a sort of heaven to which he aspires and to which he thinks he may one day go, if he is very good—although not in this world, and not for a long time yet. But he would like to be talked to, and does what he can to remind the world that he exists.

Since I have been in the village, I have gone every day to talk to this dog, and it is quite clear to me that I ought to do something about him. By the end of my visit, the weather growing hotter every day, the dog is on my mind. I talk to him three or four times a day, bring him water, and think about him at night before going to sleep. But I have done nothing to secure his release. Why not? Because I am afraid. If I ask in my halting French for the temporary release of the dog, my motives will certainly be misunderstood. Or rather, since no motive at all can be conceived for such a request, I shall be thought to be a little weak in the head, and the owner of the dog will stare at me with the hard curiosity that one bestows upon some strange natural phenomenon. A little crowd will gather to listen to the mad Englishman; probably they will laugh at me. In any event the request will almost certainly be refused, and I shall have to endure the humiliation of being stared at daily by a hostile and victorious butcher, coupled with the shame of knowing that I have done nothing to help the dog.

All these considerations and many more weigh with me. Why, then, do I not leave the matter alone? Because of my conscience! My conscience nags me continually, telling me that it is my duty to interfere and that I shall be a contemptible coward if I neglect my duty. And every day that passes finds me more humiliated, more ashamed of myself, more lacking in self-respect. I experience that lowering of moral tone which is historically recorded as the fate of those who struggle unsuccessfully against temptation. Presently I begin to suffer remorse. And so on the last day of my stay I go boldly up to the house and let the dog off his chain. He barks deliriously and jumps all over me. The woman of the house comes out and to her I expatiate upon the wickedness of keeping dogs on chains, calling her to witness his present happiness, and beseeching her not to chain him up again except at night. She looks dubious—the point of view has not, it is obvious, previously occurred to her—but is not unsympathetic. She does not even bring forward the usual arguments to the effect that the dog unchained will bite children, consume chickens, get run over by cars, disappear, fall a prey to thieves, get into any and every sort of mischief and fail to guard the house. After the first surprise is over, she nods and smiles at me pleasantly enough, even, I think, a little indulgently. And then I go away; I leave the village altogether never to return. Thus I do not see the future fate of the dog; I escape the humiliation of his probable speedy return to the chain. My conscience, you observe, is strong enough to compel me to make the protest, not strong enough to compel me to see it enforced.

The Marston Ferry Linnet. Outside a country inn at which I was having tea—the Marston Ferry Inn near Oxford—there was a linnet in a cage. It was a very small cage; the linnet had lived in it for about a year, and I had never heard it sing. I was told that it never sang much. My conscience beginning to work, I struck up a conversation with the odd man of the place and gradually brought it round to the linnet. He was a Mr. Pollyish sort of person, and among his multitudinous tasks was that of providing the bird with food and water. This he did with praiseworthy regularity, professing himself very fond of the linnet and anxious to do the best he could for it. 'Why then' I said 'do you keep it in a cage?' 'Why not?' he asked. The bird had always been in a cage, since he caught it a year ago, and was, he said, quite happy there. How did he know that it was quite happy? Would *he* be happy confined in a small room? He admitted that he would not. 'Very well, then,' said I, 'admitting that it is very difficult for us to know what the bird feels, admitting even that it is just possible that it is happier where it is, I can't help thinking that it ought to be given the benefit of the doubt. But after all, it is quite easy to put the matter to the test. Open the cage and let the linnet choose for itself. If it prefers its cage, it will stay where it is; if freedom, it will fly away.'

I went on in this strain for some time and finally persuaded the man, who was simple-minded to a degree, to make the experiment. So convinced was he of the happiness of the bird that he stoutly maintained that it would not take advantage of the opportunity of escape and had just mounted a chair to open the cage door, when the proprietor and his wife came out. It was some little time before they could understand what was taking place, and, when they did, they were very angry indeed. The linnet, they said, was a valuable bird; it sang very sweetly and, if let out, it would be pecked to death by the other birds. And then they began to abuse me for imposing on the simplicity of the odd man. Anybody could see, they said, that he was not 'all there', and I had no business to persuade him to do such a silly thing, which amounted to downright robbery. I bowed before the storm. I did not attempt to argue with them; I did not defend myself; I did not plead for the bird's liberty; I did not even offer to buy it; I turned tail and fled. My conscience was not equal to the task of compelling me to a second effort, and I went away thoroughly ashamed of myself for my failure to stand up for what I knew to be right. You are, I told myself, a child of your generation; there are few things about which you feel morally and feel strongly, few things of the rightness of which you are sufficiently convinced to be justified in imposing your views on others, and this is one of them. Yet, when it comes to the point, you are afraid to testify: you are hopelessly lacking in moral courage. And this, I suppose, is the truth of the matter. In regard to the few, the very few matters on which I feel morally at all, I am a moral coward. I am prepared to do what I think right, provided that it is not too difficult and that I do not meet with too much opposition. Otherwise I leave it undone.

The Magpie at the Inn. Or, I do it and am so ashamed of doing it that I do it in an underhand way and try to avoid the consequences. When this happens, most people would call my conduct morally blameworthy. For example, I stayed once at an inn where they kept a magpie in a large wooden cage suspended from the ceiling of the passage. The passage was dark in the daytime but lit with electric light at night, and the unshaded bulb shone right into the cage. Also people were always passing, and the passage was very noisy. A more unsuitable place for a bird could not well be imagined, and the magpie had been there for three years, during which he had not been more than half a dozen times, according to the landlady's computation, out of doors in the sunlight. The reason for this was that his cage had no top. It was a home-made affair, consisting only of a bottom and four sides, the ceiling of the passage supplying its roof. Hence, before it could be taken down, the bird must be caught or he would fly out of the top and be at large in the house. Catching the bird, suspended as he was high up above people's heads, was a troublesome affair, and the consequence was that the cage was hardly ever taken down. The magpie appeared to me to be wretched; his eye was dull, he was listless in his movements and his whole attitude suggested a dreadful boredom. He seemed to wish to get away as far as possible from the people beneath, and from always straining upwards on his perch had rubbed a smooth, hollow patch in the ceiling with his head. I tried to speak to him several times, but he would take no notice of me. The thought of this magpie made me miserable, but the landlady to whom I spoke about him said that she was very attached to him, and could not think of letting him go.

And so one night I got out of bed, went downstairs, opened the window of the bar parlour, took down the bird's cage and let him out. I had previously ascertained that his wings were uncut, and there seemed to be no reason why he should not fly. And sure enough he did fly out of the bar window into the night, and that was the last I saw of him. In the morning there was a great fuss about the magpie, but I was too ashamed of what I had done to own to it, and, if the landlady suspected me, she did not say so. After I left I sent her a letter confessing my misdemeanour and a five-shilling postal order to compensate her for the bird.

But into what a hole-and-corner affair has the mighty Victorian conscience degenerated, that it should drive a man to such furtive steps!

CHAPTER XII

On being not so Black as I have Painted

This book misleading. Looking back through the pages of this book, I cannot but be conscious that they are invested with a certain gloom. Something, it seems, is always wrong; something is always being suggested as an object of ridicule or contempt, and, whether it is the old, the countryside, the cinema, the convention of decency, war, unreason or women which is being abused, the reader must have gained the impression that I am a disgruntled person out of touch with the trends and movements of the time, and impotently grumbling at a society in which I have failed. Were it not, indeed, for the literary turn of my sentences and the occasional suggestions of intelligence and even culture which grace these pages, I might well have seemed to him just another letter-writer to the *Morning Post*, one of those verbose failures who

> Compound for sins that they're inclined to
> By damning those that they've no mind to,

compensate for their own lack of success by deprecating the achievements of everybody else, and conceive that the world is going to the dogs because the movement of evolution has passed them by. Or, simpler still, this autobiography of ideas may be written off as the mere literary expression of spleen and a bad liver.

On being not so Black

No suggestions could be further from the truth. I am in the main a good-tempered person; my liver is in admirable order and always has been; I like my fellows, am fond of company, singularly lacking in malice or uncharitableness, have plenty of acquaintances, some of whom I like to think are friends, and on the whole enjoy myself very well. The intransigeance of my youth has mellowed into the tolerance of middle age. I still think that the world is badly and stupidly run, and that the application of a little intelligence would improve it out of all knowledge; but I no longer believe that world improvement is my life's job. I can enjoy the company of my friends without trying to convert them to Socialism, and, so far from being an ill-tempered and disgruntled bore, I am, so far as I can see, tolerated pretty well. Also I have had a fair measure of success, which is always good for a man and makes him more able to bear the successes of others.

Way of Life. For sixteen years I was in the Civil Service, a square peg in a round hole and miserable in consequence; but I did little work there in my later years, so little, that the only important differences brought about by my resignation are that I write my books and articles and prepare my lectures in a library at home instead of in a room at an office, and say what I choose about politics. Since then my lot has been cast in pleasant places. I live in Hampstead in an ugly but comfortable house overlooking the Heath. The situation combines many of the advantages of town and country. London is only twenty minutes away by Tube, and the Heath stretches for three or four miles from the door. I am not claiming that the Heath is the country, any more than I am claiming that the Tube journey is not a trial. Once, indeed, I found it intolerable. Nowhere do the faces of one's fellow-beings appear so featureless and depersonalized;

nowhere is our comparatively recent animal origin more disconcertingly apparent than in those rows of tired people, the men for the most part hidden behind their papers, the women peering at each other with that look of curious, slightly hostile interest that is liable at any moment to harden into a glare of downright disapproval, should a smart turn-out or daring dress declare a competitor for male attention. A few indefatigables are even trying to make their voices heard above the prevailing din. Men and women alike are irritable and dispirited, dulled by the memory of innumerable Tube journeys in the past and the prospect of Tube journeys stretching away in an endless perspective into an eventless future. Nobody should make light of this horrible convenience of civilization, a convenience which, as I have already pointed out, we have insisted on turning into a necessity. But the horrors of the Tube are considerably mitigated for those who need not travel in the rush hours, and, when all is said and done, it forms an admirable background to the reading of the daily paper. I have read the morning paper for so many years to the obbligato of the Tube, that it has become an indispensible accompaniment to my learning from the *News Chronicle* the particular beastlinesses upon which the world has been engaged during the preceding twenty-four hours, and learning too from that admirable paper how to a deeper view and a maturer judgment the beastlinesses are not beastly at all. So large a part has the *News Chronicle* played in forming my middle-aged mind, that I regard this autobiography as a last despairing attempt to avoid complete mental suffocation by the vaguely aspiring platitudes which it wraps every morning in soul-comforting cotton-wool.

As for the Heath, although it is a passable substitute, it is not the country. There are no flowers, and, except for the grey squirrels and the owls, very little wild life; but there is a mass of blossom in spring, and a great variety of trees which assume all the colours of a gorgeous decay in the autumn. Also, as I have noted elsewhere, there is an excellent swimming-pool; in fact, there are three. On Bank Holidays, and in a lesser degree at every week-end, the citizens of London descend upon the Heath. The effect is disastrous; it is exactly as if the place had been raided by a swarm of locusts and then subjected to a heavy snowfall, so complete is its investiture of newspapers and bags. I used to know, but forget, how many hundreds of tons of paper are collected from the Heath after every Bank Holiday; but I do know that, if tacked together, they would produce a *Daily Mail* large enough to cover the whole surface of the globe from the North Pole to the South, to be perused with amazement and dismay by the Gods, the Man in the Moon, the Holy Ghost and whatever other celestial personages may have a curiosity to know what is happening on the earth. The wiser residents of Hampstead always absent themselves on Bank Holidays and usually at week-ends.

Why Not in the Country? If after all the fuss I have made about the country in previous chapters, you are not yet convinced that I care for it, I cannot help it. But your conviction, if it exists, impels you to ask the obvious question, 'Why, if the author really feels for the country all that he says he feels, does he not go and live in it?' I will, if you will permit me, answer your question with the care it deserves. In the first place, let me assure you that my feeling for the country is not assumed. The feeling, however, is parochial; it is the English country and no other that moves me. I am never away from England for more than a fortnight without suffering acutely from nostalgia. I never return without a thrill of excited pleasure. The food is at first uneatable, the restrictions on drinking are childish, the papers are obviously written for children; yet the

On being not so Black

first sight of the Sussex Downs and of Southease and Rodmell nestling at their foot, as you pass through the Gap of the Ouse on your way from Newhaven to London, banishes all such trifles from the mind, and convinces you that nowhere is there such another sight in the world. Nor is it necessary to go abroad to enjoy the thrill. I can recapture it every time I get out of the London train at a wayside station for a country week-end. And having said so much, I can proceed to tell you why, nevertheless, I do not live in the country.

Although I truly care for it, I care for it only in regulated and not very large doses. My feeling, if it is to be kept fresh and vivid, must not be dulled by familiarity. I must not be encouraged to hold the country cheap. Yet this, if I stay in it for any considerable length of time, is what I invariably do. The beauty is taken for granted, the view is never looked at, the details of leaf and tree and soil and flower are ignored. Presently I begin to think the country dull. And that the country is duller at some times than it is at others must be admitted. There is August, for example, when the birds no longer sing and everything is coloured the same shade of uniform green; or there is that long period of waiting from mid-February to mid-April when the spring, eagerly expected, still hangs fire; for weeks on end there is no perceptible change, and we are all telling each other, as we do every year, what a late spring it is. If at such times I am tied to the country, I begin to hate it; I long for the town and the society of my fellows, and fly from the mud and the rains of not-yet-spring to some stuffy chop-house, full of men and smoke, to eat a porterhouse steak, talk nineteen to the dozen and bask in the society of my kind. Mind, I am not excusing myself for this, or claiming what I know to be a limitation as a virtue. It is myself I am censuring, not the country. The plain fact of the matter is that we are no longer fit, most of us, to live in the country simply

or for any length of time. We are too far gone in civilization and sophistication. We are no longer in nature; we
are out of her, having made our own non-natural conditions. And our conditions in their turn have reacted
upon us, making us what we are, artificial creatures,
unable to come easily to terms with nature, or to be long
alone with her without feeling ill at ease.

Gregariousness. About those of us who seek artificially
to return to her, taking her as it were by violence, there is
something indefinably wrong; we live in little staring houses
dumped down upon the protesting land, subsist on greens
and nut butter and brown bread, do our housework for
ourselves and are thoroughly dull and uncomfortable, with
all our windows open and perpetual trouble over the oil-
stoves and the drains. The root of the matter is, I suppose,
that I am too fond of the company of my fellows, and by
now too dependent upon them for interest and amusement,
to stand the monotony of a country life. Solitude, like
the country, I can manage very well in small doses; and
not only manage but demand, occasional short periods
of solitude among country sights and sounds having,
indeed, become almost a necessity of my nature. Also I
like to be alone in the morning. The morning is, it is
obvious, the time for work, for work by oneself. Most of
us are not fit for the society of our fellows until midday,
and those of us who have the sense to know it insist on
avoiding human contacts until lunch-time. More happy
marriages have split upon the altar of the family breakfast-
table than upon any other single rock. But in the afternoon I begin to need the society of my fellows, and by the
evening it has become a condition of my happiness. The
evening is the time for sociality; one talks, one relaxes,
one expands, one lets oneself go, and, if these things are
denied one, depression sets in. I at least begin to feel
that I am a hopeless failure, that nobody likes me, and

On being not so Black

that I shall decline to an obscure, unloved and lonely old age.

Nor is it enough that I should have society; it must be changing and varied society. I said above that I am on the whole given to liking people; other things being equal, my instinctive feelings towards them are those of approval and welcome. I enjoy the society of my kind, and I like to think that I enjoy more varied kinds of society than most of my fellow-intellectuals who write and lecture in London. It is my ideal to be able to talk with ease and opportunity to all sorts and conditions of men, to be as much at home in a miner's cottage as in a business-man's week-end country house. I do not, I am afraid, live up to this ideal, and, as time goes on, I live up to it less and less. Inevitably, as one gets old, one stiffens, hardens and narrows, and I am now conscious of a definite barrier of shyness, which amounts in some cases almost to antipathy, to be overcome before I can be at ease in the company of working-class folk. Yet, starting as I did, with an initial predisposition in favour of my fellows, and having been brought through my apprenticeship in the Socialist movement into touch with more social strata than falls to the lot of most middle-class people, I am, I humbly believe, more catholic in my tastes. When Mr. Priestley's *Good Companions* first appeared, it was highly and de-servedly praised by the critics. When later it became a colossal popular success with sales running into hundreds of thousands, literary persons changed their tone and began to decry it. It was, they complained, so fright-fully hearty, so determinedly cheerful; it insisted so un-blushingly on the fact that the world was a good place; it was sentimental, shallow, superficial; it was imitation Fielding; it was bad Dickens. So the highbrow chorus with a unanimity which presently saw in appreciation of *The Good Companions* the hall-mark of bad taste. As with the book, so with the play. Bloomsbury scoffed at what the suburbs loved, the contempt of the few being the inevitable obverse of the approval of the many. In this matter my sympathies are with the suburbs. I derived more pleasure from *The Good Companions* than from any work of literature since the great days of Shaw and Wells. I liked it because it was a good story brimming over with fun and high spirits, because of its inexhaustible fertility of incident and invention, because through its pages there walked, ran, strutted and danced a procession of real individual characters, all alive and kicking. I liked it, in a word, for its rich and varied humanity.

Demand for Variety. Now I think this book a very fair test of a man's attitude to people and to life. To like it is to like people and to like life; to scorn it, to dislike people and to distrust life. Most of the intellectuals I know maintain a fastidious attitude to their fellow-beings. They very carefully select their acquaintances, strictly limit their numbers, and pass their lives in a little closed circle of the intelligent and cultured. I, on the other hand, like people too much to be content with a few of them, however carefully chosen. I like to think that, in Terence's famous phrase, '*Nihil humanum a me alienum puto*', and to take my acquaintances from all classes of society. Naturally I have a preference for intelligence, wit and culture, but it is far from being exclusive, and some of my oldest friends have been unable to muster an original idea between them. But, to please me, people must be not only varied but varying. I want new acquaintances so much that, to make them, I am even ready to ignore old ones. This desire for novelty in people proceeds to such extremes as to become a positive nuisance. I will find interest and entertainment in a new acquaintance who I know to be infinitely inferior in respect of both to the old friends to whom I am temporarily preferring to him. New people stimulate me. I like to

show off before people, to amuse and to entertain them;
I desire to dazzle them with my mental agility and
to impress them with an apparently limitless fund
of anecdote and information. I have seen many men
and cities, and known a fair proportion of the famous
people of my time. I like to 'come it over' new acquaintances with the fruits of these contacts and to see myself
exalted in their eyes. In a word, I like to evoke admiration. There are only five or six people with whom I
have been able to transcend the need to stimulate and to
be stimulated, people whom I have known so long and
like so well that with them I can afford to be dull. But I
do not see them very often and, like most of us, pass my
time not with friends but with acquaintances. And these,
I find, must be renewed.

This vice, if vice it is, is a harmless one—at least, I
cannot see that it harms anybody. On the contrary, it
may even add to the world's amusement, since, as Aristotle pointed out, we all tell a story with exaggeration
in the belief that we are giving pleasure; but its indulgence demands an audience perpetually renewed. It is
this need that I feel for a constant and constantly changing stream of new acquaintances which effectively deters
me from living in the country.

If I am thrown upon the society of a few people, I
rapidly become as intolerable to them as they are tedious
to me. Having no incentive to make myself amusing
or interesting before those who know my parlour tricks
and have explored the necessarily limited resources of
my mind, I become dull, moody and silent. It is for this
reason that I have never been able to make a success of
walking tours.

In my youth, under the spell of a literary tradition, I
used, as I have already recounted, to go on walking tours
with a few carefully selected friends, one or two or at most
three. In almost every case the walking tour killed the

friendship. As day succeeded day, we grew so bored, we grew so to hate the sight of each other, that we never wanted to see one another again. On reflection I have come to the conclusion that what was the matter with these tours was simply the continual proximity. We simply could not get away from each other. As with walking tours, so with marriage. For marriage is like a walking tour indefinitely extended and prolonged into the night, with the result that I have made even less of a success of marriage than I have of walking tours. The continual familiarity, the everlasting 'dailiness' of marriage, is, indeed, its most distressing feature. It causes married people to treat one another with a rudeness which they would never dream of extending to their most casual acquaintances; it leads them to appear before each other in postures and attire which they would sooner die than reveal to their neighbours—the mere sight of his wife cutting her toe-nails in a dressing-gown and curl papers has killed the love of many a good man; it renders them unwilling to amuse and incapable of being amused by each other. In the end it engenders a fatty degeneration of the mental and moral being, an atrophy of the higher faculties brought on by the feeling that there is no need to take any trouble to be at one's best before the wife, and it destroys affection so surely that, if love is a disease, marriage is the best sanatorium that has yet been devised for the cure of it. So, at least, it has been with me, and, so far as my observation goes, my case is extreme rather than unusual.

Objections to Country Life. What is true of walking tours and true of marriage is true also, *mutatis mutandis*, of living in the country. There are many among my acquaintances, intellectuals like myself, who have chosen a country life. Bucks teems with them; the Surrey hills are dotted with their residences; more recently they have taken flight before the invading stockbrokers and retired to Essex. They have no country contacts except with emigrated Londoners like themselves, and they rely for society upon the friends they invite for week-ends. Granted that the dearth of people during the week might be rendered tolerable by social week-ends, there seem to me to be three objections to this course. First, it is expensive; perpetual entertaining is a drain upon the income and a strain upon the wife. Secondly, it means that one's relation to one's fellows is always that of host to guest. This may be all very well for those who are nature's hosts; but, apart from the fact that many people, like myself, are not by nature hosts at all but guests, it destroys the basis of monetary equality upon which people can most easily meet. I would sooner sit with a party of friends in an inn where each man pays his own footing, than at any man's table where I am beholden to another for my meat and drink. It is difficult to tell the man whose bread one is eating what one thinks of him, and the perpetual host grows eccentric through social coddling.

Thirdly, the man who lives in the country and relies for his society upon the week-enders he entertains from town, lives on his social capital. He makes no new contacts, but perambulates the same circle of friends, whom he invites at carefully spaced intervals all the year round. Presently the circle becomes a clique. The vice of cliques is intellectual inbreeding, and intellectual inbreeding soon leads to intellectual sterility. It is the desire to keep my contacts keen and fresh, to meet new people and different kinds of people, and to go on meeting them, that has finally decided me against living in the country. I like to wander socially as well as territorially.

The question is often discussed in the sillier papers whether husbands should take their holidays with their wives. A change, it is said, does good to both; on the other hand, there are possibilities of unfaithfulness when the parties are separated, which do not arise when each acts as watchdog to the other. And so on . . . I cannot abide spending my holidays with people, let alone with wives, whom I meet and know in my work-a-day life. I like to dump myself unknown and unrecognized among a crowd of people I have never seen before, and gradually to find my own level. Hence, I find myself in my element at summer schools, conferences and festivals, where the constant impact of new personalities keeps me up to the scratch, and I am saved the infinite boredom and fatigue of the restful holiday in the company of friends with whom I need not take trouble.

Life in Hampstead is admirably adapted to my needs and limitations. I write all the morning, bathe or play tennis in the afternoon, lecture or dine out in the evening. The first half of my day is solitary; the second social, and I can vary the proportions at will. Moreover, it is my good fortune to be visited by a fairly continuous stream of callers. Young men who are clerks and would be writers want to know whether they should kick over the economic traces and live by their pens; young women, how to fill their unoccupied lives. There is a fairly constant trickle of visiting philosophers from India, America and occasionally Germany; there are newspaper people who want to know what a philosopher thinks about love or lotteries, American lecture agents and Americans *tout court* who have a nose for celebrity, even when it does not exist.

Writings: Their Nature and Motive. I have written books upon a considerable number of subjects. There was, for example, a book on religion which evoked a brood of protesting parsons, the apostles of half a dozen esoteric creeds anxious to claim me as a convert, and even a few indignant rationalists outraged by my suggestion that, whatever one might think of the Church, religion need not necessarily be written off as nonsense. Of recent years I have dabbled in politics. Religion and politics are subjects admirably adapted to the making of enemies and the attracting of disciples. Between them they have brought me a host of new acquaintances and a dozen new interests, inserted my finger into a number of new pies and brought me a bag of from ten to twenty letters a day.

But religion and politics are far from being my only interests; indeed, they are little more than side-shows, which I only mention here because of their special value in enlarging my circle of acquaintances and interests. It is, indeed, my good fortune to be interested in a great number of things, in philosophy and psychology, biology and physics, music, literature, the state of the world, public opinion, politics. My interests for the most part express themselves in strong and extreme views which I find it difficult to keep to myself, so I write a book, or a pamphlet, or a series of articles to give the world a piece of my mind. On academic subjects I find that the best way of understanding the import of other people's ideas and ordering my own is to arrange and write them down. I have a certain gift of lucidity, and the arrangement is generally praiseworthy. Once the data are clearly arranged, I find that they give rise to fairly definite opinions in my own mind. It seems a pity to withold the benefit of the arrangement and exposition from others, and there seems to be no reason why they should be denied the expression of my own opinions. Hence a book follows, which is a testimony less to a mastery of the subject than to the fact that, for me, to write about something is usually the best way to understand it. 'How'—I agree with my daughter, reproved for speaking without thinking—'How can I know what I think, until I see what I say?'

In this way I have written a prodigious number of books—I am only forty and there are already twenty-six of them—on a considerable variety of subjects. I

have written half a dozen or more books on philosophy.
In addition to religion and politics, I have written about
morals, leisure, literature and the countryside. I have
written a critical biography of Samuel Butler and a
critical estimate of America. I have even written a novel
and a book of short stories. I am aware of the fact that
this incursion into many fields precludes distinction in
any. This is not because it is impossible for a writer to
combine versatility with depth, but because the critics are
unwilling to concede eminence in more than one sphere.

Drawbacks of Versatility. All really big men have been
versatile. Voltaire wrote tragedies, epic poems, polemical
tracts and political treatises, while Shaw, not content with
being the best playwright since Shakespeare, contrives to
be a political theorist, an economist, a biologist and a
philosopher, in all of which capacities he has profoundly
affected the thought of the age by original contributions,
which he has expounded in the best prose style and platform speeches of his time. But most versatile men are
not of the class of Voltaire and Shaw. If you are big
enough to win through on all fronts, well and good; your
reputation in each sphere will increase your reputation
in all. If not, the common envy of talent in any sphere,
reinforced by the shocked horror of academic persons
for anyone who ventures to express himself on matters of
current interest, and the contempt of the man in the
street for the incursions of the mere intellectual into
practical affairs, is apt to ensure that the work of the
man who refuses to be bound by any one subject will
be damned in advance. It is grudgingly received, denied
serious notice, and praised faintly or not at all, while
such recognition as it may achieve is won in the teeth of
public hostility and indifference. Just as there is no post
in the country which a man cannot hold, if he can only
hold his tongue, so inability to restrain the utterance of

one's views on several topics is thought effectively to rob them of importance on any. The biologists say that Mr. X is, no doubt, an original and highly stimulating social critic, but that he cannot be taken seriously as a biologist, while the critics and journalists dismiss his views on current affairs as palpably absurd and remark what a pity it is that eminent scientists will not keep to their own province.

Trade Union Spirit in Philosophy. For myself, my reputation has fallen between two stools of public esteem. The majority of my books are on philosophical subjects. Some are popular and seek to make the thought of modern philosophers intelligible to those who have no previous acquaintance with the subject; others, two in particular, are intended as serious contributions to modern philosophical thought. Neither sort of books has been altogether successful. Philosophers, like scientists and doctors, are animated by a strong Trade Union spirit and deprecate the admission of outsiders to the mysteries of the profession. When an outsider manages to find out for himself what the insider professes to teach him, the prestige of the insider is proportionately diminished. Explanations of philosophical ideas stripped of technical jargon such as I have endeavoured to give, have the effect of black-legging the philosophers' union by instructing outsiders in an intellectual technique which has previously been the preserve of members of the craft, and are, therefore, inevitably unpopular. The fact that no philosopher can be brought to admit even to himself what the reason for his objection to them is, does not prevent him from crabbing them whenever he can on the ground that they are superficial, inaccurate and misleading. As for my supposedly original works, they suffer in two ways. First, it is not thought that one who has a facility in expounding the ideas of others can possess original ideas of his own; in the second place, the view is taken that anybody who wishes to be regarded as a serious philosopher must make philosophy a wholetime job, and not give his thoughts to matters that may lie outside the strict confines of the subject. If his mind does stray in this way, he will do well to keep quiet about it and not lower his dignity as a philosopher by revealing the weakness to the world. He must not, indeed, speak to the world at all.

Not only have I spoken, but I have spoken out. As I hope I have sufficiently indicated in the preceding pages, events from time to time occur which seem to me to be the outcome of a quite unnecessary degree of folly and hypocrisy on the part of society. When this happens, I find it difficult to keep quiet; I am moved, as I have said, to give society a piece of my mind. Thus, most of my non-philosophical books are in the nature of social criticism, or even of social satire. I have made fun of conventional morals and hay of conventional religion; I have held up conventional politics to ridicule and the conventional method of settling international disputes to shame. Apart from the books, there has been of recent years a continuous stream of articles on all sorts of subjects. During the fortnight, for example, in which I am finishing this chapter, I have written on 'A Charter for Walkers', 'The Politics of Youth', 'The Plight of Marriage in Modern Society' (for an American symposium), the use and misuse of the powers of science, and the character of the English, as well as a semi-technical article on a discussion on 'Physics and Free Will' at a philosophical Congress, and three or four fairly technical reviews. These literary activities are conceived and carried out in a light-hearted mood, which cannot but seem to the academic world a sad derogation from the grave dignity of the philosopher. Many eminent persons have, I fear, come to regard me in the light of an obstreperous little boy cocking snooks at what society regards as established

On being not so Black

and reveres accordingly. Socrates, it is true, went down to the market-place, but then Socrates was Socrates, and even he made himself such a nuisance that the Athenians had to poison him to get rid of him.

I am sorry for all this, but I cannot help it. Whatever trouble is brewing in the world, I must, I feel, have a finger in the pie, and, if the plums I pull out are few enough, I get a good deal of fun out of the pulling. Nor, in spite of the scrapes into which it has got me, the missed professorships and the lectures on indiscretion, do I feel disposed to apologize for or to regret this diversity of activities.

Function of Philosophy. It is the business of philosophy, as I conceive it, to seek to understand the nature of the universe as a whole, not, as do the sciences, some special department of it, but the whole bag of tricks to which the moral feelings of the Puritan, the herd instinct of the man in the street, the religious consciousness of the saint, the æsthetic enjoyment of the artist, the history of the human race and its contemporary follies, no less than the latest discoveries of science contribute. Reflecting upon this mass of data, the philosopher seeks to interpret it. He looks for a clue to guide him through the labyrinth, for a system wherewith to classify, or a purpose in terms of which to make meaningful.

Has the universe, for example, any design, or is it merely a fortuitous concourse of atoms? Is mind a fundamental feature of the universe, in terms of which we are ultimately to interpret the rest, or is it a mere accident, an eddy in the primeval slime, doomed one day to finish its pointless journey with as little noise and significance as it began it? Are good and evil real and ultimate principles existing independently of men, or are they merely the names we give to the things of which we happen to approve and to disapprove?

As I have Painted

Duty of Philosophers. Now it is difficult to concede
the purpose without feeling some obligation to further
it. It is difficult to conclude that human life is designed
without concluding also that society, as we know it, is not
realizing the design; difficult to believe that the object of
evolution is the achievement of truth, goodness and
beauty, without lamenting the rise of the talkies and the
fall of the countryside; difficult to hold as an ethical principle that people ought to behave with kindliness towards
each other and not to break out against war. Most philosophers, I know, succeed in doing these things; succeed,
that is to say, in discerning a purpose and recognizing an
ideal without feeling an obligation to further the purpose
or to remove obvious impediments to the realization of
the ideal. Most, but not all; for the greatest thinkers
seem also to have felt the impulse to act. Inevitably their
actions were such as to get them into trouble with society.
Plato ignominiously turned out of Syracuse, Christ dying
on the Cross, Tolstoy hounded from pillar to post by the
Russian Government, Voltaire taking refuge with Frederick
the Great, and, when Frederick could not stand him
any longer, at Ferney, all bear witness to the persistence
of the philosophers' interventions in affairs and to their
uniformly disastrous results; and, if you object that
Christ and Tolstoy and Voltaire were not philosophers,
I can only beg you to wait until you know as much
philosophy as I do before venturing to contradict.

Now I do not wish to suggest that I am in the least
like any of these great men, but what is good enough for
them is good enough for me, and with such precedents
to back me I feel no call to apologize for my frequent
and no doubt ill-timed emergences from the philosophic
shades to tell the world what I think of it. At any rate,
to return to the point from which I digressed, this variety
of writing upon a multiplicity of subjects, the enemies it
makes for me, the controversies in which it embroils me

and the friends and advocates it brings me, prevent me from becoming slack and complacent; and, for me, to become slack and complacent is to become bored. For, I had better confess it here and have done with it, boredom is my great enemy. To confess to boredom is to confess to failure in life, and, were I often to succumb to it, this chapter on enjoying life would never be written. On the whole I do not succumb; on the whole I defeat the enemy; but eternal vigilance is the price of victory, and it is only by means of a series of very carefully planned devices, an elaborate structure of outworks and fortifications, that I keep boredom at bay.

Of these devices the two most important and successful are writing and games. Of my writing I have already spoken; it remains to say a few words about games.

Love of Games. Considering that I am an intellectual, I am rather good at games. Unlike many of my 'highbrow' friends who carry the heads of athletes on the bodies of thinkers, I have been endowed not only with a broad fore-head but with a good eye and a reasonably athletic body—at least, it was reasonably athletic until, owing to greed, I developed a paunch. I have always been fairly good at hockey and tennis, and was a competent scrum-half at rugger, until I grew too short-sighted to see the ball in the scrum. The high-water mark of my athletic prowess was a trial for Oxford University at hockey: I was only tried once, but I was tried. I am too old now for hockey, but I still play a good deal of tennis, averaging two or three games a week all the year round. I consider tennis to be the best narcotic yet invented for persons of intelligence who are fattening. It brings forgetfulness no less surely than opium or heroin, and, unlike them, it leaves no ill effects. To confess that such an escape from life, or the self, or boredom, call it what you will, should be necessary is perhaps, a confession of failure—that an enlightened and intelligent race, lord of the universe and heir to all the ages, can only make existence tolerable to itself by continually whacking little round bits of matter with long thin bits of matter in the shape of bats, cues, clubs, mallets, polo sticks and rackets, does, no doubt, appear to require some explanation—but, if confession it is, I freely confess that, if I could not be assured of escaping from the atmosphere of the English Sunday in winter by playing tennis from eleven to four, and from its midday meal by taking a cold wing of chicken and a flask of claret on to the court for my lunch, I should tear myself in pieces with restlessness and boredom. In summer-time in the evenings I play in tennis matches; if it begins to rain in the afternoon, I can do no work at all, but must be every minute at the window watching for possible signs of the rain stopping. I am doing this at the moment and the continual interruption is, I observe, reponsible for a certain scrappiness and lack of coherence in the writing of the last two pages!

Campaign against Boredom. What with writing and lecturing—I write on an average two books a year and in term-time give nine lectures a week, sometimes more—seeing editors, reviewing a couple of books a week, entertaining visitors, meeting old friends and attracting new ones, making the thousand and one contacts which are necessary to keep my mind fresh and bright, attending meetings and conferences, answering from ten to a dozen letters a day, playing games—chess and bridge, as well as tennis and a little vestigial hockey—keeping my eye on my children, making love, overeating and sleeping off its effects, I am pretty busy and on the whole succeed in keeping the enemy boredom at arm's length.

I have settled down to a middle-age medium kind of existence, which finds in effort and endeavour the chief happiness of life, and bases itself on the maxim that the

On being not so Black

only way to avoid being miserable is not to have leisure enough to wonder whether you are happy or not. The defect of the method is an inability to rest. I never dare leave myself with nothing to do for fear of an attack of boredom, and, no doubt, I am wearing out very rapidly in consequence. I never go anywhere but I take a book, and I never pass a day without writing. To write in the morning after breakfast has for me become as habitual as . . . well, as a physiological function; perhaps it *is* a physiological function, and books should be regarded as the excrement of the brain.

I map out the day, often the week, in advance. Every hour, every moment must be occupied. And the occupation must be as varied as possible. If it is tennis from two to four to-day, it must be the cinema to-morrow; if I am going to a theatre to-night, I must dine out to-morrow and the next night spend quietly at home. If it is Miss X and a French lunch in Soho on Monday, it must be a party of men with beer and a steak on Tuesday. Thus my life consists of a series of tasks, engagements and planned diversions. Most involve effort, most in one form or another require the exercise of my faculties at full stretch, demanding activity of intellect or application of will, speed of foot or quickness of eye, rapidity of decision or charm turned on tap-like for special purposes. I take even my periods of rest strenuously; I do not lounge in an arm-chair by the fire, or in a hammock on the lawn; I go to bed. In fact, I do not know how to rest; I can only sleep.

Industrious Automatism. I cannot at present even let myself read very much. Working in the bad old days of the Civil Service, when I could never bring myself to regard interviewing and drafting letters as real work, meant for me reading philosophy and writing. I read and wrote like a galley slave to make myself a name to earn me an income when I left the Service. Always

As I have Painted

I said to myself, 'Once you are out of this, you will have time to read and write what you please; time, in fact, for real work'. But, now that I am out of it, I cannot shake off the habit of feverish industry I acquired in order to get out of it. Now that I have leisure for what I call work, for reading, I find that I am restless with somebody else's books; I feel all the time that I should be writing myself, making money or fame, or contributing to the world's store of knowledge or enlightenment. I have, of course, to know what is going on in the world of letters, and I have developed in a high degree the capacity for knowing what is in a book without reading it.

I have, for example, a good reviewer's nose. It is with the sense of smell rather than with that of vision that the skilled reviewer acquaints himself with the contents of books; and, when my reviewing nose is working properly, I have only to smell a book to know what to say about it. I comfort myself for this slipshod attention to current literature with the reflection that a day will come when I shall be too old to write any more books, and then, I tell myself, I can read a few. Perhaps some of my own, for, as Samuel Butler pointed out, nobody can tell what one wants to read as well as one does oneself, and to write books while my powers are still with me in order that I may have something to read later on, is merely to make prudent literary provision for my old age.

In spite of, or, as I should prefer to say, because of all this activity and effort I enjoy myself well enough, and I attribute my happiness very largely to having seen through most of the great catches of life.

The Catches of Life. (1) *Love.* The great catches of life are the snares of youth, and, until one has found them out, one's life is bound to provide a surplus of pain over pleasure. The first catch is that love will last. Strong love, especially strong first love of the romantic kind is, as is well known, a most upsetting occurrence. Love inflames the passions, intoxicates the senses, clouds the judgment, destroys the perspective. It causes the loving male to endow the loved female not only with the desirability of a Venus, but with the virtues of a Madonna, the intelligence of an Athene and the practical ability of a first-rate house-wife, and assures him that in comparison with the possession of the person of this epitome of all the excellences, nothing in the world is of the slightest importance.

Finally, it assures the lover that his feelings are permanent. None of these beliefs is true, and all contribute to deepen the disillusionment which ensues when the hot fit passes; but none brings a disillusion quite so bitter as the discovery that it does pass. Love is the bait on the hook of life, whereby men and women are induced to take those steps which are necessary to the continuance of the species. Two people may be hopelessly and utterly imcompatible; they may have no single taste in common and share no single preference or prejudice; they may belong to different classes or countries or races; they may be of different colours; they may hate one another in their hearts. Yet, once the bait so cunningly compounded of sexual attractiveness and sentimental romanticism is presented, the infatuated pair are no more free to refuse it than a starving dog is free to refuse a proferred bone. Once the bait is swallowed, there is no further need of love, and though kindliness and affection may succeed, that is the best one can hope. Unappeased, love is a devouring hunger, a pain past all bearing. Fulfilled, it becomes its own parody, turns homely and dwindles at best into something small and gracious, at worst into something small and ugly. The shock of finding all this out is considerable but salutary. It has the effect of inoculation, and if repeated often enough, gradually confers immunity. Immunity means the exposure of the catch of love.

As I have Painted

(2) *Ideals.* Another catch is the belief that what lies over the hill or beyond the horizon is better than that on this side. The belief is instinctive and apparently ineradicable. Even when bitter experience has assured you that to-morrow is not better than to-day, the next town not better than the one in which you live, the second woman not better than the first, you continue to make experiments in the vain hope of improving the present by forcing the hand of the future, and bettering your lot by changing it. To inhibit this impulse is now so much second nature, that I no longer think that the view on the other side of the hill will be as good as I think it is. Yet I still think it is.

For this ever-renewed hope is, I take it, yet another of the carrots with which life draws us forward. That we should think and believe that what lies in front is better than what lies behind, that the future will be better than the past, is a necessary condition of our making those efforts which are necessary to forward the purpose of evolution. Once it was enough that living organisms should feel hunger. Now many human beings are too well nourished to need to make efforts to get food, and hope, or that organized system of hope's delusions known as Idealism, is the substitute for hunger. We must, it is clear, look forward with hope, despising the present in the interests of the future. There is nothing at the end of the road better than can be found beside it, although there would be an end to travelling did man believe it; and because man was made to travel, because he was contrived for the express purpose of carrying life to higher levels by the exercise of his faculties, the sharpening of his intelligence, and the strengthening of his will, no man does believe it—at any rate at first. With middle-age the true character of hope as Life's dodge to induce man to go on trying is understood, and, in the light of understanding, is exposed the catch of Idealism.

311

On being not so Black

(3) *Beauty*. A third catch is that there is meaning in beauty. A young man sees a sunset and, unable to understand or to express the emotion that it rouses in him, concludes that it must be the gateway to a world that lies beyond. It is difficult for any of us in moments of intense æsthetic experience to resist the suggestion that we are catching a glimpse of a light that shines down to us from a different realm of existence, different and, because the experience is intensely moving, in some way higher. And, though the gleams blind and dazzle, yet do they convey a hint of a beauty and serenity greater than we have known or imagined. Greater too than we can describe; for language, which was invented to convey the meanings of this world, cannot readily be fitted to the uses of another.

That all great art has this power of suggesting a world beyond is undeniable. In some moods Nature shares it. There is no sky in June so blue that it does not point forward to a bluer, no sunset so beautiful that it does not waken the vision of a greater beauty, a vision which passes before it is fully glimpsed, and in passing leaves an indefinable longing and regret. But, if this world is not merely a bad joke, life a vulgar flare amid the cool radiance of the stars, and existence an empty laugh braying across the mysteries; if these intimations of a something behind and beyond are not evil humours born of indigestion, or whimsies sent by the devil to mock and madden us, if, in a word, beauty means something, yet we must not seek to interpret the meaning. If we glimpse the unutterable, it is unwise to try to utter it, nor should we seek to invest with significance that which we cannot grasp. Beauty in terms of our human meanings *is* meaningless. It does not mean that the universe is good, that life has a purpose, that God is in heaven, or even that the human and the friendly condition and underly the alien and the brutal. The lesson is a hard one, and the learning of it brings pain and disillusion. The Victorians for the most part never learnt it at all; they gave art human meanings and insisted that beauty must be symbolic. Thus they read moral homilies into nature and moral abstractions, Faith, Hope, Charity and so forth, into the curves of female figures. So far as pictures are concerned, our own age seems to have learnt better. Victorian symbolism is out of fashion, and I am glad to note that Burne-Jones's pictures of symbolical virtues and vices, hopes and aspirations, which used to fetch hundreds and even thousands of pounds, now sell at Sotheby's for five or six. Some of Sir Edwin Landseer's vast cartoons fail to evoke a bid. . . .

But we still look for meaning in life and above all for meaning in beauty, meaning that we can somehow relate to ourselves. We still judge the universe anthropomorphically and see in events portents of hope or menace to humanity. To realize that the preparation for eternal happiness of a certain number of human souls, conceived in the likeness of twentieth-century Nordic adults, is not the purpose for which creation travails, and that the moon does not ride the clouds on a summer night with any message for us, to realize, in a word, the vast indifference of the universe to man, is the beginning of the wisdom of an adult mind. Yet the realization means the exposure of another of life's catches, the catch of beauty. Until the exposure has been made, one is apt to be taken in by beauty as completely as one is taken in by love; by beauty, and, although this happens now less frequently than it once did, by religion. Love, beauty and religion; undeniably they are important, and between them they confer upon human life such value as it has, but, if we would achieve happiness, we must be on our guard against taking them as other than they are; of taking them, that is to say, as signs of something beyond themselves, of reading between lines that are not there.

On being not so Black

(4) *Pursuit of Pleasure*. And the final catch, the cunningest and hardest to expose, is the one that set me talking about catches in the first instance, the catch about pleasure. Pleasure, it seems, is not to be pursued directly. Pleasure is not itself a state, but an accompaniment of other states; not itself a process, but, like coke, a by-product of other processes; not an object, but a grace that attends activities directed to other objects. The road to happiness is not direct but roundabout, and, much as we may desire it, we may not go straight to what we desire. In this respect happiness is like beauty and sleep. Many people hold, though falsely, that there is nothing a man may not win, if he is sufficiently determined to win it. 'Where there is a will, there is a way,' they say, and, even though there be no way to the moon, for the common run of things the proverb contains its grain of truth. But with happiness it is not so.

The kingdom of happiness, like the kingdom of beauty, is not to be taken by storm, any more than it is to be purchased by dollars.

Set out to seek happiness and it will elude you: throw yourself body and soul into your work, devote yourself to some cause, lift yourself up out of the selfish pit of vanity and desire, which is the self, by giving yourself to something which is greater than self, and on looking back you will find that you have been happy. Happiness, in short, is not a house that can be built by men's hands; it is a flower that surprises you, a song which you hear as you pass the hedge, rising suddenly and simply in the night and dying down again. For my part, I have found that happiness is bound up in some important way with the full development of every side of my nature. Such development is the fruit of unremitting activity and effort, and, since I have been and on the whole am happy, I had better end by giving the recipe which I have learned to follow, the creed by which I try to live.

As I have Painted

Acceptance of Body. First, I should advocate an unpro-testing acceptance of our bodies and of all that they imply. In saying that we must accept the body, I mean that we must be prepared to do justice to those instincts which, through our association with the body, we possess in common with the animals. It is from these instincts that we derive our energy and draw our vital force. They are the necessary basis of any structure that we may raise upon them; they determine the pattern which life has traced for us, and we mutilate them at our own peril. It is of such mutilation that I conceive the ascetic to be guilty. He would strive to subdue the body and the instincts of the body as though it were the enemy of the soul, from whose humiliation the soul would reap the benefit. The better course is surely that of Plato, not subjugation but discipline; not, that is to say, to trample upon the forces of our animal nature, refusing to avail ourselves of the energy and passion which flow from them, but harmonizing them one with another, to dedicate them to the service of a dominant purpose, which is the good of the whole. So utilized, they may be of inestimable benefit to the mind itself. An intellect that is divorced from the interests and affections of common men is apt to be dry and pedantic; it becomes a logic-chopping machine engaged in the elaboration of systems which have no contact with life and no relation to fact. More than this, it may suffer from the distortion of a definite bias. You cannot starve one side of your nature and expect to produce no effect upon the rest; and to see life steadily and to see it whole, we must be whole men and women. If we are less, if we have achieved a supremacy of intellect or will and drained ourselves of blood and passion in the struggle, our outlook upon the world will reflect the partiality and lopsidedness of our natures.

But, and this is the second article of my creed, there

is more in the recommendation to cultivate a healthy mind
in a healthy body than that health is a good thing, and
that it is better to have two good things than one. For
the healthy body rightly utilized may strengthen and
enthuse the healthy mind. It seems to me to be possible,
as it is certainly desirable, to enlist the humours and energy
of the body in the service of the mind. Professor G. M.
Trevelyan has coined a phrase in description of the soul,
which exactly expresses the view that I have found to be
right, right that is for me. He advocates 'the flushing
of the brain with the blood, of the cold intellectual with
the hot animal'. It is the personality so conceived, a blend
of mind enthused by passion, and of passion inspired by
mind that we may perhaps regard as the highest type of
product which life has hitherto succeeded in evolving.
It is not in terms of massiveness and force of intellect alone
that we must assess success in life, but of a compound of
faculties in which the mind, in the narrow sense of the word,
while remaining directive and supreme, is quickened and
sensitized by the forces of the body. To give practical effect
to these beliefs, I try to observe the doctrine of 'The Mean'.

Doctrine of 'The Mean' If we are to regard the different
faculties and parts of our being not as antipathetic but
as complementary, if the health of one part is in some
sense dependent on the health of all, we must give to
each and all their proper exercise: to the body not
asceticism but athletics, to the brain not meditation but
work, to the emotions not atrophy but discipline. For
the rest we should obey all the demands of our nature,
yet let none command our nature. We should not only
know where to stop; we should learn to stop, while we
still wish to continue. Thus will all our faculties be kept
at cutting edge, and our tastes remain fresh and unsated.
For a guide to the demands of our nature we should
refer to the pursuits of our fathers. For what mankind

has done uninterruptedly for thousands of years, we may be assured, there is a natural itch in the blood. In all ancestral and customary pursuits, then, we should indulge, but in none of them overmuch. We should pray a little, compete a little, play a little, dig a little in the ground, and go on the sea in ships; we should make love, speak to our fellows in public, and expand in the company of our friends in private. Above all, we should recognize that we have an instinctive desire for occasional solitude and a need for country sights and sounds. Of this desire and of this need we may not be conscious, yet none the less are they instinct in the blood; they are needs which the conditions of modern civilization render hard to satisfy, yet, unless satisfaction is found for them, the development of the man as a whole will suffer and symmetry will be lost. Symmetry, poise, and balance: these are the marks of the fully developed man, and they will not be achieved by neglecting the unconscious needs of his nature.

To the exhortation to develop every side of our natures I should like to add the qualification that we should develop them not in isolation but together. Our faculties are not allotted by nature to watertight compartments, although they may be so relegated by practice. The best of them are always blends of less-developed constituents, love a blend of sentiment and lust, wit of humour and sense. We should bring to our playing all the cunning of the mind, and to our thinking all the passion of the body.

Importance of Here and Now. It is not, then, by regarding this world as a vale of tears and suffering, a temporary habitation of the spirit whose real home lies elsewhere, that we shall live happily, nor, if the consolations of religion achieve their end by belittling the significance of what happens here in comparison with the transcendent importance of what awaits us else-

317

where, shall we be wise to avail ourselves of the comfort they bring. Such comfort destroys our sense of the importance of the actual, and paralyses effort; it is an endeavour to support our dignity under the realization of our own insignificance, by assuring us of the equal unimportance of our admired fellows and of the world that makes much of them. This is an easy doctrine, at once a snare and a justification for the slack and the comfortable, bidding them take not overmuch thought for the present, because of the imminence of a heavenly future. In opposition to it, I urge that the present does matter here and now; that we matter in it in a sense in which we shall never matter at any other time or place, and that we exist in the present for the fulfilment of certain purposes, which will be furthered neither by an indifference to the calls and needs of the world as we find it, nor by an attitude of resignation to the evils with which a hypothetical providence may have thought fit to surround us. We are here to remove those evils.

But if we refuse to belittle our existence in the present because of the importance of an imagined life in the future, we shall equally reject a fatalistic attitude which destroys hope and saps effort by assuring us that we are helplessly entangled in the web of destiny. It is of the essence of my belief that life is free and changing; it is not an incidental and unimportant offshoot of matter, but an independent principle controlling matter and moulding it to its purposes. Life, then, is the maker of its own destiny, nor is there any other principle in the universe that can interfere with its accomplishment; neither a brooding and ineluctable fate, nor a capricious and irresponsible chance. We are not strangers straying naked and forlorn across an alien environment, mere targets for the shafts of doom, nor are we puppets twitched into love and war by an invisible showman, indifferent alike to our weal and woe, who pulls the strings; but servants and

messengers of life, created by life to carry aloft the torch
of evolution, entrusted with a charge which it lies with
us to neglect or to fulfil.

Effort and the Good Life. We neglect this charge at
our peril; yet its fulfilment depends upon effort and
achievement in the present. I have tried, then, to make
the texture of my life one of unremitting effort. If I
were to seek for the most appropriate human activity to
illustrate my belief, it would be the activity of man as
a mountaineer. We should struggle always, even if, as
Meredith puts it, 'we should only struggle to be wise'.
But, though ours is a steep upward path, there is no peak
in sight; nor is it in the achievement of a goal, but in the
efforts we make towards it that we carry forward the
purpose of life.

Effort is what is valuable; but, and this is the paradox
which besets us, it is valuable only if it is not valued.
Just as, when we make pleasure our end, we find that
nothing pleases, so, if we make effort our aim, we find
that no effort satisfies. First and foremost we must
desire things, both material and spiritual, and strive to
obtain them; on reflection we may admit, and as philosophers we must insist, that it was not what we wanted that
mattered, but the effort we made to get it; yet, if such an
admission were entertained for one moment in the heat
of the struggle, it would blight our endeavours and take
all the savour from our success. We must, in a word, be
busy, not because 'busyness' is a good, but because (and
this is what we may not realize at the time) it is the
condition of other goods being added to us; so true it is
that the only way to avoid being miserable is not to have
leisure enough to know whether you are happy or not.

Above all, I should insist on the belief that we are free;
free, within limits, to make of our lives what we will.
But though we may go the way we choose, life has pointed

On being not so Black

out to us a way of its own, and we shall be well advised to follow it. There are signposts on the way of life, and our satisfaction is dependent upon our taking the course they point. This course, however it may vary from individual to individual, will always be found to involve unremitting effort in pursuit of those aims and ideals which as conscious individuals we find on reflection to be valuable. We should give all sides of our nature their due, but we should do this not in the interests of self-development, but in furtherance of a life given to the pursuit of external things and the cultivation of objective ideals. We do not rightly begin to live until we forget ourselves, and learn to look not inwards upon the self, but outwards with all the eyes of the soul.

Self-Forgetfulness. Herein lies the justification of my description of the self as a little pit of vanity and desire from which it is our duty, so far as possible, to avert our eyes. The Greeks advocated knowledge of the self as the end of life, and the psycho-analysts have given to their advocacy a pseudo-scientific backing, bidding us perpetuately dig up the seeds of our nature that we may the better attend to the growth of the plant. For my part, I would praise not self-knowledge but self-forgetfulness. Such happiness as I have known has resulted not from preoccupation with myself, but from an oblivion of myself in concentration upon some external thing. And, if you care to remind me that an autobiography is the most flagrant form of self-culture, that it is the fruit of self-absorption presented in a sustained act of self-revelation, I can only reply that this of mine is a poor sort of autobiography, and point out to you that in degenerating, as it has insisted upon doing, into a series of essays upon war and the countryside, music and the body, morals and the old, it affords the best testimony to the self-forgetfulness of its author.

320